AF543159

Swapna Liddle's abiding love for the history of Delhi has translated into a PhD as well as several books and articles on the subject. She also seeks to raise awareness about the city's historic precincts through her work for the Indian National Trust for Art and Cultural Heritage (INTACH). For the past twenty-five years, Swapna has been leading walks through the city's historic precincts.

ALSO BY SWAPNA LIDDLE IN SPEAKING TIGER

Chandni Chowk: The Mughal City of Old Delhi

Connaught Place and the Making of New Delhi

The Broken Script: Delhi Under the East India Company and the Fall of the Mughal Dynasty (1803-1857)

14 Historic Walks of Delhi

SWAPNA LIDDLE

SPEAKING
TIGER

SPEAKING TIGER BOOKS LLP
125A, Ground Floor, Shahpur Jat, near Asiad Village,
New Delhi 110049

First published by Westland Ltd in 2011
This edition published by Speaking Tiger Books 2023

Copyright © Swapna Liddle 2023

All images courtesy Madhulika and Swapna Liddle,
except where mentioned otherwise

Maps © Devashish Verma

ISBN: 978-93-5447-643-3
eISBN: 978-93-5447-645-7

10 9 8 7 6 5 4 3 2 1

Typeset by SÜRYA, New Delhi

Printed at Shree Maitrey Printech Pvt. Ltd., Noida

All rights reserved.
No part of this publication may be reproduced, transmitted, or stored in a retrieval system, in any form or by any means, electronic, mechanical, photocopying, recording or otherwise, without the prior permission of the publisher.

This book is sold subject to the condition that it shall not, by way of trade or otherwise, be lent, resold, hired out, or otherwise circulated, without the publisher's prior consent, in any form of binding or cover other than that in which it is published.

For my mother, from whom I learnt a love for language, and my father who taught me that anything worth doing is worth doing with a passion.

CONTENTS

COME WALK WITH ME

THIS BOOK WAS the outcome of years of walking through historic areas in Delhi. When it was first published it received a very gratifying reception, but soon after went out of print. Since then I have received many queries as to when the book would be available again. For one reason or another that did not happen, but in the meanwhile I continued to walk these and many other routes. I have walked alone, with friends, leading organized heritage walks, or on walks led by others. Many of these places have changed in that period, with new site orientations and new restoration projects. My own knowledge and understanding too has changed over time. Clearly an updated version of what had proved to be a popular guidebook was required.

I am happy that the new edition of *Delhi: 14 Historic Walks* is finally ready. Over the years, with the growing popularity of heritage walks, the demand for a guidebook has only increased. I hope this book will help those who want to explore the city's main historic sites without having to either join an organized walk, or having to do extensive research for reliable historical information. The fourteen walking routes in Delhi included in this book are tried and tested. Some are through areas that are very well known and are ticketed historic attractions, including the three World Heritage Sites—the Qutub Minar complex, Humayun's Tomb and Red Fort. Others, such as Khirki or the Mehrauli village, are less well known.

The walking routes charted out here will lead you clearly through an area, helping you find your way around, and identify each building. Each walk will tell you about the historical background of the site that you are visiting, quite apart from the individual buildings within it. At each building, the walk will tell you the building's history to the extent that it is known. It will also point out significant architectural and decorative features, and the concepts and techniques that lay behind them. *14 Historic Walks of Delhi* intends to go further than the average guide book; I have tried to incorporate insights that are rarely known beyond academic publications. Before this frightens off the lay reader, I hasten to add that I have done this in an easy-to-read style.

The walks are arranged in a roughly chronological order—oldest areas to newest. I say 'roughly', because in most areas there are buildings dating from different eras. On the whole, however, the idea is that if you proceed from one to the next in an orderly fashion, you will get a systematic history of the development of the city and its architectural heritage. Of course this is not essential. Each walk stands alone, and if you have the time or inclination for even just one, go ahead and pick any.

At the beginning of each walk, I have included some practical information such as timings and the rate of tickets. Please note that these are correct at the time of going to press, but are liable to change. Ticket prices are as per online booking rates. Charges at monuments may be higher for on-site cash purchase of tickets. Other helpful tips to ease your way through particular areas include maps—an essential tool for navigating the areas—for each walk. Ordinarily, the walks can be accomplished in a duration ranging from one and a half hours to two and a half hours at the maximum. I have also pointed out the highlights of each walk so that if you have less time you can finish in an hour or so.

While designing this book, it was felt that keeping it light and easy to carry around was a priority. For this reason, only a limited number of photographs has been included. These are generally of features that may not be otherwise easy to spot, instead of general photos of the buildings being described. The latter can easily be found online if required, and an explorer will end up taking their own photos! Some photos of buildings have been included, and in some cases these were taken for the first edition of the book. The reason for including them is to point out changes that may have taken place at the site since that time. Photographs of some important architectural and ornamental features have also been included in the glossary.

1

QUTUB MINAR COMPLEX

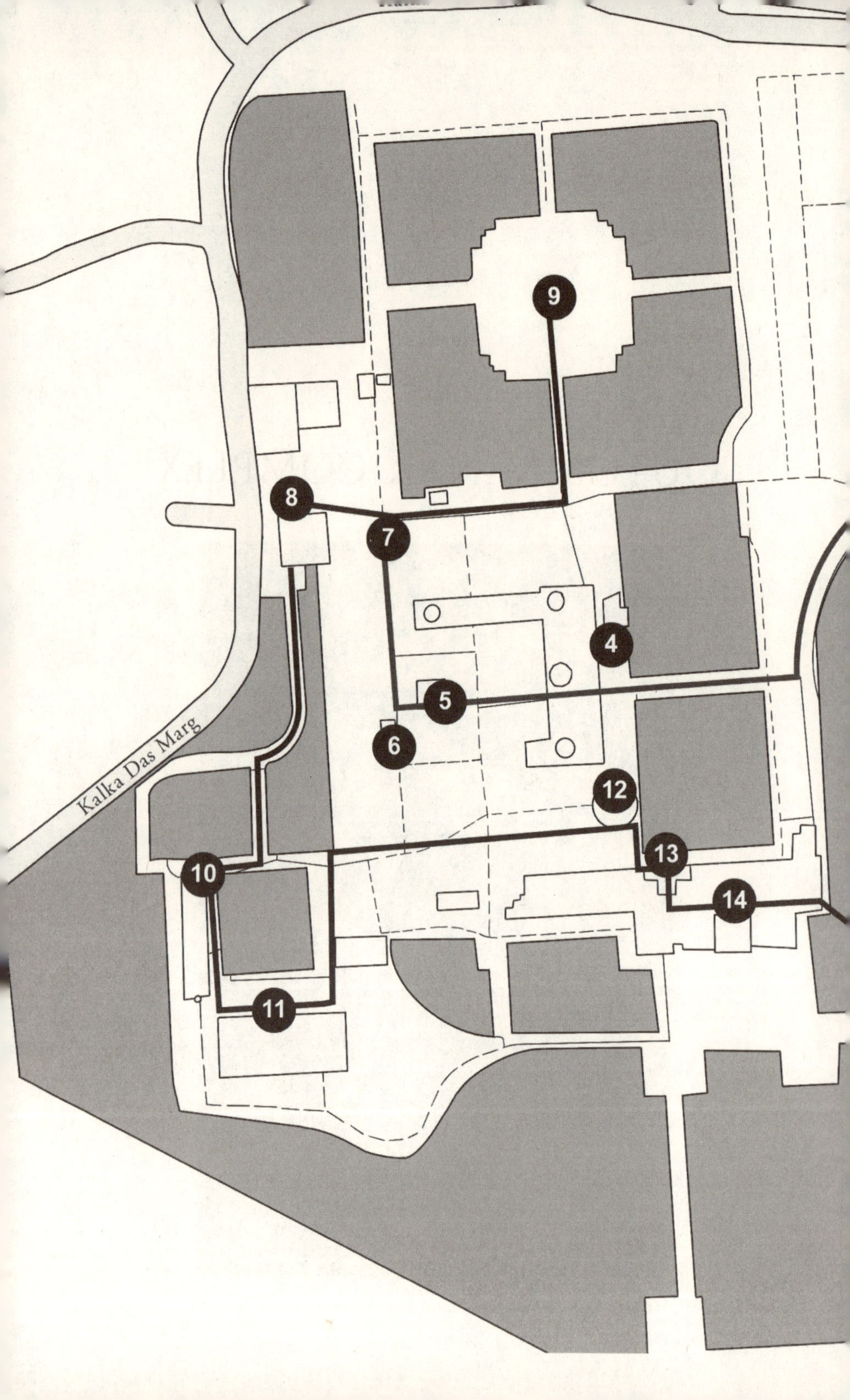

Kalka Das Marg
4
5
6
7
8
9
10
11
12
13
14

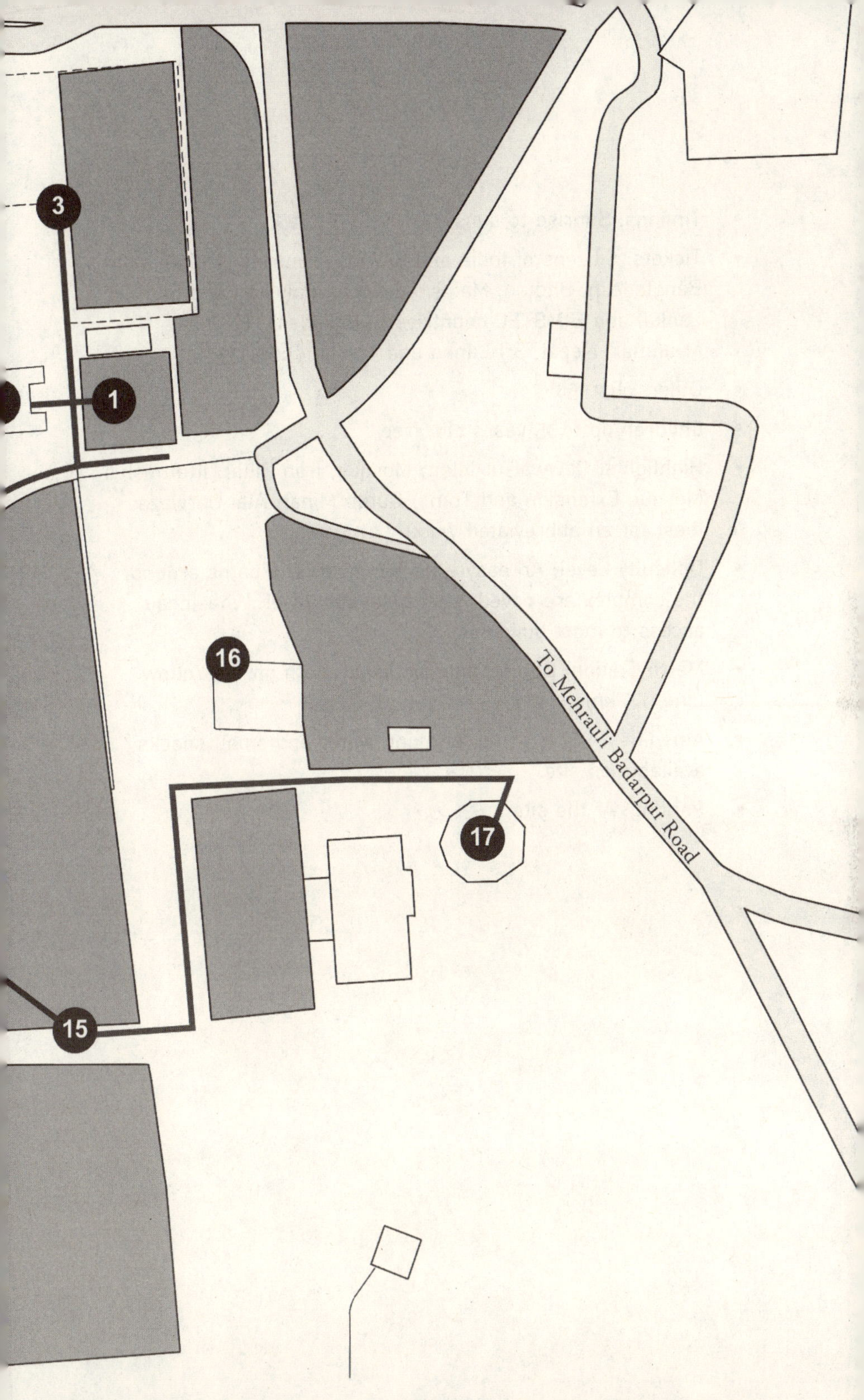

3
1
16
To Mehrauli Badarpur Road
17
15

- Timings: Sunrise to sunset.
- Tickets: Citizens of India and SAARC countries (Afghanistan, Bangladesh, Bhutan, Maldives, Nepal, Pakistan and Sri Lanka) and BIMSTEC countries (Bangladesh, Bhutan, Myanmar, Nepal, Sri Lanka and Thailand): Rs 35
- Others: Rs 550
- Children up to 15 years old: free
- Highlights: Quwwat-ul-Islam Mosque, Iron Pillar, Iltutmish's Mosque Extension and Tomb, Qutub Minar, Alai Darwaza (best for an abbreviated walk).
- Difficulty Level: An easy walk for most. The paths around the complex are paved and reasonably level. Wheelchair access to most buildings.
- Metro Station: Qutub Minar or Saket, both on the Yellow Line, 1.5 kms.
- Amenities: Washrooms, drinking water and small snacks available on site.
- Parking: At the site.

LAL KOT

The Qutub Minar—a massive tower with a distinctive silhouette, is today the most readily recognized visual symbol of the city of Delhi. It is one of three historic locations in Delhi to have received the status of World Heritage site from UNESCO, and is one of the most visited tourist attractions of the city. Moreover, the historic, aesthetic and cultural importance of this structure and those immediately around it, more than justifies its reputation as an awe-inspiring place.

The Qutub Minar complex stands at the core of an early fortified city of Delhi—Lal Kot. This name literally means 'red fortress', due to the red bricks out of which the upper part of the walls is built. The lower part of the walls is built of stone rubble. Lal Kot was built around the middle of the eleventh century by Anangpal II of the Tomar dynasty. The Tomars were one of the many ruling clans of north India in the early medieval period that were collectively known as Rajputs.

In the middle of the twelfth century, Delhi came under the rule of the Chauhans, another Rajput clan, which ruled from Ajmer. It appears that under the Chauhans, the original Lal Kot was expanded, though some historians credit the expansion to later rulers. A new line of fortifications was built towards the north and east of Lal Kot, which increased the earlier perimeter of 3.6 kms to about 8 kms. The resulting fort is now popularly known as 'Qila Rai Pithora', after Prithviraj Chauhan, the last Chauhan ruler.

In 1192, the Chauhans were overthrown by a conqueror from Afghanistan—Mohammad Ghori. The Indian territories of Ghori were controlled by his generals who were mostly ethnic Turks who came from Central Asia. They were followers of Islam and brought to India an Islamicate culture and new techniques in building and ornamentation. From this time, Delhi became the capital of a substantial kingdom and soon an empire, whereas under the Rajputs it had been at best a city of regional importance. Most of the remains seen within the Qutub Minar complex date from this early period of the history of Turk rule, known as the Delhi Sultanate.

As one approaches the Qutub Minar complex, the road climbs up to a slight rise, which tells us something important about the location of Lal Kot/Qila Rai Pithora. The site is a small rocky outcrop that is a part of the northern limits of a very old and eroded mountain range—the Aravalis. This location—on a height—was of strategic significance for the fort.

The Walk

You enter the complex through an arch with a scalloped edge, and as you come through it, you see a similar one ahead. These were the two entrances to a **late Mughal sarai complex**[1]. This sarai is one of the more recent buildings in the complex, dating from the eighteenth century. It would originally have consisted of a large enclosure entered through the two gates—both made of thin bricks typical of the late Mughal period—with an open space in the middle. Most of the enclosing walls have disappeared, but a section (on your right as you enter) remains, where you can see a row of arches leading into rooms to house travellers. Within the sarai there is also a **mosque**[2] from the same period, which was built for the convenience of the travellers who used the sarai. It is built of rubble and plaster, and is surmounted by three bulbous domes, characteristic of the late Mughals. It is still in use.

Attached to the northern wall of the sarai is an enclosed **late Mughal garden**[3]. The enclosing wall has at each corner a bastion surmounted by a domed chhatri, or kiosk. Midway in the west wall there is a ruined pavilion. The garden itself has considerably changed and is not representative of what the original Mughal garden would have been.

By the eighteenth century, the capital of the empire had shifted far northwards (to what is now called Old Delhi) and so had much of the population. But people still visited Mehrauli for recreation, for pilgrimage to the shrine of Qutubuddin Bakhtiyar Kaki or even while enroute to the neighbouring town of Gurgaon. The sarai and its attached structures would have provided a convenient resting place among beautiful surroundings.

Move beyond the sarai in the direction of the Qutub Minar. Just beyond the gate of the sarai, you will see a platform with graves and a small wall mosque. This is one of several late Mughal burial site scattered about the complex, some with attached wall mosques.

Now go right up the path to the **Quwwat-ul-Islam Masjid**[4]. The name literally means the 'power of Islam mosque', but this name appears to be a much later one. It was originally known simply as the Jami Masjid or the congregational mosque. This is one of the earliest mosques in India. The core of it was built in 1192 on the orders of Qutubuddin Aibak, immediately after the conquest of Delhi. Aibak started out as

Look out for the bright green parakeets that like to perch on the buildings.

the slave and general of Mohammad Ghori, the ruler who conquered North India, but in time became the independent ruler of many of Ghori's North Indian territories. Aibak and the other early rulers of what became the Delhi Sultanate are popularly known as 'slave sultans', so called because many of them were originally slaves, purchased when young and raised to be very competent soldiers and administrators.

This is a large congregational mosque, built over different phases. As you stand before the eastern doorway, look at some of its distinctive features. The structure of the arch itself is quite intriguing. It has the shape of an arch but not in its architectural form. A true arch consists of a number of stone blocks arranged in a semicircular formation so that the weight of the masonry above compresses each stone against its neighbour and distributes the weight fairly equally between them. The arch of this doorway is different as it is built on trabeate principles. This means that the shape of an arch has been achieved by placing stones flat, one on top of the other, instead of side by side. Each stone projects out a little further than the one below it, until the gap at the top is closed. An arch made in this way is not as strong as a true arch and therefore the builders thought it prudent to add a lintel—a horizontal beam support—below the arch.

Before the establishment of the Delhi Sultanate, Indians had not used the arch in construction. Arcuate construction that is based on arch-making principles was first used in ancient Mesopotamia and later popularized by the Romans. The Turk soldiers, newly arrived in Delhi, who commissioned the mosque, were familiar with arches in their homelands, but were not builders themselves. It seems that they were able to tell Indian builders what the shape of an arch looked like, but could not explain its structural distinctiveness.

The Indian builders realized that the 'false arch' which they were building was not very strong, so they placed a lintel under it, to give support for the doorway. Look closely at the slab between the arch and the lintel. It has an inscription in the Persian language, telling us that this mosque was built by Aibak on the orders of his master Mohammad Ghori. Below this there is some decorative carving in a horizontal band. In the middle of this decorative horizontal band, you will see a somewhat fierce face. This is a 'kirtimukha', used in traditional Indian temples, and even homes, to keep away the evil eye. Evidently the Indian builders believed that it was required even for a Muslim place of worship.

'This fort was conquered and this Jami Masjid built in the year 587 (hijri) by the Amir, the great and glorious commander of the army, Qutubuddin Aibak Sultani, may God strengthen his helpers.'—Inscription on the lintel of the eastern gate of the mosque.

After you go through the doorway, look overhead and you will see the inside of a small dome. A proper dome would of course have been based on a true arch, so this one is not a true dome. It was built by stacking concentric rings of stones until the gap on the top was closed. The effect on the outside is of a wide conical shape rather than a proper round dome.

You will notice that you are now at one end of a large courtyard. This courtyard is the main body of the mosque. Around much of the perimeter runs a pillared colonnade. Most of the pillars are elaborately carved, and on close inspection, one can see many human, animal and divine figures. Such sculpture seems out of place within a mosque since depiction of human or animal figures is unacceptable to orthodox Islam and akin to idolatry. The answer to this mystery lies in the fact that these are reused materials from twenty-seven Hindu and Jain temples that had stood in the vicinity and were mostly destroyed by the invading Turks as an act of war. The aim of this destruction was to discredit the previous regime, which had probably built most of these temples. Some other temples, which were shrines revered by the common people were spared. Two of these lie elsewhere in Mehrauli—the Dadabari Jain Mandir and the Jog Maya temple.

Walking forward into the courtyard, you will see some graves, which are not inscribed but probably belong to individuals associated with the mosque. A little further on, you will come to the **Iron Pillar**[5], which is the oldest structure in the complex. It dates back to the fourth century and was erected to commemorate the victories of Chandragupta II, one of the Gupta dynasty of kings who ruled over a major empire at the time. The pillar is made of very pure cast iron and is remarkable from a metallurgical point of view because it has continued to be virtually free of rust through the centuries.

'By him, the king...having the name of Chandra and a beauty of countenance resembling the full moon...this lofty standard of the divine Vishnu was set up.'—Gupta inscription on the Iron Pillar.

Some historians believe that the Iron Pillar was originally located somewhere else, as the original inscription talks of it being placed on top of a hill. One of the other inscriptions on the pillar dates from the eleventh century and refers to the Tomar king, Anangpal. A popular tradition associated with the pillar is to be found in the Rajasthani epic, *Prithviraj Raso*. This story is called the 'Kili Dhili Katha' or 'the tale of the loose nail'. It says that Anangpal was told by a holy man that the pillar was driven into the hood of Vasuki, the serpent king, who supports the earth from below. It was also prophesied that Anangpal's kingdom would survive as long as the pillar remained firm in the ground. Anangpal unwisely insisted on uprooting the pillar to verify this truth, which resulted in the pillar permanently becoming loose or *dhili*. Simultaneously of course Anangpal's rule also became unstable. According to this story, the name of Delhi—originally Dhilli, has its origins in the *dhili kili* or loose nail.

Just beyond the Iron Pillar, at the western end of the courtyard, is a tall and imposing **screen of arches**[6], parts of which have fallen down. This screen is placed so that while facing it, the worshipper faces west, the direction of Mecca, which a Muslim must face while praying. The arches of this screen too are not true arches and this is the main reason for their collapse. Though the basic structure is built of rubble masonry, the surface of the arches is decorated with beautifully carved sandstone in variegated colours. The pattern contains many captivating elements. It was the work of Indian stone carvers, who tried to create what the Turk soldiers wanted the mosque to look like. They incorporated inscriptions in the Naskh style of Arabic script, one of which tells us that this screen was built in 1198. Interwoven with the script is a design of naturalistic creepers bearing lotus buds—an Indian touch.

They also included other motifs that were very Indian, and were inspired by the temples that these builders had been constructing for generations. Typically, temple doorways were flanked by images of the river goddesses, Ganga and Yamuna. Though Islam did not permit the carving of such images, they carved the symbols of these rivers, in the form of vertical panels, on the arches. The scroll-like pattern symbolizes Ganga, as it is a representation of the tail of the makara, or crocodile, which is her vehicle. The wave-like pattern represents Yamuna. Towards the base of the structure you can see, carved in stone, the shape of a kalash, a Hindu ritual vessel.

You can leave the main courtyard of the mosque through the north gate (it is best to orient yourself through the screen of arches, which is at the western end of the courtyard. This will make it easier to navigate through the enclosure), which brings you to **Iltutmish's extension**[7]. This part of the mosque, of which not much remains, was built in 1230 by the then ruler Shamsuddin Iltutmish. Iltutmish had been Qutubuddin Aibak's slave, and on the latter's death had managed to assert his dominance not only in opposition to other the slaves and generals of Aibak, but also his son. To further legitimise his position, he married Aibak's daughter. He ruled from 1211 to 1236. If you look at the screen here, in scale and treatment, it is quite similar to the one inside the courtyard, though there are important differences. For one, a fairly uniform colour of red sandstone has been used, which tells us that the Sultanate could now command the resources of larger territories to procure better construction materials.

Secondly, the carved motifs now are not naturalistic but stylized and geometrical. In the intervening three decades, between 1198, when the older part of the screen was built, and when this part was constructed in 1230, the 'imported' elements of design had come to be better understood by the craftsmen creating the structure. You can see sophisticated calligraphy in the inscriptions, which suggests that calligraphers and other artists from Central Asia were now settled in Delhi, contributing to the design. It is a curious fact however, that the true arch was still not used in construction, though no doubt among the immigrants from Central Asia in Delhi, there would by now also be architects and builders. A possible explanation is that the building trade was firmly in the hands of the Indian master builders and masons, and they were not yet convinced of the soundness of the new technology, and therefore reluctant to adopt it. The continuing importance of the Indian hand in the construction is evident in the motifs of the lotus and the kalash, which were still used, and in fact, from now on became fairly constant features of Sultanate architecture.

Immediately north-west of this screen is the **tomb of Iltutmish**[8] built probably after the sultan's death in 1236, or possibly during his own lifetime. It consists of a square chamber that is open to the sky. A dome was probably never built because the builders, as has been noted before, were not confident enough to build a large dome without the use of arcuate principles. Inside, the surface of the walls is covered in sandstone, carved in a style similar to that of the screen placed outside, with a profusion of carving. The western wall, which indicates the direction of prayer, has no opening and instead has a closed arch, richly decorated with carved marble. This is the oldest building in Delhi to use a combination of red sandstone and white marble, which we can see in so much of the historic architecture of Delhi. Just outside the northern doorway, one can see an opening in the ground, which leads down to the grave chamber. While the actual grave is in the ground beneath the tomb structure, a large marble cenotaph stands in the middle of the chamber.

Before leaving this part of the complex look to the northeast of Iltutmish's tomb. You will see a large circular structure built of stone rubble masonry. This is the **Alai Minar**[9], built by the emperor, Alauddin Khalji, who ruled between 1296 and 1316. Around 1310, Alauddin commissioned a major expansion of the Jami masjid. The colonnades of that expansion towards the north have now disappeared, except for the foundations, but the remains of a partly built enormous pillar can still be seen. This pillar was designed to be twice as big as the Qutub Minar, but its construction was abandoned after the death of the emperor.

Going back to the tomb of Iltutmish, go through its southern doorway. A pathway leading through an open stretch will lead you to a group of plain but elegant buildings in grey stone. This is the **madrasa of Alauddin Khalji**[10], dating to the early fourteenth century. The buildings are constructed from dressed grey quartzite, without any decorative carving.

Note the perfectly formed arches. The stones lining each arch lie side by side against each other, and a keystone at the top holds the structure together. It is evident that by this time Indian builders had adopted the technique of building arches. The rooms are arranged on three sides around a grassy court, and halfway down the middle wing. About halfway down the latter wing is a large room believed to be the **tomb of Alauddin**[11], though no trace of the original cenotaph now remains in it.

From the madrasa one gets a good view of the most prominent building of the complex—the **Qutub Minar**[12]. Minars or towers are frequently found attached to mosques and they serve to provide an elevated place from where the faithful can be called to prayer. Nominally this too is such a tower (called a maznah), but practically speaking, even if the muezzin had breath left after climbing up to its top to give the azan or call to prayer, it would have been difficult to hear it. At 72.5 m high, the Qutub Minar is definitely overdone as a maznah. It is however a prominent and unmistakable political statement. It was consciously designed to be a symbol of the Turk conquest of north India.

'Om! Hail, during the victorious reign of the illustrious Suratarana Pherojsahi [Sultan Firozshah] in the Samvat year 1426, the fifth day of the bright half of Phalguna on Friday, the minar was renovated. The work was completed by the grace of Sri Visvakarma.'—Sanskrit inscription on the fifth storey of the Qutub Minar.

The first storey of the Qutub Minar was built during the reign of Qutubuddin Aibak (1206-11) and the rest under Iltutmish (1211-36). The name 'Qutub' suggests many different things. It could have been named after the revered Sufi saint, Qutubuddin Bakhtiyar Kaki, who at this time lived in the vicinity. The word 'Qutub' literally means the

Pole Star, around which the heavens revolve. This would also underline the importance of the structure and the new political power it stood for. Finally the name also brings to mind Qutubuddin Aibak, who commissioned it.

Decoration on the minar consists of finely carved sandstone and some marble. The tower is divided into five storeys, each of which is topped by a projecting balcony, the underside of which is richly carved. Bands of calligraphy encircle each storey and are embellished in the same style that is found on the screen of arches in the Quwwat-ul-lslam mosque. The inscriptions consist of verses from the Quran as well as the history of the construction and repairs of the structure. For instance on the fifth storey, there is a Persian inscription that reads 'this minar was injured by lightning in the year 770 (hijri). By the Divine grace, Firoz Sultan, who is exalted by the favour of the most Holy, built this portion of the edifice with care. May the inscrutable Creator preserve it from all calamities.' There is also a Sanskrit inscription, written by the master builders who executed the repairs. It invokes the blessings of Lord Vishvakarma, the God of architects, on the work.

The Qutub Minar has seen many rounds of repairs.

Originally, the tower consisted of only four storeys. Lightning struck it in 1368, damaging it. The ruling emperor, Firoz Shah Tughlaq, who is known to have repaired many other buildings around the city, ordered it to be repaired. (He genuinely seems to have been interested in buildings for their own sake rather than as relics of previous rulers or dynasties.) In the process certain fundamental alterations were made to the structure. The fourth and final storey was rebuilt as two storeys and decorated using marble. Another round of repairs were executed in 1503 and both these events are recorded in the inscriptions on the minar. The artists, Thomas and William Daniell, who saw the tower in 1789, have depicted it with a small pavilion on top, which was destroyed some years later, probably by an earthquake that occurred in 1803.

In the late 1820s, when Delhi was under the rule of the British East India Company, Major Smith, an army engineer was assigned to carry out repairs. Unfortunately many of the facing stones that had fallen down were put back without regard for the original order, so that the inscriptions became unreadable. Major Smith also added a balustrade in the Gothic style to the projecting balconies. It stands out as it is in a different shade of stone and of an incongruous design. A new cupola was placed on top of the tower which was widely condemned and finally taken down in 1848.

To the south of the Qutub Minar, lies the colonnade that was a part of Iltutmish's extension to the mosque. The pillars here are not reused from earlier structures but were purpose-built. They are much plainer than the carved temple pillars in the core of the mosque.

Attached to the colonnade is a large red sandstone building which is known as the **Alai Darwaza**[13], a gateway built by Alauddin Khalji in 1311. This gateway would have provided access to the mosque and minar from the south, where the

'Lord of the kings of the world, the king of Darius-like splendour, the Sultan of perfect justice and abundant benevolence, the emperor whose orders are universally obeyed.'—Praises of Alauddin inscribed on the Alai Darwaza.

population was concentrated at that time. The structure consists of a large square room with four arched doorways on each side, and covered by a large dome. The arches as well as the dome are perfectly formed. The surface decoration consists of carved marble and sandstone. The inscriptions are mainly praises of Alauddin Khalji, who is referred to, among other grandiose epithets, as a 'second Alexander'. The motifs are geometric and harmonious. A distinctive feature is the horseshoe-shaped arches with lotus buds forming a fringe along the edge. The northern arch is smaller than the others and of a different design. Another notable feature is the dome, which has an opening in the top that is capped by another small white marble dome. The gateway represents a sophisticated stage in the coming together of indigenous and imported features to create a unique composite, medieval Indian style of architecture, often called Indo-Islamic.

Going through the eastern arch of the Alai Darwaza, you will come to the **tomb of Imam Zamin**[14]. Imam Zamin, who died in 1539, built this tomb in his lifetime. He probably held some important official position in connection with the congregational mosque, though not much is known about him. The tomb is in the form of a pavilion with stone lattice screens for walls. Polished white limestone plaster covers many of the surfaces of the building. The grave of Imam Zamin, which is within, is still revered. Look at the finial on top of the dome, as well as the partly damaged finial on top of the Alai Darwaza. These were modelled on finials typical of Indian temples.

Step out through the doorway which leads eastwards

off the platform on which the tomb of Imam Zamin stands. Before you is a stretch of lawn, at one end of which stands the red sandstone structure known as **Major Smith's folly**[15]. When Major Smith carried out repairs to the Qutub Minar in the 1820s, he designed this pavilion and placed it on top. A wooden pergola in a Chinese style was placed over this, and over that was a flagstaff. The wooden portion was soon after destroyed by lightning, and later this pavilion was removed and placed here, at some distance from the minar.

After you exit the gate of the Qutub Minar complex, towards your left you will see a **stepped square structure**[16], somewhat like a pyramid. A little further, to your right, is a similar **circular stepped structure**[17]. These curious constructions date from the 1840s and were commissioned by Thomas Metcalfe, the highest British administrative official in Delhi at the time. He used to visit Mehrauli occasionally and lived in a tomb that he had converted into a home. He built these 'false ruins' as a picturesque addition to his view, in the typically English tradition of constructing 'follies' which were meant to resemble exotic ruins.

2

TUGHLAQABAD

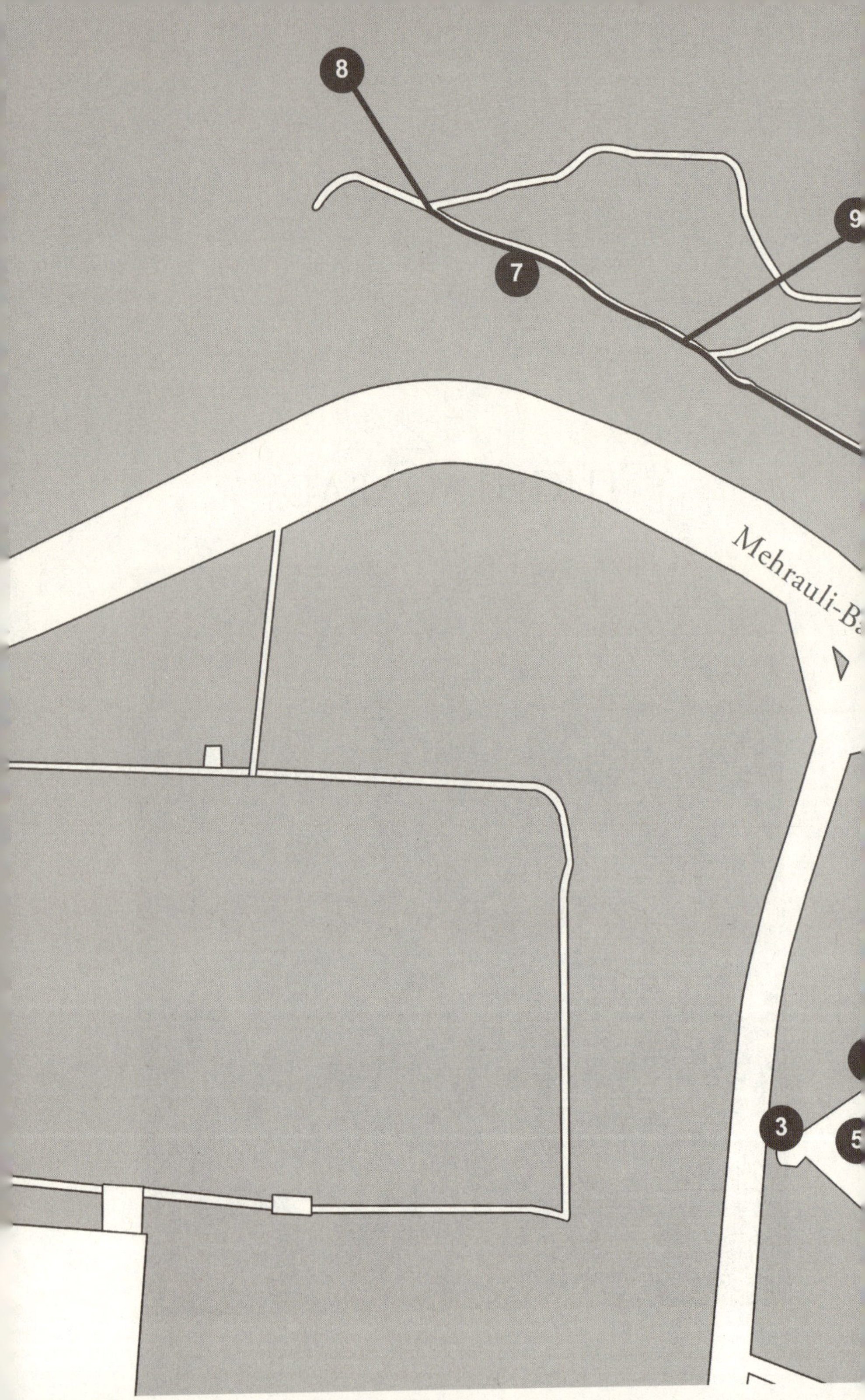
8
7
9
Mehrauli-Ba
3
5

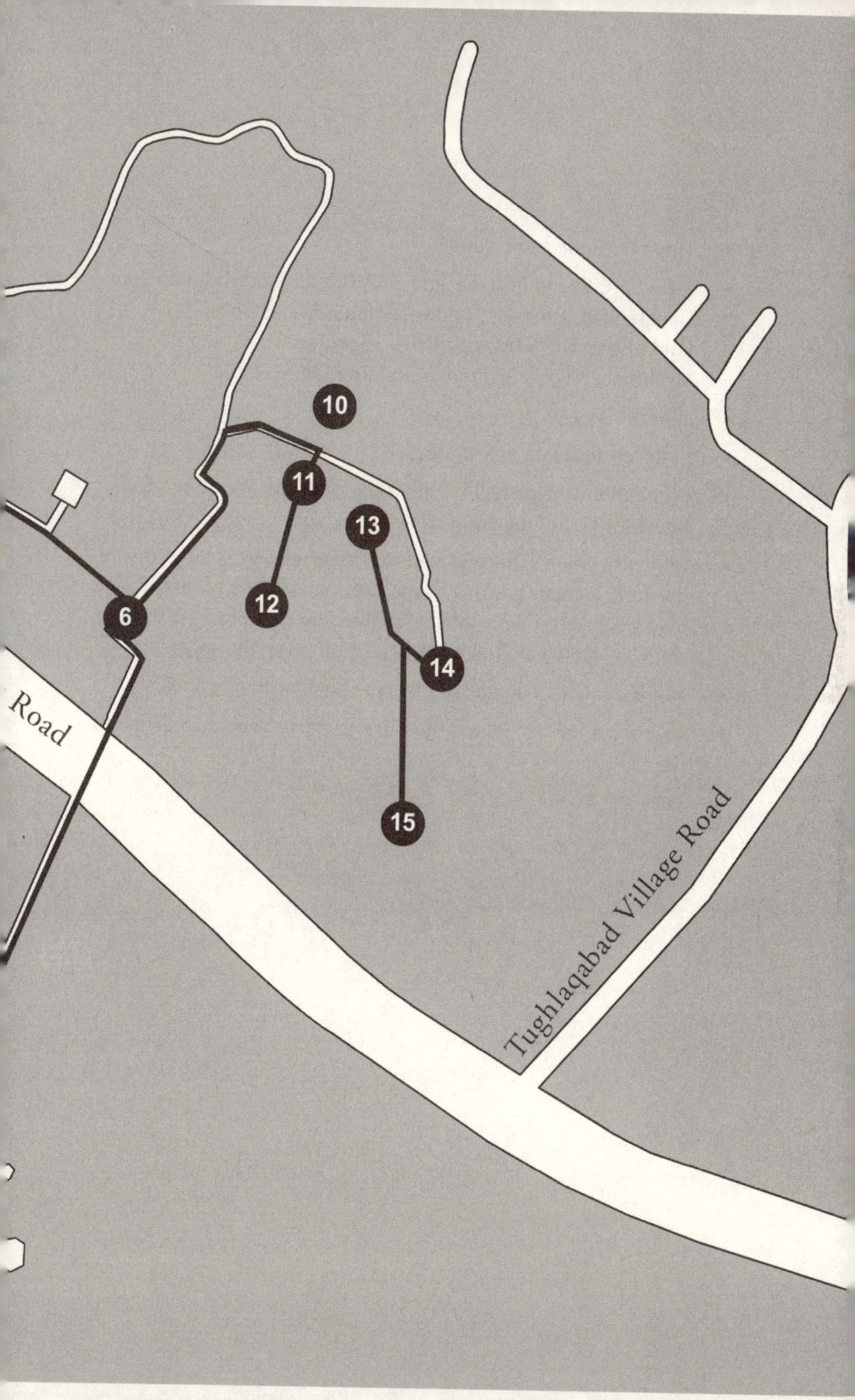

10
11
12
13
14
15
6
Road
Tughlaqabad Village Road

- Timings: Sunrise to sunset.
- Tickets: Citizens of India and SAARC countries (Afghanistan, Bangladesh, Bhutan, Maldives, Nepal, Pakistan and Sri Lanka) and BIMSTEC countries (Bangladesh, Bhutan, Myanmar, Nepal, Sri Lanka and Thailand): Rs 20
- Others: Rs 250
- Children up to 15 years old: free
- Highlights: Ghiyasuddin Tughlaq's tomb, palace ruins, Burj Mandal (for an abbreviated walk).
- Difficulty Level: There is considerable uneven ground inside the fort, including a few moderate inclines. Some areas may be covered with thorny bushes, so it is prudent to wear sensible footwear and garments that cover the legs.
- Metro Station: Tughlaqabad, on the Violet line, 4 kms.
- Amenities: None. Please be sure to carry your own drinking water.
- Parking: At the site.

FORT IN THE WILDERNESS

TUGHLAQABAD IS A truly amazing place. The fortress walls are taller and more formidable than any other in Delhi. For a city that has more than its fair share of forts, this is saying something. When you enter the fort, there are further walls, bastions and picturesque ruins of what was once an imperial capital city.

The context of this monumental construction is worth recounting. In the early years of the fourteenth century, the charismatic emperor, Alauddin Khalji, was on the throne of the Delhi Sultanate. He managed to not only extend the empire to the central and southern parts of India, but was also able to fend off the Mongols, who repeatedly attacked north India, on occasion coming right up to Delhi. In keeping the Mongols at bay, an important part was played by Alauddin's general Ghazi Malik, who had spent the major part of his career at the frontier, fighting the Mongols.

'One day as he stood before the Sultan Qutb-al-Din he said to him "O master of the world, it were fitting that a city should be built here." The Sultan replied to him ironically, "When you are Sultan, build it." It came to pass by the decree of God that he became Sultan, so he built it and called it by his own name.'

—Ibn Batuta

The death of Alauddin in 1316 was followed by a period of turbulence for the Khalji dynasty. A series of weak rulers came to the throne and were unceremoniously dispatched in palace coups, until an individual called Khusro Khan usurped the throne and put to death all potential heirs of the Khaljis. Khusro Khan was not entirely popular and in 1320, Ghazi Malik, who had managed to hold on to the province of Multan on his own, defeated Khan in battle. Historians of that time have recorded that after the defeat of Khusro Khan, since no Khalji heirs remained, the nobles decided to put Ghazi Malik on the throne, and he became emperor with the title Ghiyasuddin Tughlaq.

Though he ruled for a very short time, till his death in 1325, he managed to commission and probably see the completion of this massive project. The location of the fort, some 7 kms east of the earlier cities of Lal Kot and Siri, was entirely dictated by strategic concerns. To Ghiyasuddin, the possibility of Mongol invasions was an ever-present threat. And so this rocky outcrop was picked because it was surrounded by ravines on the north, east and west, and bounded on the south by a flat plain, which could be turned into a vast lake by carefully blocking up the three rocky defiles further south.

The building of the fortress was not uncontroversial in its time. The emperor felt he was all-powerful and had no hesitation in ordering the entire labouring population of Delhi to devote their energies to this project. There were however important competing interests in Delhi. The revered and influential Sufi saint Nizamuddin Auliya was building a baoli or step well near his khanqah, much further north. Contrary to the ruler's orders, workmen continued to report for work at the saint's well, clandestinely at night. When he heard of Nizamuddin's defiance, Ghiyasuddin was out on a military campaign and is said to have sent word back that he would punish Nizamuddin on his return. Though urged by his followers to leave the city, Nizamuddin simply said *'Dehli dur ast'*, Persian for 'Delhi is yet far'.

Sure enough, Ghiyasuddin did not enter the city alive—he was killed in an accident when a pavilion, constructed for his reception under the orders of his son Mohammad Tughlaq, collapsed. There were insinuations (reported by the traveller Ibn Batuta), that the collapse had been deliberately engineered by Mohammad who was in a hurry to be emperor. Moreover, Mohammad was a devotee of Nizamuddin. In the course of his tussle with Ghiyasuddin, the Sufi saint also cursed the new city of Tughlaqabad, saying, *'ya base gujar ya rahe ujad'* that translated means 'either it will be occupied by Gujars, [a semi-nomadic tribe], or it will be a wasteland.' Sure enough the fort was abandoned soon after Mohammad Tughlaq came to the throne and even today, a large part of it is a wilderness. The saint's prophecy, *'Dehli dur ast'*, is still a popular proverb which means something like—'there's many a slip between the cup and the lip'.

The Walk

After you have bought your ticket it is best to first visit the **tomb of Ghiyasuddin Tughlaq**[1-5] on the opposite side of the road. It is approached via a causeway that originally connected it to the fort but was broken to accommodate the road. You can see that you are walking towards a small and independent fortification. In fact this is also built on a natural rise in the ground. When Tughlaqabad was built, it was felt that this rocky outcrop too needed to be fortified to prevent an advancing enemy from occupying the height. Later, Ghiyasuddin Tughlaq decided to locate his own tomb there as well.

Look at the walls of the fort. There is a pronounced slope, which makes it difficult for intruders to lean ladders against the wall to scale its height. Towards the top there are rows of arrow-slits, which enable archers standing in tiers within the fort to discharge arrows to the outside. At the very top are a row of merlons, or kanguras, as they are known in Persian. They too give an archer cover while still allowing him to shoot at the enemy. These kanguras, though picturesque, look a bit crude and is difficult to imagine how they could adequately shelter a man. As you enter through the **gateway**[1], notice that it leads to a passageway with sharp turns and twists, designed to slow down an advancing enemy.

In the roughly triangular space within, you might like to explore the edges of the enclosure first, which will give you time to admire the tomb from different angles too. At the narrow end of the triangle is a **bastion**[2] which has two openings in the floor. These are grain pits, intended to be stocked so as to last a siege. On the wall that encircles this spot, note the ledge on which the archers could stand while shooting through the arrow-slits.

Make your way along the side of the triangle opposite to where you entered. There is a covered verandah all along the wall, and a little way down, there is an opening in the floor, closed to the public, which leads to the grain pits. Further on there are two more similar-looking openings. Each of them leads to an underground passageway. One leads to the crypt under the main mausoleum, where the actual grave is located; the other goes similarly to a subsidiary mausoleum that will be described later.

At the end of the wall, there is a fairly elaborate **pillared verandah**[3] which leads into a room that is open to the sky. This, along with other pillared verandahs positioned at various points against the enclosing wall, is believed to have housed a madrasa. It was not unusual to have an institution of learning attached to a tomb. There was a precedent in the case of Alauddin Khalji's tomb and was later repeated with Firoz Shah Tughlaq's tomb.

In the final corner of the triangle is a **tomb chamber**[4] topped with a marble dome. Of the two graves within, the marble one in the centre belongs to a man; the other is a woman's. Notice how the small niches on the top let small shafts of light into the room. The inscriptions over the doorways say that the person buried here is Zafar Khan, a successful general who conquered the territory up to Lakhnauti (in Eastern India), but died at a young age. It also says that the emperor Ghiyasuddin built this tomb, known as Dar-ul-Aman or 'abode of peace', for him. Maybe the grave next to his is that of his wife.

Now come to the **main tomb**[5], in the centre of the enclosure. You can see that this has sloping sides not unlike the walls of the fortification. This however was not needed as a defensive device. In this case, it was simply an element of design that was quite common, particularly in Multan, where Ghiyasuddin had spent much of his time. A perceptible slope on outer walls, known as 'batter', became a hallmark of Tughlaq architecture and can generally be taken to identify buildings from the time of the Tughlaq dynasty.

Another feature, which was to become a characteristic of Tughlaq buildings, is the plainness of the surfaces. There is minimal carving, though the expanses of good marble show that there certainly was no skimping on materials. The use of a lot of red sandstone and marble is however unusual for Tughlaq buildings, which tended to be finished in plaster. In the use of these decorative stones, it is more like the earlier Sultanate structures such as Alauddin Khalji's Alai Darwaza in the Qutub Minar complex. Another point of similarity with that building is the lotus bud fringe along the inside of the entrance arches.

Even the mihrab is quite plain, and it is hard to say if it had some decoration originally. Anyone visiting the tomb, who wished to pray for the peace of the soul of the occupant, would know which way to face. Many tombs therefore have this mihrab, as of course do all mosques.

The centrally placed cenotaph inside is that of Ghiyasuddin. It is believed that the male tomb (identifiable by the rectangular ridge shaped 'qalamdan' on it) next to his is that of his son Mohammad Tughlaq, and the other that of Ghiyasuddin's wife, Makhduma Jahan. Mohammad Tughlaq is one of the most controversial figures in history. He has been criticized sharply by historians of his time as well as more recent historians for

'In spite of all his extraordinary liberality, the Sultan was far too free in shedding blood... Every day there are brought to the audience hall hundreds of people, chained, pinioned, and fettered, and those who are for execution...those for torture...and those for being beaten.'
—Ibn Batuta

his revolutionary schemes, which failed gloriously, causing misery and chaos. One of these was the introduction of a token currency, an idea before its time. He is also reputed to have had a quick and cruel temper.

His cousin and successor, Firoz Shah, was a much milder man. In the memoirs of his reign, it is recorded that he further embellished this tomb by installing sandalwood canopies over the graves and hanging curtains like the Kaba shrine from them. He also took measures towards some posthumous atonement on Mohammad's behalf. All the people who had been mutilated by the orders of the latter, or the heirs of those who had been killed, were approached. They were paid compensation, and in return, asked to sign deeds of forgiveness. These were then put in a box and buried at the head of the grave of Mohammad Tughlaq.

From the tomb enclosure, go back over the causeway, cross the road, and climb up to the main fortress of Tughlaqabad. You can see the wall stretching a long way on both sides. This southern wall is nearly 2.5 kms long. The other three walls are much shorter, creating a half-hexagonal shape. The total perimeter of the fort is almost 6.5 kms, and the wall in places rises more than twenty-five metres above the ground. The wall is punctuated by several bastions, curved outworks that provide a vantage point and cover for the wall itself.

As you enter through the **gate**[6] you will get an idea of the vast size of the space within. This however is not the best point to get a bird's-eye view—you have to wait a bit for that. For now, turn left and walk along the wall for a bit. Notice the rooms that make up the bastions, from where archers could command a view of the surrounding area. You can climb up into them, and walk along the wall some distance. Climb back to ground level and continue.

You will soon come to a large **reservoir**[7]. It is built on the same principle as baolis or step wells, with steps leading down to the level of the water. At the top there was also provision for drawing the water up via a pulley—the stone supports can still be seen at the edge. The baoli/reservoir has no water now, and probably had little water at any time. Groundwater at such a height would have been difficult to reach, particularly in such stony ground. It might have been possible to store some rainwater, but maybe never enough.

Climb out and continue a bit further in the same direction. You will soon come to a broad, stone-paved carriageway that slopes down to another gate on the left. Don't take that, but get off the path and continue further. Just beyond is a slightly raised mound-shaped patch of land. Go up it but with care because the mouths of many deep pits dot the area. These, lined with stone walls, are most likely **grain pits**[8] for enough stock to withstand a siege. Grain is best stored away from light, damp and air, so these were the ideal storage.

Walk back the way you came till on your left you see some ruined buildings, extending quite a way inside the fort. These appear to be various **public buildings**[9], and some of them were part of a palace with rather large grand halls.

Pick your way through these ruins. One room has a pool sunk in the floor; another large hall has the remains of pillar bases. Along the top of some walls are brackets, which once supported a chhajja that has now disappeared. They are all built of stone and the surface plaster has in most places fallen off. Where it still exists it is quite black, but here and there you can see some incised ornamentation.

Keep a lookout for the wildlife inside the fort. There are birds, including the pretty green bee-eater, and nilgai or blue bull, a large blue-grey antelope-like creature.

These buildings occupy a very large area and there always seems to be one more interesting structure looming ahead; explore as much as your energy and inclination will allow. The next destination is the high citadel to the east, past the gate through which you entered. Its large round bastions dominate the skyline in that direction. If you have gone quite far north in your explorations, you can approach it from the north too. When you get close you will walk up a formal pathway, probably designed for ceremonial processions by the emperor and his entourage. Alternately you can go back to the entrance gate, go past it, and up the steps to the citadel. This is the way the emperor would have entered after a trip out of the city.

The citadel was probably the more private living and working area for the emperor, and he went to the palace below only for public appearances and court. As you go through the entrance within the walled citadel, on your left is a jumble of **ruins**[10], mostly broken walls of small rooms. These date from the Mughal period, as is evident from certain typical architectural features such as cusped or scalloped arches and numerous small niches in the walls. This was evidently a small but reasonably prosperous settlement that grew up here long after the capital city of Tughlaqabad had been abandoned.

On the other side of the entrance to the citadel is a small **mosque**[11]. If your idea of a mosque is a grand, elaborately ornamented edifice, it is easy to miss this squat blackened building. It looks like a simple pillared verandah with arches, but if you stand facing it, you are facing Mecca, and nothing more is required of a mosque. It has certain stylistic features that mark it out as a Mughal building—notably its vaulted bangla or 'Bengal' roof, modelled on reed huts with curved roofs found in rural Bengal. The Mughal buildings in this part of the fort date from the late sixteenth and early seventeenth centuries. During this time, a settlement existed here, and some of the structures in the fort were commissioned by Sheikh Farid, the bakshi or the paymaster of the army of the Mughal emperor Jahangir. Sheikh Farid was also the founder of Faridabad.

From behind the mosque a path leads south to another large **reservoir**[12]. In size and construction this is comparable to the reservoir outside. It was probably thought prudent to supply the inner citadel with an independent water supply, just in case it ever had to hold out against forces outside.

Roughly parallel to the path leading from the mosque to the reservoir, and best accessed from near the mosque, is long row of curious **underground chambers**[13] arranged on either side of a gallery. Though regular openings overhead let in air and light, it is too dark to really see into the underground rooms. It is possible that these were storerooms of some sort, or maybe since they were cool, they were converted into living quarters during the hot weather.

If you choose not to enter the underground chambers, you can take the path to the left which goes up to a building on a height, quite close to the row of chambers. If you go through the chambers you can access this from the other side. Climb up the steps and you will emerge on the flat top of a building known as **Burj Mandal**[14], but which has also been referred to as Jahan-numa or 'that which shows you the world'. The name is apt to an extent because this gives probably the best view of Tughlaqabad. Look back over the fortress. You will notice that the citadel you are within is a walled space set in the south-eastern comer of the fort. On your left, where you saw the palaces and grain pits, is another larger walled area. Both are in turn set within the much larger, walled city of Tughlaqabad. Much of it is green wilderness, and you can make out the long line of the wall that forms its limits. Close to the citadel, to its right, is a space covered with buildings. This is Tughlaqabad village, one of Delhi's many 'urban villages'!

To the south of Burj Mandal, against the outer wall is an easy-to-miss opening leading into a **secret passage**[15]. Though it is not wise to try and explore it, excavations have revealed it to be complete with storage chambers and a disguised exit. Though many forts are reputed to have secret passages leading to other cities and forts, this is probably the only one that has definitely been found in Delhi.

3

SATPULA AND KHIRKI

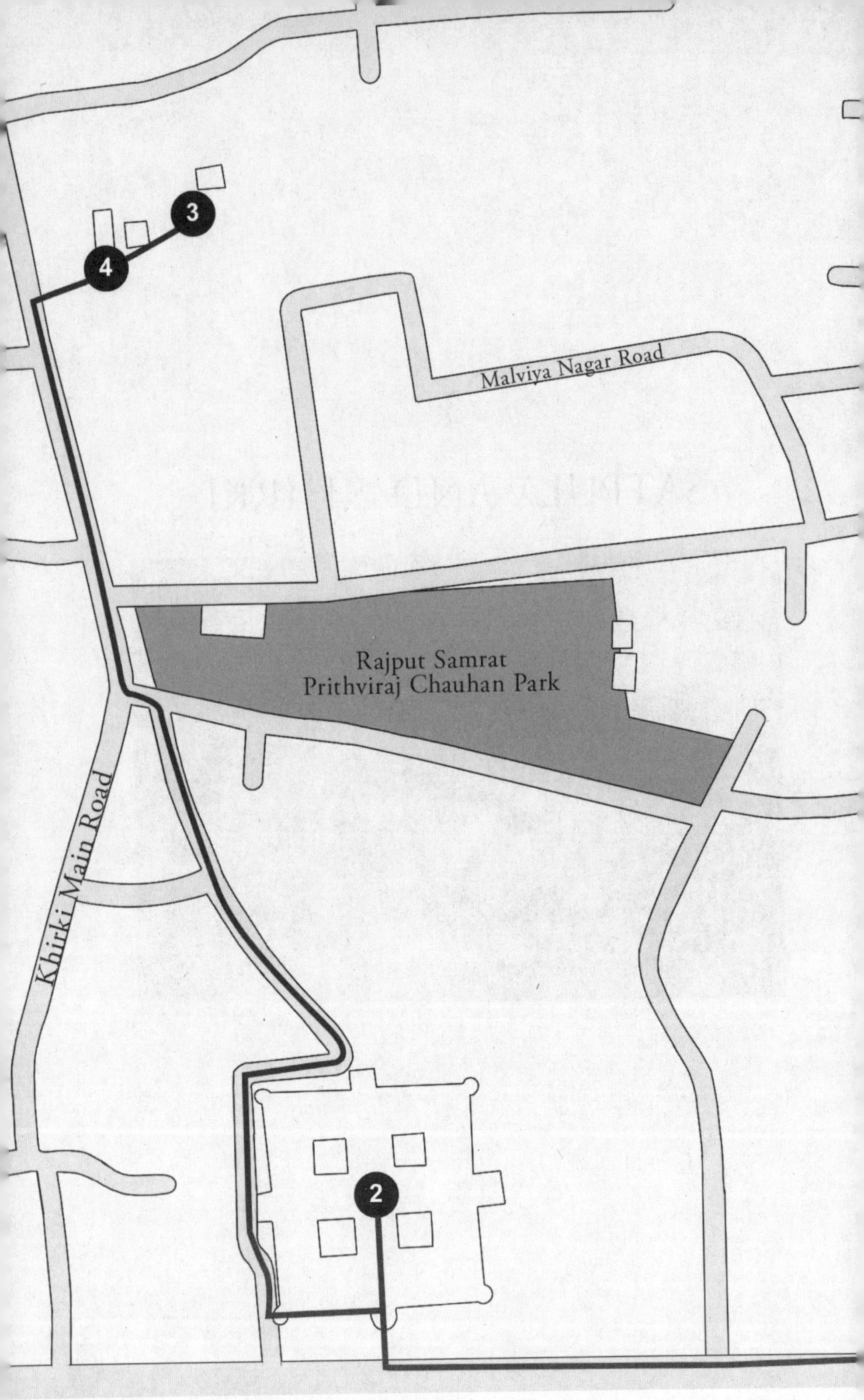
3
4
Malviya Nagar Road
Rajput Samrat
Prithviraj Chauhan Park
Khirki Main Road
2

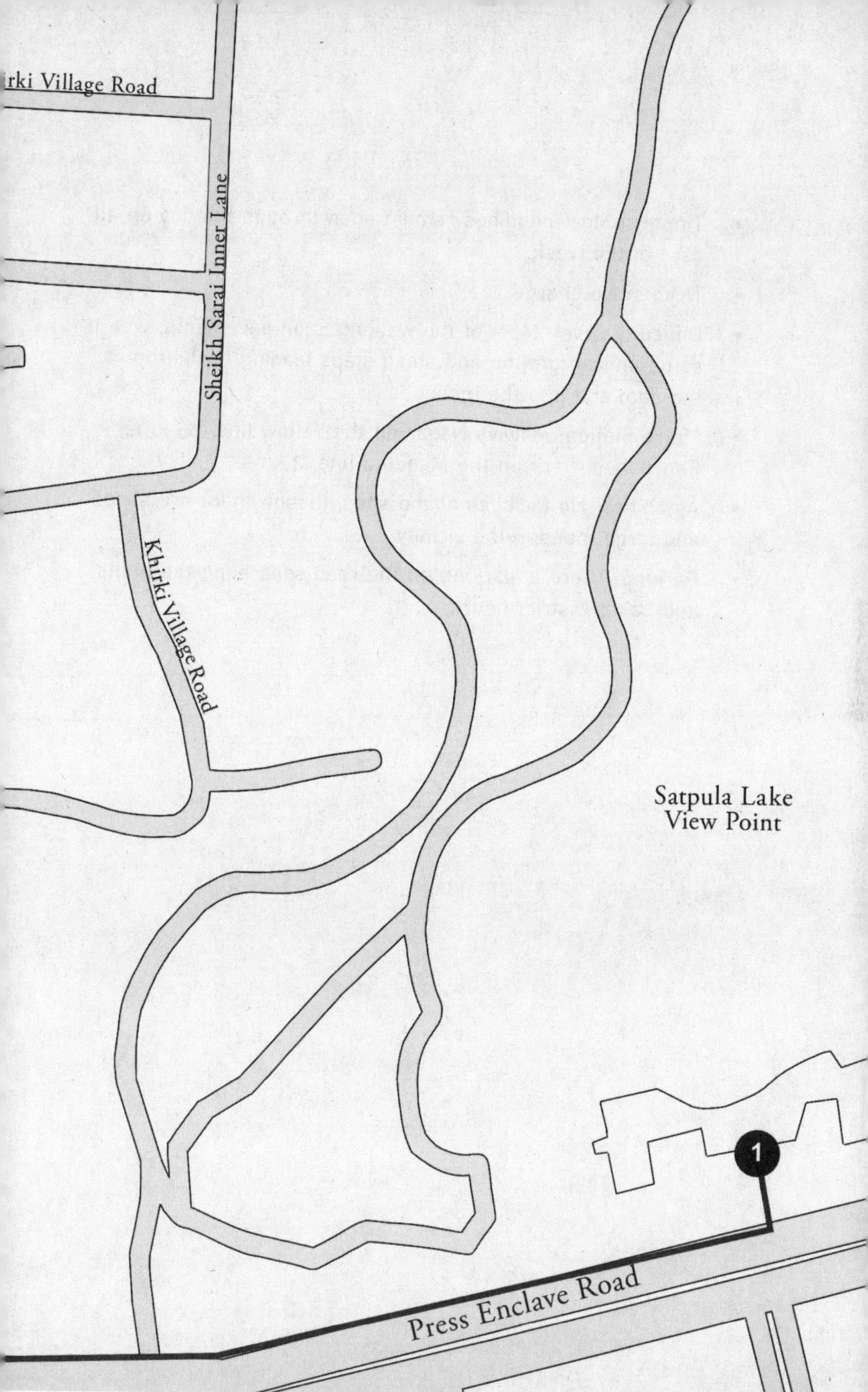

Khirki Village Road
Sheikh Sarai Inner Lane
Khirki Village Road
Satpula Lake View Point
1
Press Enclave Road

- Timings: Most buildings remain open through the day on all days of the week.
- Tickets: No charge.
- Difficulty Level: Most of the walking is on pavements, with some uneven ground and steep steps leading to the top of the dam and into the mosque.
- Metro Station: Malviya Nagar on the Yellow line, 1.5 kms; Panchsheel Park on the Magenta line, 2 kms.
- Amenities: No facilities at the sites, though there are shops and large malls in the vicinity.
- Parking: There is parking on the road separating the malls and Saket District Court.

JAHANPANAH

THE BUILDINGS IN this area are mostly the remains of the fourteenth-century city of Jahanpanah, founded by Mohammad Tughlaq. The Tughlaq dynasty came into power at a time when the Mongol Empire was a major threat to north India. The first Tughlaq emperor, Ghiyasuddin, had in fact spent most of his previous career as an army commander under the Khaljis, fighting against the Mongols, who on occasion came up as far as Delhi. Not surprisingly, a major project of Ghiyasuddin, even in his short reign from 1320-25, was the building of the imposing fortress of Tughlaqabad.

His son and successor, Mohammad (reigned 1324-51), while expanding the empire further into south India, also perceived the Mongols as a shadow and a threat constantly looming over the northern part of the country. When he came to the throne, the highest concentrations of population in Delhi were in the old fortified area of Lal Kot and Qila Rai Pithora, and in Siri, which had been fortified by Alauddin Khalji. In fact there was a considerable growth of population even outside the walls of these two areas, and the land between them had also become fairly populated. Mohammad Tughlaq felt it was wise to enclose this area within defensible walls. He therefore ordered the construction of two lengths of wall connecting Qila Rai Pithora and Siri, and in the process enclosing the area between these two. This newly enclosed area was named Jahanpanah—'the refuge of the world'. Mohammad built within it a palace complex and a large congregational mosque.

The site that is covered in this walk is the area just within the southern wall of Jahanpanah. Though the wall has now disappeared, its foundation can be discerned as a long low ridge of ground running parallel to Press Enclave road. At the western end of the road, where it runs into Aurobindo Marg, you can see the high wall of Qila Rai Pithora. Travelling eastwards on Press Enclave road, after a while the Qila Rai Pithora wall on your right comes to an end. Henceforth the foundation of the wall of Jahanpanah is on your left, but you will only be able to make it out as a raised area if you are on foot. The walk begins somewhat further east, on the same road roughly across from the Saket District Court.

The Walk

Along the line of the wall, and therefore just beside the road, you will see a large masonry structure. This is the **Satpula dam**[1], which was built across a stream that entered the wall of Jahanpanah at this point. You can see a stream of rather dirty water immediately to the east of the dam. This stream originally flowed under the dam. It was deliberately diverted sometime during British rule, to protect the dam from the effects of the water. One branch of the stream originates in the slightly hilly area to the south, another in the rocky area around Qila Rai Pithora. Just south of Nizamuddin it meets up with the Barapulla Nullah which drains into the Yamuna river. In the fourteenth century, the volume of the water in these channels was almost certainly much greater and cleaner.

In the 1340s, when Mohammad Tughlaq was building Jahanpanah, not only was Delhi threatened by the Mongols,

but a series of famines and plagues had caused discontent among the population. The need to protect habitation and agriculture within a defensive wall, as well as to provide an accessible and reliable source of water for irrigation was felt greatly. Both objectives were met by the construction of Satpula. It allowed the entry of the stream into the walled area, so that its water could be used to irrigate the fields and orchards of the flat plain within. At the same time, it needed to do this in a way that would not compromise the safety of the defensive wall by allowing intruders to enter along the same route. A closer look at the construction of the dam can tell us how this was done.

The lowest part of the dam consists of seven water tunnels that span the central part of the bed of the stream. A view of these can be had by clambering down a part of the sloping side of the dry bed on the side closest to the road. These seven tunnels give the structure its name—*Sat* (seven) *pul* (bridge). On either side are two more water tunnels spanning the shallower part of the stream. Climb out and go around the other side of the structure that is the inner part of the dam where there is a fairly broad terraced area. In the part immediately above the water tunnels, you can see arches with grooves along the sides. This is where heavy sliding wooden boards would have fitted. A rope and pulley system operated from above would have been used to move them up and down. The main aim was probably to close the gap between the water and the wall. When the water level was low during dry seasons, the tunnels could have provided an easy entry into the walled city, unless the heavy wooden gates were lowered.

There were additional defensive features in the dam. On either side of the row of eleven water tunnels are solid-looking bastions. Inside each, there is a circular room surrounded by smaller rooms, which give a view of the dam and the bed of the stream through strategically placed arrow-slit. Guards would have been stationed here round the clock to keep a watch for possible intruders. In this part of the building, you can see some ornamental features too. For instance, the limestone plaster that covers the walls has been decoratively incised or carved.

From the sides of the bastions there are steps that lead up to the top. This will give you a good view of the surrounding topography. Along the narrow walkway that connects the two bastions you can also see the openings where the rope and pulley system for raising and lowering the sluice gates would have operated.

The water, which flowed from south to north, was slowed down by the dam and formed a pool just within. Though this is now dry, we can imagine its original ambience with the water and the greenery. This beautiful spot was given an additional sanctity when the Sufi saint Nasiruddin Mahmud took up residence just north of this area in the fourteenth century. Nasiruddin was the disciple of Nizamuddin Auliya, and was the last of the great saints of the Chishti 'silsila' or order. He went by the title 'Chiragh-e-Dehli' or 'the lamp of Delhi', and his shrine and the area around it is still called Chiragh Dilli. It is said that Nasiruddin used the water of the pool at Satpula to perform his ritual ablutions just before prayer, and thus sanctified the water.

Jahanpanah was soon abandoned as a capital city, as Mohammad Tughlaq's successor, Firoz Shah, built a new capital at Firozabad, in the area we now know as Firoz Shah Kotla. Satpula ceased to have a defensive importance, but it continued to be significant in its new role. For many centuries, the water of the pool was considered holy and was believed to cure many illnesses. Bathing in the water was also believed to protect against evil spirits. Till late into the nineteenth century, there used to be a big annual fair here just before Diwali, when people would come for a holy dip and even take some of the water away with them.

The rooms in the bastions were for some time also used as a school, giving the building an alternate name—the Madrasa. By the early twentieth century, the Archaeological Survey of India took it upon itself to protect and conserve the building, at which time probably the local ritual practices and social functions associated with this building were stopped.

Climbing down from the dam, and leaving the building behind, turn right and walk along the main road. You will notice that to your right, there is a slight rise in the ground, forming a ridge that runs parallel to the road. This is the remains of the city wall. Soon you will come to Khirki village, and to your right, you can glimpse a fort-like stone building set somewhat back from the road. This is the **Khirki mosque**[2].

The Khirki mosque is the most unusual mosque in Delhi and has some unique features. From the outside, the corner towers look like the bastions of a fort. The pillars on either side of each gateway remind one of the Qutub Minar (particularly those flanking the eastern entrance)—a fairly common device that was carried into later Lodi times. The heavy jalis of the windows give it a barred appearance. There is an overall suggestion of defensive architecture and it reminds us of how the Mongol invasions had coloured the view of the Tughlaq builders.

No date is to be found inscribed on the mosque or mentioned in histories of the period, so one has to make educated guesses about its possible date. It is most probable that a mosque of this size would have been built to serve a large population, which puts the date within the heyday of Jahanpanah. We do know that Mohammad Shah Tughlaq built a large congregational mosque, the Begampur mosque, in the heart of Jahanpanah, next to his own palace. He is not likely to have built another large mosque so close to the congregational mosque. It is therefore more likely that the Khirki mosque was built in Firoz Shah's reign but when Jahanpanah was still flourishing. This was probably in the early 1350s or the first few years of the emperor's reign, before the establishment of Firozabad.

The mosque is built in two storeys. The lower one consists of arched cells running all around the building, opening to the outside. On three sides of the building—north, south and east—steps lead up to the second storey, which is the mosque proper. The entrance of the mosque closest to the road is the southern one. Inside, the mosque continues to surprise. It is mostly filled with pillared arcades. There are just four open courtyards, occupying less than a fifth of the total area. Such an arrangement is unusual in India where the typical plan for a mosque is a large open courtyard. Drains slope away from the open courtyards to the edges of the building, to carry away rainwater entering the open court. There are carved brackets that support a chhajja all along the edge of the roof around each courtyard. The screen windows and the open courtyards let in some light, but the western side which is in the direction of Mecca is entirely closed and therefore particularly gloomy.

In the north-eastern corner of the building, the roof has fallen in as a result of a fire in the late eighteenth century. At that time of the fire, the building was not functioning as a mosque. Those were politically troubled times in Delhi. The Mughal Empire was weak and the city and the surroundings were prey to marauding bandits. This led the population from the surrounding villages to take shelter within the solidly built mosques and tombs of the older cities of Delhi. This happened to the Khirki mosque too, which had long ceased to be used as a place of worship—probably when the Tughlaq dynasty came to an end in the early fifteenth century. In the middle of the nineteenth century, it was reported that 134 people and 147 head of cattle were living in the mosque. The north-western corner was used to store fodder that had earlier caught fire, which led to the damage. Sometime in the second half of the nineteenth century, the local British government ordered the inhabitants to be evicted from the mosque.

Just within the eastern entrance there are steps that lead to the roof. The sight here is spectacular, as the roof is covered with domes, arranged in nine clusters of nine, and one extra dome over the middle of each of the four sides of the mosque.

Leave the mosque by the southern entrance, turn right and walk around the perimeter of the enclosure to the northern-western corner of the mosque. Here, there is a narrow lane that goes off to the left. Take this and it will eventually bring you to Khirki Main road. Turn right onto this road and walk about 250 metres. You will come to a fenced area on your right which contains some old buildings. The most prominent among these is the **tomb of Yusuf Qattal**[3].

Yusuf Qattal was a Sufi saint who died in 1526-27. (The years are usually given according to the Hijri calendar, and each year can overlap with two possible Gregorian years, unless the day and month are specified.) He probably lived in this area because he is believed to have performed ablutions at Satpula too. The tomb is an attractive structure. Notice the beautifully carved, red sandstone pillars and jalis. The design of the parapet around the roof is derived from kanguras. Here of course the merlon is only suggested in the very stylized design. Above, around the dome, there is a band decorated with blue tiles.

Inside is the grave of Yusuf Qattal that is still revered. On the western wall is the mihrab and on the panel above it, the kalima or Islamic creed is written—'There is no God but Allah, and Mohammad is his Prophet'. The script of this writing is the angular Kufic style, a particular variant of the Arabic script.

To the west of the tomb of Yusuf Qattal is a **mosque**[4] that was probably built at the same time. It has some nicely executed, though recently re-touched plasterwork, which is typical of the high quality incised plaster of the Lodi period. There are several other graves around these buildings, of persons now unknown. One of these is a ruined tomb to the south-east of Yusuf Qattal's tomb, which was originally a hexagonal pavilion, the roof of which has disappeared.

It appears that the tomb of Yusuf Qattal was built on a raised platform, but the ground level of the surrounding area rose over the centuries through the deposition of silt brought by a stream in the area. The lower levels of some of these buildings, including the mosque, were revealed when the earth was removed during conservation work some years ago.

4

HAUZ KHAS

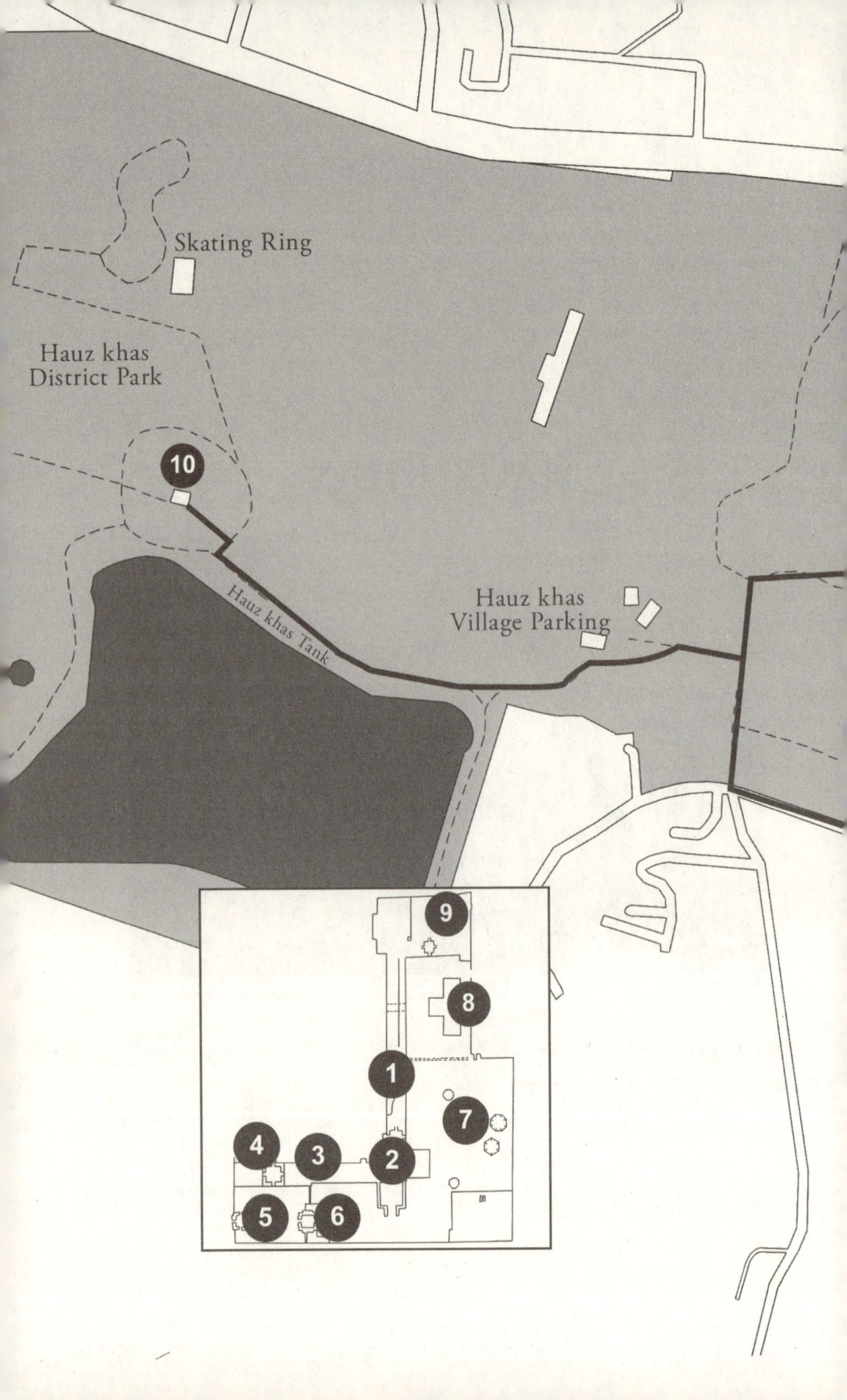
Skating Ring
Hauz khas
District Park
10
Hauz khas Tank
Hauz khas
Village Parking
9
8
1
7
4
3
2
5
6

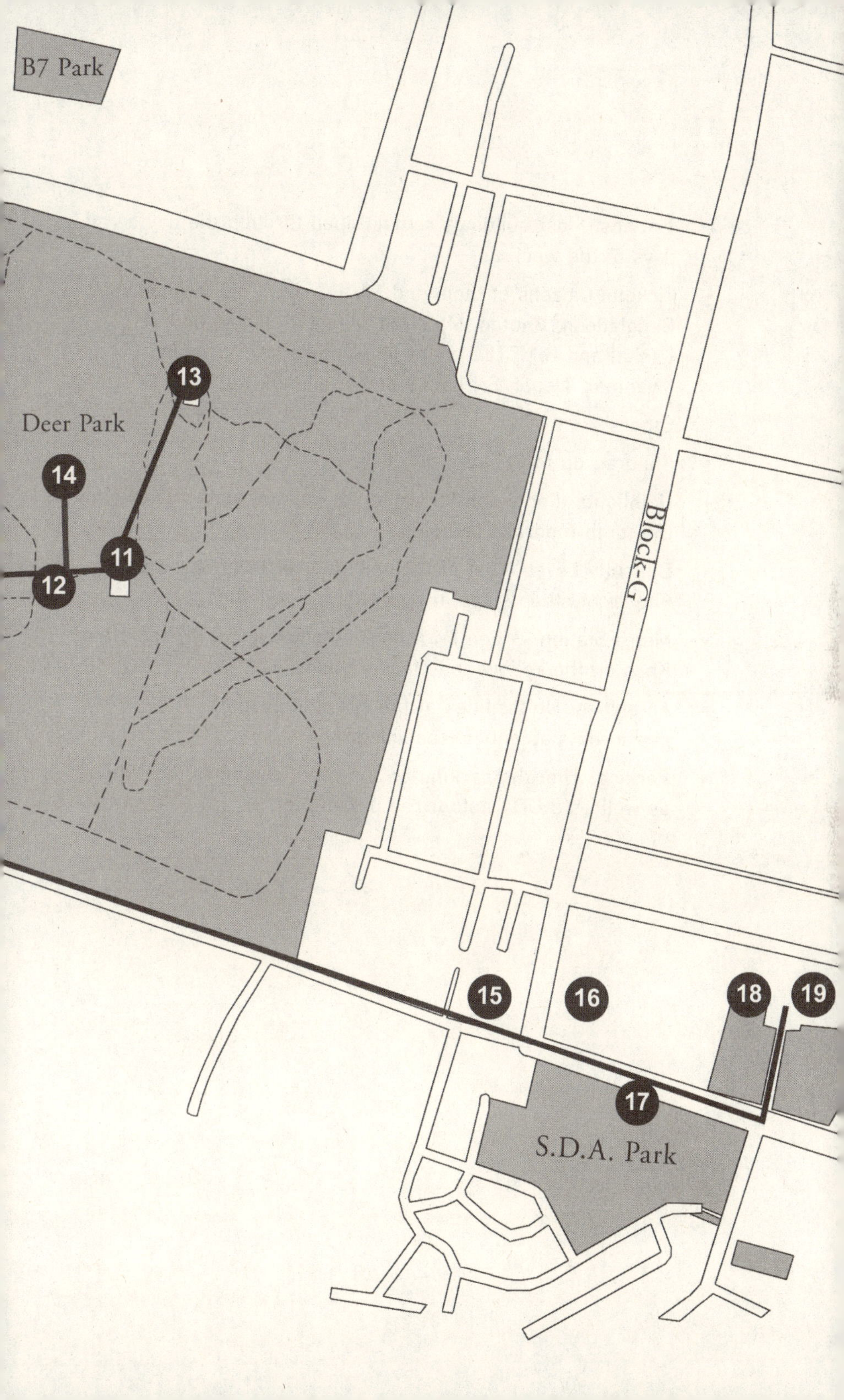
B7 Park
Deer Park
13
14
11
12
Block-G
15
16
18
19
17
S.D.A. Park

- Timings: Most buildings remain open through the day on all days of the week.
- Tickets: Citizens of India and SAARC countries (Afghanistan, Bangladesh, Bhutan, Maldives, Nepal, Pakistan and Sri Lanka) and BIMSTEC countries (Bangladesh, Bhutan, Myanmar, Nepal, Sri Lanka and Thailand): Rs 20
- Others: Rs 250
- Children up to 15 years old: free
- Highlights: For a shorter walk just see the buildings within the tomb-madrasa complex.
- Difficulty Level: Most of the walk is over level paved paths. Flights of steep steps in the madrasa buildings.
- Metro Station: Green Park on the Yellow line, 1.75 km; Hauz Khas on the Yellow and Magenta lines, 1.75 km.
- Amenities: No facilities at the site, but shops and restaurants aplenty in the village.
- Parking: There is parking on the road leading to the village, as well as a DDA authorized parking lot.

ROYAL TANK AND COLLEGE

HAUZ KHAS VILLAGE is one of the first of Delhi's 'urban villages' to reinvent itself as a commercial space with fashionable boutiques and restaurants. The place itself has a long history. In the thirteenth century, there was a large plain in this area, known by the name of Siri. This was where certain important battles were fought, notably towards the end of the thirteenth century against the Mongols by Alauddin Khalji. Though the major concentration of the population at the time was in Mehrauli around the Qutub Minar, orchards and cultivation were spreading northwards to Siri.

At the end of the thirteenth century, Alauddin Khalji decided to have a large reservoir constructed, to serve the needs of this growing population. The tank, known as Hauz Khas (the special tank) or Hauz-e-Alai (the tank of Alauddin) was spread over a huge area—some twenty-eight hectares. Monsoon water collected here in a large enough quantity to last till the following year.

Soon, in the early fourteenth century, the nearby camping ground of Siri (to the east of Hauz Khas) was fortified and declared as the new capital of the empire. The heads of eight thousand defeated Mongols are said to have been buried in its foundations or built into the walls. Suitable buildings were constructed in it, including a magnificent palace known as

'Hazar Sutun' or 'thousand pillars'. Today only the remains of the outer walls of Siri, or Siri Fort are visible, within which are the village of Shahpur Jat and the Asian Games Village. The reason for this is that in the middle of the sixteenth century, the ruler Sher Shah dismantled the building materials within Siri Fort for use in his city of Sher Garh (near the Purana Qila).

By Sher Shah's time Siri had been lying abandoned for a while. After Alauddin Khalji, the focus shifted away from Siri as his dynasty collapsed and the Tughlaqs shifted the capital to Tughlaqabad and then Jahanpanah. The reservoir too fell into disrepair, the water channels leading into it were silted up, and its dry bed began to be cultivated. In the middle of the fourteenth century, Firoz Shah Tughlaq ascended the throne. In Firoz Shah's time, the capital shifted further north, as the new city of Firozabad was built. However Firoz Shah had a great interest in construction projects, particularly setting up educational institutions, laying out gardens and commissioning water works. These were spread far and wide in Delhi and around. Among the many projects undertaken under direct orders of that emperor, the one at Hauz Khas was constructed in the 1350s and combined all these characteristics. The tank was desilted so that it could again hold water, and it was at this time that it was renamed Hauz-e-Khas, 'royal tank'. Along its eastern and southern edge, a madrasa was built, and set amidst beautiful gardens. Firoz Shah in fact had such an attachment to this spot that he decided to build his own tomb in the midst of this college. Other people from the city also built houses along the banks of the reservoir.

This idyllic state did not last very long. Firoz Shah died in 1388 and the Tughlaq dynasty did not last long after that, beset by internal strife and the devastating invasion of Timur, or Tamerlane, in 1398. Once royal patronage for the madrasa was discontinued, it soon ceased to function. The tank silted up once again. The surrounding buildings were abandoned. The area came to be inhabited by a rural population that grew into the Hauz Khas village. Some of the historic buildings were even used by the villagers to live in or to store fodder until it was taken over for protection by the Archaeological Survey of India.

'The tank is filled by the rains in the rainy season, and it supplies the people of the city with water throughout the year. When I had pitched my camp here, the princes and amirs...generals and officers, came to wait upon me to pay their respects.'—Timur, 1398

Much has changed around Hauz Khas from Firoz Shah's time, but it is still a charming place. The buildings are fascinating and picturesque and the tank once again has water. The surrounding parkland is green and teeming with bird-life, which incidentally includes migratory birds that visit the tank every year.

The Walk

Begin the walk by going to the end of the main street of the village, where you will find a gate leading into the madrasa compound. Once inside the gate, turn right and you can walk up to the **eastern wing**[1] of the madrasa. If you climb up to the broad platform you can get a good view of the tank below. If from here you move to your left, you'll find yourself alongside the upper storey of the madrasa. It is raised slightly above the level of the garden and there is a long hall with pillars joining two rooms that have domes. On the inside, it has the look of typical functional Tughlaq architecture—built of solid quartzite beams and square pillars, with very little else by way of ornamentation. The pillared hall has an open plan looking out on the garden on one side and the tank on the other. There is evidence that some kind of protective grill work might have existed between the outer pillars.

It was clearly a beautiful setting to engage in scholarly pursuits and this was a prestigious institution of higher learning. A curriculum broadly based on a teaching of the Quran and Islamic law and jurisprudence was probably taught, along with mathematics, astronomy, medicine, grammar, rhetoric and calligraphy. It was a royal institution funded by the emperor himself, and so the best teachers were appointed, with probably a very good teacher-student ratio. Students received generous stipends, so in theory at least, economic background was not a bar to receiving a good education. If later traditions of the Indian system of education are anything to go by, an aspiring student would have had to convince his prospective teachers of his sincerity as well as ability.

The pillared hall leads into a domed room. This has a jharokha. Such jharokhas were a popular feature in indigenous Indian architecture from before the founding of the Delhi Sultanate. They became a popular feature of the composite style of architecture that evolved under the Sultanate. It combined elements peculiar to India, with imports like the arch and dome, brought in by Turk immigrants. The Mughals later continued with the tradition of the composite style, with some modifications of their own. Another such element was the chhajja, which you can see below the parapet on the wall overlooking the garden.

The domed room leads through a connecting passage to a much larger domed chamber. (If the passageway is closed, you will have to come around from the front). This is the **tomb of Firoz Shah**[2]. The inside of the room is finished in plaster, which is decoratively incised and painted. The arches over the doorways and the squinch arches in the four corners are decorated with verses from the Quran. The drum, the circular band on which the dome rests, is inscribed with the ninety-nine names of Allah. The ceiling of the dome is particularly elaborate. The prominent motif is that of the eight-pointed star. The medallions between the lines of the star contain further verses from the Quran and the hadith (traditions or sayings of the Prophet Mohammad). All this decoration is in the form of incised and painted limestone plaster. The central marble cenotaph marks the grave of Firoz Shah, the other two marble cenotaphs are believed to be that of his son and grandson. Another unknown person is buried alongside.

To the south, a doorway leads into a small, paved yard surrounded by a stone railing. This kind of stone railing was another typically Indian feature that was enthusiastically adopted by Sultanate builders. On the outside, the tomb wall has the distinctive slope of Tughlaq architecture called 'batter'. The inscription around the entrance arch tells us that repairs were carried out on this building in 1508 under the orders of the emperor Sikandar Lodi. It was fitting that Firoz Shah, who himself paid considerable attention to the repair of pre-existing buildings, including the Qutub Minar, should have had his own tomb repaired by a later emperor.

Today, the exterior of the tomb has a cream limestone plaster finish. There are however accounts of travellers in the fourteenth century, which suggest that the exterior surfaces of the tomb and the madrasa buildings were painted in different colours including red, with golden domes. Much of the exterior of the buildings of the madrasa is now quite blackened. This is because of the growth of fungus on the plaster surface, encouraged by various organic materials that were traditionally added to the plaster to make it strong, like pulses and the pulp of the bel fruit. The mortar, holding the stones together had an even richer mix including limestone, brick dust, greens, cowdung and gur (jaggery), which made for a mixture that was strong but could also breathe.

Inside Firoz Shah's tomb you will notice that there is no qibla wall with a mihrab, the usual practice with tombs as well as mosques. Instead, in the west wall there is another opening into a passageway that leads into the **southern wing**[3] of the madrasa, mirroring the arrangement on the north of the tomb. There are identical domed buildings and a pillared hall. At the end of these you will find stairs that lead you to the lower level.

The lower storey, now much ruined, contains what was evidently the residential quarters for the students. Small narrow cells, with small openings for light and air and small shelves for storage, indicate a fairly spartan lifestyle. Steps lead down from this area to the water, and are quite distinct from the broader steps leading down—in the style of a ghat, from the emperor's tomb.

Beyond the students' rooms is a **tall building with a dome**[4]. The room on the ground level has a flat roof, with a large and clumsy pillar in the middle for support. Narrow stairs built into the wall lead up to the upper level which has a domed roof and consequently a much more open look. This is in fact the great benefit that the invention of the dome conferred—it enabled the bridging of a wide space without the need to use intervening pillars for support, such as a flat roof made of beams would have needed. The precise functions of this building are not known but maybe one can find a clue.

If you emerge from it into the garden, you find yourself in what might have been a sort of entrance courtyard, of which the enclosing walls have disappeared. There are two buildings which now stand in the garden in front of this domed building, which might have formed gatehouses. The **western gatehouse**[5] may have given access to this entrance courtyard, with the tall domed building serving as an impressive focus or even a reception area. From here one could move on to the **eastern gatehouse**[6] which led, via a small enclosed court, into the garden in front of Firoz Shah's tomb. The garden which ran in an L-shape all around the madrasa and the tomb buildings would have been a sight in itself, planted with colourful and scented flowers and fruiting and shade-giving trees.

Within the garden you can see several graves and some **pillared tombs**[7]. Mainly in the form of open pavilions, the tombs are constructed of quartzite stone with decorative details in carved red sandstone. In particular, look at the decorative battlement pattern (kangura) on the parapet

'Because this madrasa is a monument of good works and benefaction, prayers, obligatory and superogatory, are constantly being offered within its precincts.'—Ziauddin Barani, 1357)

and around the dome. There are no imposing cenotaphs; instead the site of the burial is marked by a shallow decorative indentation in the floor. It is probable that it was the teachers of the madrasa who were buried in these garden pavilions, and it is not far-fetched to see their tombs doubling as areas for students to study in. (A possible reason for the flat floor unencumbered by a raised cenotaph.)

Two of the smaller pavilions have disproportionately heavy beams projecting out from under the dome, which has led to a suggestion that they may have been connected as part of a larger building. They do not appear to be tombs.

This part of the garden is separate from another open space further to the north. Here you will see a large **T-shaped building**[8]. From its size and location, it is likely that this was an assembly hall of sorts, though it has been designated as a tomb in some books. The open pavilion structure was ideal for a public building, to make the most of the surrounding views and the fresh air.

On the other side of this building is the entrance to a section on the extreme north of the madrasa. Though in a ruined state, it is apparently a **mosque**[9]. Entering through the doorway, on your right is the eastern side which has some ruined chambers. The western side, which is on your left, is the qibla which in this mosque is an unusual one. Traditionally the qibla wall of a mosque would be denoted by mihrabs, the central one often larger and more elaborate than the others. Here the central mihrab takes the form of a jharokha with a flight of steps on either side leading down to the tank of water. The secondary mihrabs are windows with jalis. Thus the faithful would be praying towards Mecca but in the process looking out over the tank which brought blessings in its own way into their lives—through water which they used for their everyday needs, for irrigating crops and gardens, and for providing a cool micro-climate; in sum, for life itself.

If any of the several flights of steps leading down to the water is accessible, you may like to go down to the level of the water now. Else, you will need to exit this complex and approach the water from the other side of the village. For this you must trace your steps out through the village, till you reach the entrance to the park, which will be on your left, just across from the official parking lot. Enter the park and walk down for a bit and take the first turning to the left. Keep to this path and it will lead you over a bridge, through a shady path and then up a slope to a mound with a ruined building on top.

There is considerable birdlife in the park, both in the wooded area and over the water. Look out for peafowl, barbets, hornbills, sunbirds, babblers, parakeets, red-wattled lapwings, hoopoes, and water birds like kingfishers, spot-billed ducks, pond herons, pochards and northern shovelers.

This is called the **Munda Gumbad**[10], literally the 'headless dome'—reference no doubt to a domed, pillared pavilion on top of the building, which has since fallen down. This recreational building used to once stand on an island in the middle of the reservoir, which will give you some idea of the original extent of the tank. Now it is situated across the water from the madrasa buildings and from here if you go down and walk along the water's edge you can get a good view of the madrasa from below. You can see that to some extent the two wings of the madrasa are symmetrical—with the tomb of Firoz Shah, as the highest dome, forming the junction and focal point. Beside this on either side there would have been a pair of two lower domes separated by two levels of pillared halls—with trabeate or rectangular openings at the upper level and arched openings at the lower. Some of this has now fallen down, notably the second dome on the eastern wing. At the extreme ends the symmetry is somewhat lost. On the southern wing the vertical element is emphasized, with the tall, domed, two-storey building. At the extreme end of the eastern wing is the wide qibla wall of the mosque that projects a good deal beyond the line of the other buildings and has its distinctively large jharokha (the mihrab) at the top of the double flights of stairs.

Go back but not all the way back to the Munda Gumbad. Just a little past the mosque building, a few steps will lead you into the park and eventually to the bridge over which you came. Trace your way back, and when you come to the main path leading from the gate, turn left. You will soon come to a modern building and to its right a path leads off into a wooded area. Take this path and walk till you come to a large, square, domed building.

This building at some point in its history acquired the name **Bagh-e-Alam ka Gumbad**[11]—'the domed building in the Garden of Alam' (Alam literally means 'the world' but it is also a man's name). It is in fact a tomb dating from the year 1501—which is apparent from a Persian inscription on the outside of the western wall. Though the language of the inscription is not very clear, it seems to suggest that it was built over the remains of Miyan Shaikh Shihabuddin Taj Khan by one Abu Syed. Nothing is known of either of these persons.

The building however is a fine one, typical of Lodi period architecture. On the outside are many arched niches, arranged in layers to suggest separate storeys, though inside there is only one large room. The use of neatly dressed quartzite with some marble, red sandstone and blue tiles for ornamentation has produced a beautiful effect. Inside, there is typical incised plasterwork, a closed mihrab on the western wall to indicate the qibla and several cenotaphs.

To the west of the tomb is a smallish **wall mosque**[12], with a large number of graves before it. It was in fact quite common to build a wall mosque on one side of a burial. The mosque also dates from the Lodi period as is apparent from its style—the incised plaster decoration, particularly in the battlement pattern of the top and the delicate niches. It has rather distinctive bastions in the corners.

If you take the path that goes in a north-eastern direction from the Bagh-e-Alam ka Gumbad (orient yourself with the western wall of the tomb and mosque), you will soon come to the **Tohfewala Gumbad**[13]. This is probably a Tughlaq period tomb, much plainer than the previous one, but with large cenotaphs inside.

On the way back to the park entrance, just past the Bagh-e-Alam ka Gumbad, there is another small tomb to your right, called **Kali Gumti**[14] ('black, domed building') because of the blackening of its exterior plaster. It also probably belongs to the Tughlaq period and is very plain.

When you exit the park and make your way out to the main road, just before you get to Aurobindo Marg, there are a few buildings on either side of the road that you may like to visit. On your left, you will first see **Chhoti Gumti**[15] ('small, domed building'), a tomb with a red painted medallion in the centre of the domed ceiling.

Soon after this, again on the left, is **Sakri Gumti**[16] or 'the narrow, domed building', which archaeological historians speculate may have been a gateway. The names of both these buildings are purely descriptive, and from their construction, these buildings appear to be from the Lodi period.

Across the road from Sakri Gumti is a large, pillared, square tomb, known as **Barah Khamba**[17] literally 'twelve pillars', that belongs to the Tughlaq period, and is the tomb of some unknown person.

A little further, in a small green park on the same side of the road, stand the two buildings known as **Dadi-Poti**[18 & 19] ('grandmother and granddaughter') or **Biwi-Bandi** ('mistress and maid'). The names are entirely an imaginative construction, prompted by the fact that the buildings stand close to each other and one is clearly bigger than the other. The smaller one, Poti, with its plastered and battered walls may be from the Tughlaq or Syed period and has a distinctive lantern crowning the dome. Make it a point to go around to the back (the northern side)—the façade has the remains of some very beautiful incised plasterwork.

The larger tomb, Dadi, is more typically Lodi, with arched niches arranged in rows. Look at the elaborate plan by which the corners of the square room are bridged by arches, called squinch arches, to create a row of eight arched niches. The corners of these are then topped by short beams with carved brackets and then another row of beams until a sixteen-sided drum is produced and a circular dome can easily be constructed on it.

5

LODI GARDEN AND SAFDARJANG'S TOMB

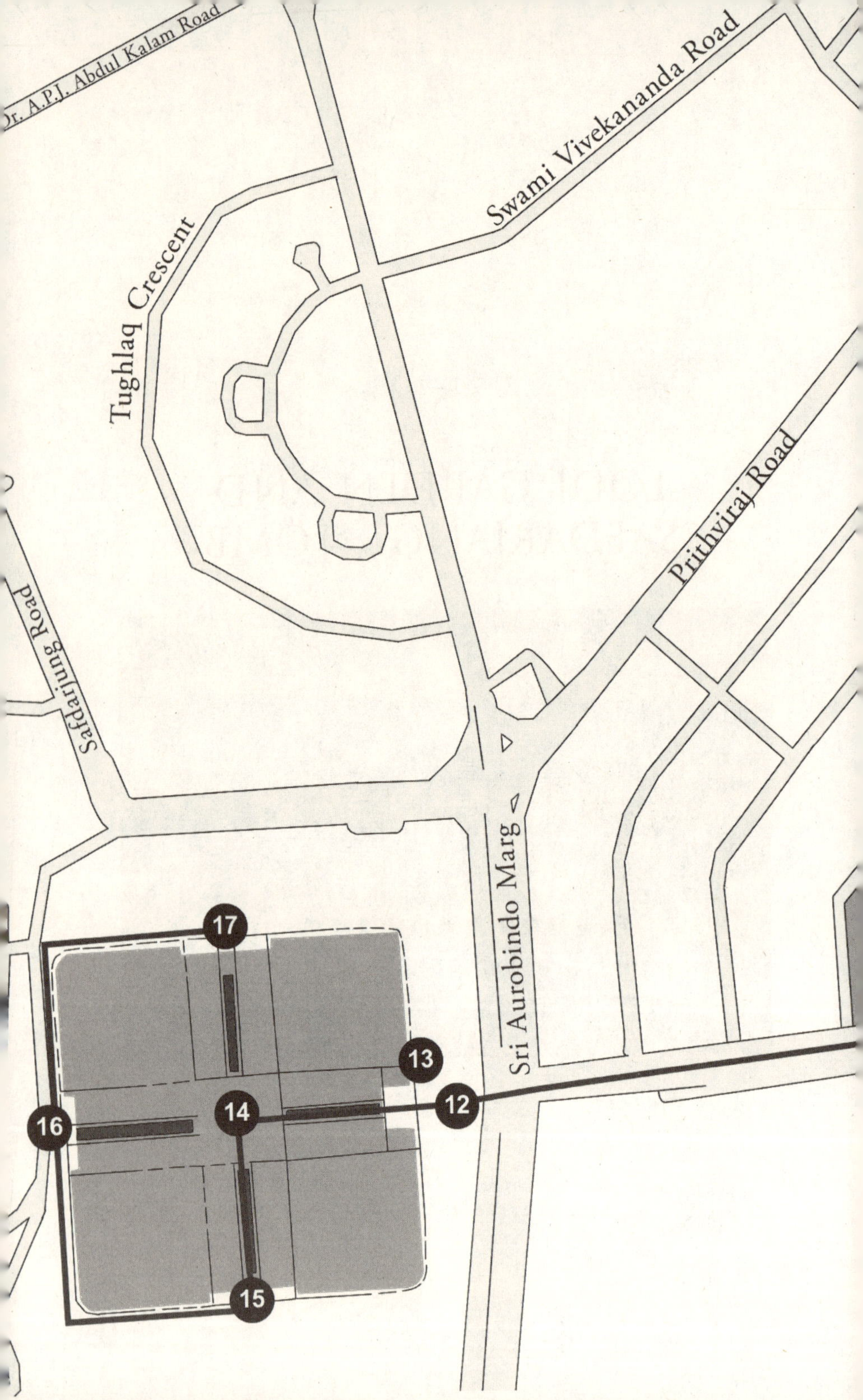

Dr. A.P.J. Abdul Kalam Road
Swami Vivekananda Road
Tughlaq Crescent
Prithviraj Road
Safdarjung Road
Sri Aurobindo Marg
17
13
12
14
16
15

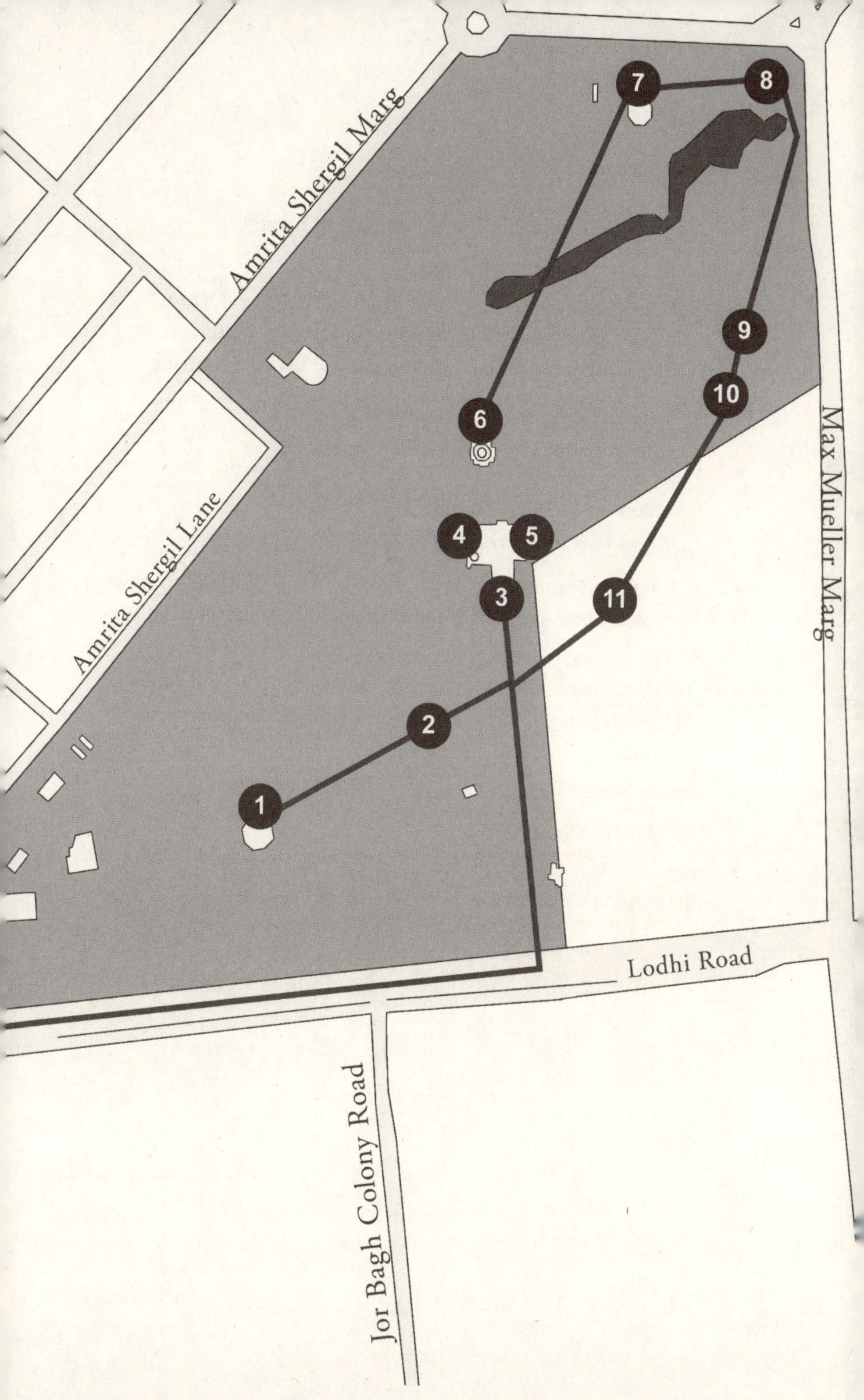

Amrita Shergil Marg
Amrita Shergil Lane
Max Mueller Marg
Lodhi Road
Jor Bagh Colony Road
1
2
3
4
5
6
7
8
9
10
11

- Timings: Safdarjang's tomb: Sunrise to sunset.
- Lodi Garden: Daylight hours.
- Tickets: Safdarjang's tomb: Citizens of India and SAARC countries (Afghanistan, Bangladesh, Bhutan, Maldives, Nepal, Pakistan and Sri Lanka) and BIMSTEC countries (Bangladesh, Bhutan, Myanmar, Nepal, Sri Lanka and Thailand): Rs 20
- Others: Rs 250
- Children up to 15 years old: free
- Lodi Garden: Entry free.
- Highlights: Mohammad Shah's tomb, Bada Gumbad, Sheesh Gumbad, Sikandar Lodi's tomb (best for an abbreviated walk).
- Difficulty Level: There are even paths through Lodi Garden and Safdarjang's Tomb, though no wheelchair access to buildings.
- Metro Station: Jor Bagh on the Yellow line, 1 km.
- Amenities: Washrooms.
- Parking: Near Gate no. 1 of Lodi Garden, and at Safdarjang's Tomb.

HISTORIC GARDEN

Lodi Garden is also worth visiting for its plant life. It contains a bonsai garden, a herb garden, a rose garden, a lily pond, and a butterfly conservatory.

LODI GARDEN IS a large landscaped park in the heart of New Delhi. It is a green space with a wealth of natural and built heritage. This includes a considerable variety of trees and birds, and some buildings of great architectural and historical significance. In historical accounts we first come across this area as being referred to as Bagh-e-Jud, as early as the thirteenth century. Since the word 'bagh' means garden, we can assume that this space was even then occupied by a garden, maybe with orchards. The name Bagh-e-Jud lives on today in the area just south of the garden, known as Jor Bagh. This was a good location for a garden in medieval times because right through this area flowed a stream which was a tributary of the river Yamuna. The stream has long since dried up, but the bed is still discernable as a depression in the ground towards the north-east, part of which has been turned into an artificial water body.

From the middle of the fifteenth century to the beginning of the sixteenth century this area came to be chosen for the location of the tombs of some important personages, including emperors of the Syed and Lodi dynasties. Apart from the beautiful ambience of the place in the midst of gardens and beside a stream of water, the nearby shrine of the Sufi saint Nizamuddin Auliya might have influenced the choice of location. While the Syed and Lodi dynasties did not last long, the garden was still visited by many people over the sixteenth and seventeenth centuries. A possible reason was that it was next to the main road that ran from Mehrauli, an important suburb, to the Mughal capital which was at Purana Qila and then at Shahjahanabad. Some construction activity took place here during that time too.

Lodi Garden attracts many birds. Lookout for the black-rumped flameback woodpecker, brown-headed barbet, the common hoopoe, the white-throated kingfisher and the white kingfisher.

In the eighteenth century, with the decline of the Mughal Empire, Delhi and its surrounding areas became an insecure place. Plundering gangs raided isolated village communities at regular intervals. In these anarchic and unsettled times, rural populations tended to take shelter within abandoned mosques and tombs. This happened to the buildings in the Lodi Garden too, and a village called Khairpur came to be settled in it, with much of its population actually living within its historic buildings.

In the second decade of the twentieth century, this area received attention from the British government because it formed the edge of the site demarcated to form the new capital of the empire—New Delhi. During 1913-14, many of the buildings here were repaired. The newer buildings of the village of Khairpur were demolished and the villagers resettled, some in Kotla Mubarakpur and some in Punjab. By the mid 1930s, the whole space was landscaped into a garden and named Lady Willingdon Park, after the wife of the then Viceroy. Though the park was renamed Lodi Garden after Independence, the original name can still be found on a plaque outside one of the gates. The garden has seen several rounds of landscaping since then.

Not far from Lodi Garden is the mid-eighteenth century tomb of Safdarjang, set within large grounds of its own. It is most convenient to visit it at the same time as the Lodi Garden. If you are coming to the area by Metro, you might find it convenient to visit it first, before you go on to Lodi Garden.

The Walk

It is best to begin the walk at Gate no. 10 of Lodi Garden which is situated on Lodi Road. Enter and walk straight up the path to the large octagonal building in front of you—the **tomb of Mohammad Shah Syed**[1]. Mohammad Shah was the third ruler of a short-lived and relatively insignificant dynasty of the Delhi Sultanate—the Syeds. They came to power in the early fifteenth century, the period after the invasion of Timur (Tamerlane), when the Tughlaq dynasty was slowly crumbling and the former empire all but broke up. The Syeds consequently ruled over a shrunken and weakened kingdom. Due to their unstable tenure and straitened circumstances, their building activities were fairly limited. The first ruler, Mubarak Shah, is buried in a fairly grand tomb in the village of Kotla Mubarakpur (near South Extension).

The third Syed ruler, Mohammad Shah, died in 1443-44 and is buried in Lodi Garden. The tomb is octagonal, a feature of a small number of Delhi's tombs. The single chamber of the tomb is surrounded by a pillared verandah composed of arches. The corners are supported and strengthened by buttresses—you will notice that each corner pillar extends outward at the base. The tomb has a large dome on top, surrounded by eight chhatris. One chhatri is placed in the centre of each side. The domes on the chhatris as well as the large central dome are crowned by lotuses.

The Syed rulers controlled very limited territories. It was derisively said of Shah Alam, the last ruler of the dynasty: 'the kingship of Shah Alam—from Delhi to Palam'; Palam being where the Delhi airport is now located.

The building is primarily built of neatly cut and assembled grey quartzite blocks. This locally mined stone is hard and quite difficult to carve. Such carving as there is, is therefore largely confined to some details that are picked out in red sandstone. Expensive stones such as marble were not used at all. The upper parts of the building are finished in limestone plaster, the original portions of which have now developed an aged patina. In places, such as the ceiling of the verandah, the plaster has been incised to create beautiful patterns.

The doorway leading to the inner chamber is of a characteristic design. A horizontal beam set below an arch forms a lintel. The resulting opening is framed by corbels made of red sandstone carved in a decorative pattern, reminiscent of Hindu temples. That impression is strengthened by the shape of a kalash that is carved into the doorposts. Such design elements were an integral part of Sultanate architecture, which had evolved into a composite style, sometimes called Indo-Islamic. This included features that were part of a long Indian tradition as well as elements, such as the arch, that had been 'imported' when dynasties with original homelands in Central Asia had come to dominate Indian politics.

Inside, there are eight cenotaphs, the central one is probably that of Mohammad Shah and the rest belong to members of his family. The interior is decorated in incised plaster, which is made by cutting a thickly applied layer of limestone plaster while it is still workable. The patterns have then been painted, mainly in blue and red. The ceiling is particularly elaborate. In the middle there is a large circular area of fine carving, surrounded by a large pattern of ribs painted in red. The western part of the domed ceiling has a smaller circular design. This serves to indicate the qibla.

Around the drum or base on which the dome rests, there are sixteen arched niches, four of which are open so that light can come in. These are not set right above the doorways, as one would expect, but off-centre. This is understandable if one remembers that right above each doorway, on the roof, is a chhatri that would block the light. The opening that most closely faces west (the qibla), is specially decorated in red sandstone. What would have been the doorway opening to the west is blocked with stone masonry, also to indicate the qibla. The outside surface of this closed opening is of decoratively carved red sandstone. It is likely that there was a similar decorative facing on the inside too, which has fallen off. It is probable that the closing of this western opening was an afterthought, and originally the motif on the ceiling and the decorative niche were considered enough to indicate the direction of prayer.

Exit the tomb in the direction from which you entered, and take the path to the left, going east. You can go over a bridge (or cross the cycling track below). Immediately after the bridge, to the left you will see a small building hidden behind some bamboo plants. This is a **mosque**[2], and its style, with a characteristic vaulted roof, suggests that it was constructed in the eighteenth century. It is quite plain, and constructed of random rubble masonry, which essentially consists of rough stones held together with a strong mortar. The structure is covered in simply decorated plaster with an unusual red finish.

Come back to the path and proceed to the imposing square building with a large hemispherical dome you see in front. This is the **Bada Gumbad**[3], or 'big dome'. It is made entirely of dressed quartzite stone with some details in black slate and white marble creating a nice effect. The façade consists of arches, most of them are closed niches but others are open. The arches are placed at two levels which suggest a double-storeyed building. Steps on the western side take you inside through an ornately carved doorway. Before you enter, look to your left. The adjoining building has a beautifully decorated jharokha. The back wall has a very ruined but even more elaborate jharokha. The jharokha was a popular feature of Sultanate and even Mughal architecture. At the corner of the same wall, which in fact belongs to the attached mosque, there is a buttress strongly reminiscent in design of the Qutub Minar!

Inside, the Bada Gumbad is a single large room rather than the two storeys its exterior suggests. The surfaces are plain dressed stone with no signs of plaster. It is nevertheless attractive and its plainness enables us to appreciate the technique by which a circular dome was placed on a square room. The four corners of the room are surmounted by arches that match those over the entrances on the four sides. These are known as squinches, and they are the means by which a four-sided room is transformed into an eight-sided one. Two additional rows of smaller arches transform this into a sixteen-sided structure and then a thirty-two-sided one. This produces a nearly circular shape on top of which the dome has conveniently been built.

The Bada Gumbad at first glance may be taken to be a tomb, but in fact there are no signs of a grave and it is simply a grand gateway. In size, proportions and even in some structural details it is not unlike the Alai Darwaza, located in the Qutub Minar complex. What it is a gateway to, has to be guessed from the buildings that lie beyond.

A north-facing doorway takes one out of the Bada Gumbad into a courtyard. In the middle of this is a ruined platform that may have supported a chhatri and/or contained a grave. On your left is a small but spectacular mosque, commonly referred to as the **Bada Gumbad Mosque**[4]. It is lavishly

decorated with carved limestone plaster, both inside and out. Stylized foliage and geometric patterns along with calligraphy cover almost every surface. Most of the inscriptions consist of verses from the Quran. One inscription located on the southern-most bay gives us the date of construction of the building as 1494. In the days when this area was occupied by the village of Khairpur, this mosque was used as a cow shed.

Opposite the mosque on the other side of the courtyard is a much plainer building which has been called a **Majlis Khana**[5], or an assembly room. It might have been used by those attached to the mosque as readers of the Quran. Small rooms with shelving suggest living/working quarters.

Though the prevalent opinion is uncertain about the precise functions of this group of buildings, at least some historians link the Bada Gumbad and its associated buildings to the large tomb that lies immediately to their north, which is the **Sheesh Gumbad**[6]. This building is similar in size and shape to the Bada Gumbad but its ornamentation is somewhat different. There are remains of glazed tiles (which explain the name, which literally means 'glass dome') arranged in bands across the façade. It appears that the upper level was once entirely plastered and tiled because in contrast to the dressed stone on the lower level, its surface is rough and uneven. The chamber inside is plastered in a pattern quite like that of Mohammad Shah's tomb. The western wall contains a mihrab.

It is likely that the Sheesh Gumbad is the tomb of the founder of the Lodi dynasty, Bahlol Lodi. Bahlol Lodi became the Sultan of Delhi in 1451, after the end of the Syed dynasty. He died in 1488 and though many ascribe a modest tomb in Chiragh Delhi village to him, various historical sources suggest that Sheesh Gumbad is more likely to be Bahlol Lodi's tomb. It is further conjectured, that the Bada Gurmbad group of buildings was built around 1494 as an elaborate gateway to the tomb.

Interestingly, the Sheesh Gumbad and the Bada Gumbad group are slightly out of alignment with each other. In fact the qibla wall of the Sheesh Gumbad is about fifteen degrees off from the true west. This defect was corrected in the later buildings, which according to scholar Simon Digby produced the misalignment between the two, and led to the prevalent impression that they were unconnected.

Now go northwards across the lawns towards the lake, which you will cross via a small bridge. It brings you close to a walled enclosure. This is a walled garden that contains the **tomb of Sikandar Lodi**[7]. Sikandar Lodi, who reigned from 1489-1517, was a dynamic man who managed to at least consolidate the remaining territories of the Sultanate. He was also a patron of learning and literature. Sikandar moved the capital of the Sultanate from Delhi to Sikandra, near Agra. Nevertheless he was buried in Delhi, probably to be near the burial place of his ancestor.

The entrance to the enclosure is through a doorway located on a large platform which also has two ruined, square chhatris on it. Enter the garden, and you will see that the middle of the western side of the boundary wall is actually a wall mosque with a high central arch and a paved area in front. In the middle of the enclosure stands an octagonal tomb that looks very similar to Mohammad Shah's tomb, except for the lack of chhatris around the dome.

Inside, the decoration is rather different. There is a considerable use of tilework, particularly framing the door arches and band of niches just below the dome. The western opening seems to have been blocked up at a later date, but originally must have given a view of the wall mosque outside. Around the drum just below the dome, there are four off-centre openings similar to Mohammad Shah's tomb. This suggests that here too chhatris once existed on the roof or at least were planned and never built.

When you come out of the garden, turn left and proceed along the wall towards the west and then north. You will find that the lake is below you on the right. Soon through the trees you will be able to see a stone bridge over the water. This is in fact the best view of **Athpula**[8], a bridge that you will finally approach in a somewhat roundabout manner by going out through one gate and in another.

Re-enter the park and go straight to the bridge. The term Athpula (according to some, Athpala) means eight piers, and the bridge in fact consists of eight supports spanned by arches. Some of these are hard to see as they are partly buried. The entire structure is made of stone and is a particularly attractive shape. The bridge dates from the time of Akbar who reigned from 1556-1605. It would then have been roughly on the way from Akbar's early capital at what is now Purana Qila, towards the south, where older cities and suburbs like Siri and Mehrauli were located.

Take the path that goes over the bridge southwards, this will take you back into Lodi Garden. In a short while you will see a couple of buildings to your right, which are attached to what was once a walled Mughal garden. The first one is a fairly damaged **gateway**[9] made of brick and plaster, with some charming floral paintings over the entrance.

The other one is a small **mosque**[10], also made of brick and plaster. The attached garden has a modern layout, with probably little reference to the original Mughal plan. This enclosure might have served as a space for rest and recreation for those travelling on the road that carried over the nearby bridge. Continue along the path, which will come out in view of Bada Gumbad.

On your left you will see a small tower, which is probably the **corner turret**[11] of an enclosure wall that has disappeared. According to Simon Digby this enclosure may have encompassed the Bada Gumbad group of buildings together with the Sheesh Gumbad. Continue past the Bada Gumbad, and the path will take you to Gate no. 1 of Lodi Garden.

Exit, turn right, and walk along Lodi Road towards **Safdarjang's Tomb**[12-17]. Safdarjang's tomb is located at one end of Lodi Road and it can be quite challenging to cross the intervening perpetually busy road which is the Aurobindo Marg. Do so with care.

The tomb, built after Safdarjang's death in 1754, is the last grand mausoleum built in the classical Mughal style of placement within a char-bagh—a garden divided in a four-fold scheme. Safdarjang was the title of Mirza Muqim Abul-mansur Khan. He was a powerful man of his time, because he was not only the practically independent ruler of the principality of Awadh, but for a while was also the wazir, or prime minister, of the Mughal Empire. Though he died in Faizabad, his body was brought to Delhi for burial. This may have been because the family wanted to emphasize their connection to Delhi. The precise location may have been chosen for its proximity to the Dargah Shah Mardan, situated in nearby Aliganj, which is in Jor Bagh. This was the shrine where a footprint of Ali, the son-in-law of the Prophet Mohammad was preserved, and is particularly sacred to Shias, among whom were the nawabs of Awadh.

The tomb complex is entered through a **gateway**[12], which is built mainly of brick and plaster. It is quite large and has several rooms built on two storeys on either side of the arched doorway. The ornamentation largely consists of moulded plaster and striking paintings, notably on the underside of the entrance arch. All the arches are cusped.

On the right side of the gateway is a **mosque**[13] which is not normally accessible to the public. You might however be able to take a quick peek mid-morning on Fridays, as it is opened for cleaning before the midday prayer. The main body of the sandstone and marble mosque is on the upper level, and the ground floor has a pool in middle.

The gateway leads into a large garden, and in it, on a high platform, is **Safdarjang's Tomb**[14]. The exterior of this large square building is made of fawn and red sandstone, and marble. Some of the marble is said to have been taken from the tomb of Abdurrahim Khan-e-Khanan, located in the residential colony of Nizamuddin East. Interestingly, the marble has been rather unevenly applied to the dome. The shape of the dome is distinctly bulbous as it bulges out over a fairly constricted drum. This shape of dome is one of the distinctly late Mughal features that this building displays.

Inside there is one central chamber surrounded by eight others. The central chamber contains the elaborately carved white marble cenotaph of Safdarjang. Beneath, in a vault inaccessible to the public, lies the actual grave of Safdarjang and also that of his wife. The walls and ceiling are mainly finished in white stucco, in high relief, highly polished and elaborately moulded—a technique much used in the period towards the end of the Mughal empire. The lower portions of the walls of the rooms are made of marble.

In the garden outside, built against the boundary wall are certain buildings quite similar to each other. The **Badshah Pasand**[15] or the 'king's favourite' is on the south side, **Jangli Mahal**[16] or 'forest palace' to the west, and the **Moti Mahal**[17] or the 'pearl palace' to the north. You may approach them along paths leading from the tomb platform. These were arcaded pavilions meant to accommodate visitors. Now they have been enclosed and are used by the Archaeological Survey of India as office and storage space.

6

PURANA QILA

Mathura Road
1
Old Fort Lake
2
8
9
Delhi Zoo
Zoo Parking

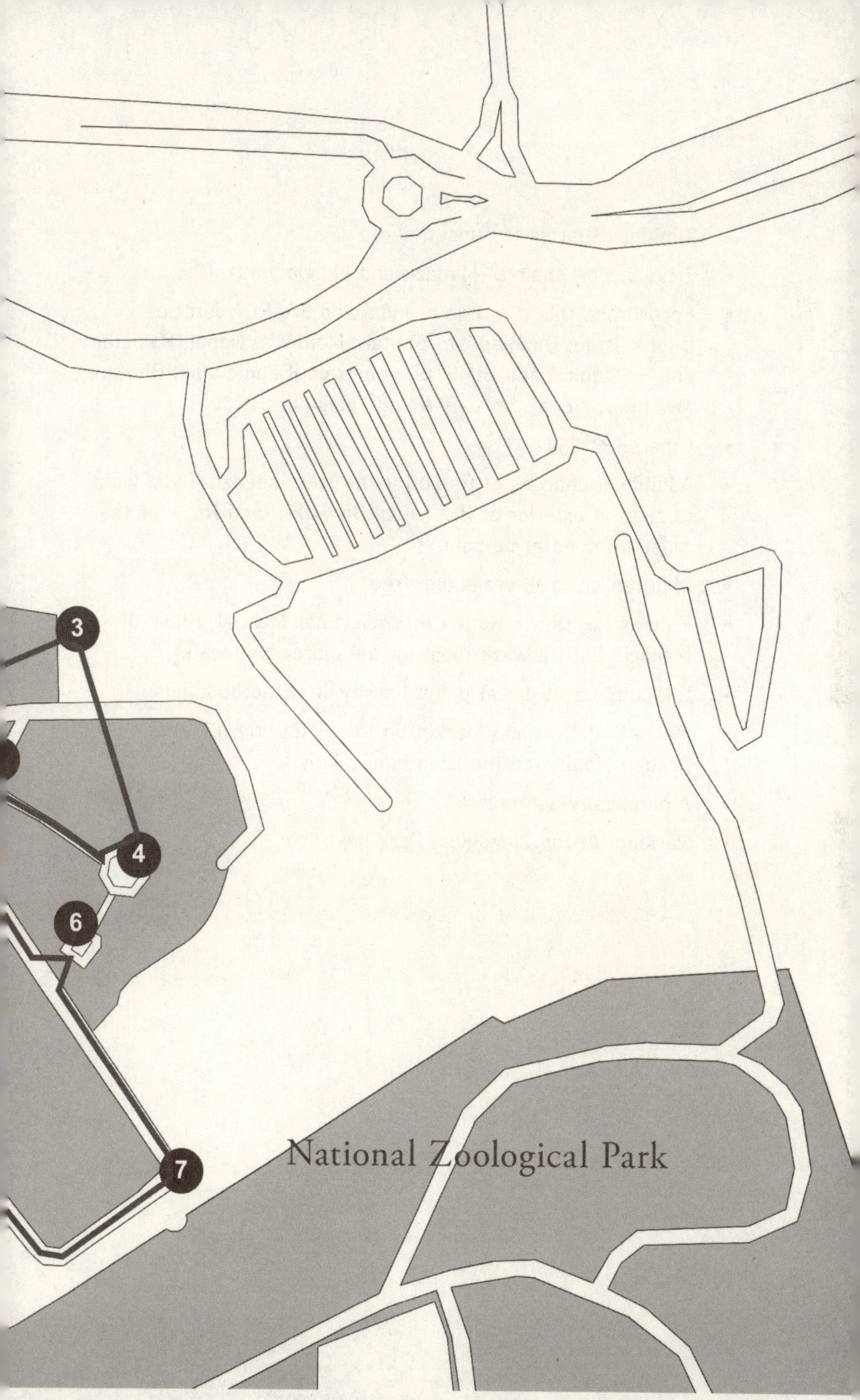
3
4
6
7
National Zoological Park

- Timings: Sunrise to sunset.
- Tickets: For Khair-ul-Manazil and Lal Darwaza: free
- For Purana Qila: Citizens of India and SAARC countries (Afghanistan, Bangladesh, Bhutan, Maldives, Nepal, Pakistan and Sri Lanka) and BIMSTEC countries (Bangladesh, Bhutan, Myanmar, Nepal, Sri Lanka and Thailand): Rs 20
- Others: Rs 250
- Additional charges of Rs 20 for the lake (needed if you want to see the exterior of the Talaqi Darwaza,) and Rs 5 for the museum need to be paid.
- Children up to 15 years old: free
- Highlights: Qila-e-Kuhna mosque, Sher Mandal, Khair-ul-Manazil, Lal Darwaza (best for an abbreviated walk).
- Difficulty Level: Level paths link most of the buildings.
- Metro Station: Khan Market on the Violet line, 1.5 kms, Pragati Maidan on the Blue line, 2 kms.
- Amenities: Washrooms.
- Parking: At the Zoological Park next door.

INDRAPRASTHA AND DINPANAH

'Jumna's dark and limpid waters laved Yudhishthir's palace walls; And to hail him Dharma-raja, monarchs thronged his royal halls.'—R.C. Dutt, *The Mahabharata Condensed in English Verse* (1899)

The Purana Qila is an imposing fortress which was built in the sixteenth century. The raised piece of ground on which it was built, however had a longer history of habitation. In popular tradition this is a site that is identified with the city of Indraprastha, built by the Pandavas, the five brothers who are the heroes of the great Indian epic, the Mahabharata. The first part of the Mahabharata, the *Adi Parva,* tells the story of the clearing of the forest by the fire God Agni, assisted by Arjuna (one of the Pandavas) and Krishna (an incarnation of the God Vishnu). The second book, the *Sabha Parva*, describes the city which was then built on the cleared land beside the river Yamuna. It talks of palaces with golden pillars decorated with precious stones, and pools of clear water.

There is no sure way of knowing if this was the site of the Indraprastha made famous in legend. All we know is that till recent times, there was a village in and immediately around Purana Qila known as Indarpat—a form of the name Indraprastha. None of the grand palaces described in the epic are visible within the fort walls, and in any case it is likely that a fairly simple material culture existed here at the time when the events related in the Mahabharata took place. Centuries of transmission of the epic by word of mouth led to an embellishment in the descriptions of the physical setting. This was the version that was recorded when the epic was finally written down. The excavations that have taken place within the walls of the fort have revealed ancient habitation, but these at most tells us that people may have lived at this site as far back as 1000 BC, the time when the events mentioned in the Mahabharata are believed to have taken place.

'...all the great mushaikhs (religious men), the respectable saiyids, the learned persons and all the elders of the city of Delhi, accompanied the King...to the spot. His Majesty with his holy hand put a brick on the earth, and then each person from that concourse of great men put a stone on the ground.'—Khondamir, *Humayun-nama* (1534)

Archaeological evidence also tells us that some habitation continued to exist here over the following centuries. In 1533, the second Mughal emperor Humayun began at this site the construction of a fortified city called Dinpanah, 'the asylum of the faith'. Within a year the outer walls, bastions and gates were complete.

Humayun's reign was rudely interrupted in 1540 by Sher Shah Sur, who became the ruler at Delhi, forcing Humayun into exile. Sher Shah in his turn established an extensive city stretching from Dinpanah northwards to the fourteenth-century city of Firozabad. Not much of this city remains; the building materials were probably utilized in later constructions such as the city of Shahjahanabad in the seventeenth century. Then, in the twentieth century, the British imperial city of New Delhi was built over the site.

Humayun returned to the throne in 1555 after defeating one of Sher Shah's successors, but died in an accident a few months later. He was succeeded by his thirteen-year-old son Akbar. After some years of ruling from Delhi, Akbar moved his capital to Agra and after a while Purana Qila came to be occupied by the village of Indarpat. The village was cleared in the early twentieth century by the Archaeological Survey of India, which then conserved the buildings and turned the fort into a tourist attraction. There was an interregnum following 1947, when the country was partitioned, and the fort for a while became a refugee camp holding mainly Muslims escaping the rioting and waiting for migration to the newly created nation of Pakistan, and then as a home for immigrants coming from there.

The Walk

The imposing walls of the fort can best be seen on the north-western side by walking along a path that leads off to the left, just beyond the ticketing and reception area. The walls of the fort are high and straight, crowned by battlements and two rows of arrow/gun-slits. The moat that once ran around much of the perimeter of the fort has now been turned into a water body. The river Yamuna once lapped against the eastern edge of the fort, but has long since changed its course eastwards.

The northern side of the fort has a tall gateway called the **Talaqi Darwaza**[1] or the 'forbidden gate'. It is not quite certain when and why this name was given to it. The commonly told story is that a certain king went out to battle through it, vowing not to re-enter unless victorious, but as he died in battle, the gate was shut forever. This account cannot be correlated to any of the historic events connected with the Purana Qila and thus has to be put down to inventive tourist guides.

The gateway itself is quite enchanting. It is very tall and actually has two doorways through it, set one on top of the other. It seems that the lower one was at the level of the water in the moat, and it was the upper one, certainly far more ornamental, that was the main entrance. Its level suggests that there must have been a drawbridge or a causeway leading to it from across the moat. The upper part of the Talaqi Darwaza has two beautifully carved red sandstone jharokhas on either side of the arched doorway. Above each jharokha is a square panel with a carved figure of a leogryph—a mythical lion-like creature, fighting a man. This motif, not uncommon in ancient Indian art, may seem surprising in such a location but has a direct reference to a legend relating to Sher Shah—that he earned the title of Sher Khan after having fought a lion single handed. The gate is topped by three chhatris or pillared kiosks, with remnants of blue tilework on them.

The main entry into the fort now is through the **Bada Darwaza**[2] or the 'large gate'. It is in fact not as tall as the Talaqi Darwaza, nor as ornate, and it has only one arched entrance. In style though it is similar, with a red sandstone facing and inlays in white and black marble providing a nice contrast. This gate too has decorative jharokhas, and above them, a row of arrow-slits. The six-pointed star—here placed on either side of the arch—is a cosmic symbol and a fairly commonly used motif in Mughal architecture.

There are two bastions on either side of the gate. The one on your left would have originally had the same kind of chhatri that you see on top of the one on the right. The battlements on top of the right bastion are also fairly intact—these consist of the parapet with kanguras on top. The kanguras along the rest of the wall have disappeared.

As you pass through the gate and walk inside, you will notice that it has quite a few cell-like chambers arranged on different levels. The gate is quite damaged and the structure immediately surrounding the arch at the entrance was probably built during the repair work carried out in the early twentieth century.

The path leading from the gate intersects with another, on which if you turn left, you can go to the inside of the Talaqi Darwaza. This too is in ruins but you can see the remains of some incised plaster work high up on the walls. If instead you continue straight, you will come to the most spectacular building within the fort—the **Qila-e-Kuhna masjid**[3]. The name literally means 'the mosque of the old fort'.

Though none of the inscriptions on the mosque tells us

either the date it was built or the name of the patron, some historical sources attribute its construction to Sher Shah and the date to 1541. This remarkable building displays a range of decorative techniques. The mosque is essentially built in grey quartzite that was locally mined, but there is a lavish use of red and yellow sandstone as well as white and black marble. Decorative techniques include stone intarsia or inlay work, beautiful stone carving, and some tile work too. As you approach, you will see the back of the mosque, which has a few projecting jharokhas. It also has two pillars set against the wall, which will remind one of the Qutub Minar. Along the top of the wall is a row of stylized kanguras. These of course would not have served the defensive function of true battlements as they are too small and placed on the roof of a mosque that is otherwise open. They are simply a decorative feature. Look closely at the prominent red sandstone turrets at either end of this back wall. The niches are framed by beautifully carved corbels.

Come around to face the façade of the mosque. There are attractive motifs that have been used in its ornamentation. The base of the slender pillars on either side of the three central arches is carved in the shape of a kalash. The use of this motif was quite prevalent in the architecture of the

Muslim rulers of India and represents the evolution of a composite cultural style. The other distinctly Indian motif that was used extensively was the lotus. Here you can see a fringe of lotus buds along the inside of the arches. There is also a large stylized lotus capping the top of the dome, in turn crowned by a finial on the pattern commonly found on Hindu temples. The lotus also appears in the form of bosses or raised medallions on various surfaces in the building. The arches at either end of the façade are simple in design but the bases, carved in red sandstone, have a Chaitya window pattern frequently used in Buddhist art and architecture.

If you stand facing the arches of the mosque, you are facing Mecca, which is to the west. This is the direction of prayer for Muslims, and if you enter through the arches you will see that there are mihrabs along the qibla wall. The mihrabs are richly decorated with carved and inlaid marble, but again, note the kalash-shaped pillar bases and the lotus rosettes. There are bands of Arabic calligraphy, mainly verses from the Quran. The other walls are profusely decorated too. An attractive feature is the black and white marble niches made in the wall to hold lamps.

In this building you can see two methods by which a square space was surmounted by a circular dome. In the central bay, the corners of the room are capped by arches, called squinch arches, constructed in quartzite. These help to create a band of eight arches and these in turn are topped by sixteen smaller arches that produces a shape that is nearly circular. Incidentally, this band of arches at the base of the dome is decorated with ceramic tiles. The brilliant colours were obtained from semi-precious stones, such as lapis and turquoise. In the bays on either side of the central one, the approach is different. Here the space at the corners of the squares is filled in by horizontal or trabeate supports which are then beautifully carved. The dome on top is very shallow. The bays at the extreme ends are rectangular and their ceilings have a very complex construction.

South of the Qila-e-Kuhna masjid is a two-storeyed octagonal building known as **Sher Mandal**[4]. Sher Mandal is a name familiar in history as a palace built by Sher Shah, though it is not at all certain if this was that building; it may have been Humayun who actually had this constructed. This is because, in style, this building is quite similar to some Mughal pavilions described in historical accounts or seen in illustrations of that period. It certainly does not look like a palace. Access to the upper floor of the building is not open to the public and the lowest level is actually solid, except for a staircase going up. The white marble inlay on the red sandstone is fairly simple compared to the intricacy at the mosque, but still quite attractive. The building is topped by a chhatri.

The Sher Mandal has an interesting story attached to it. On 20 January 1556, a few months after Humayun had recaptured the throne of Delhi, he had climbed up to the roof of this building, which incidentally he seemed to have been using as a library and astronomical observatory. He acknowledged the people who had gathered at the nearby mosque and busied himself in making preparations for some astronomical observations. Suddenly, he heard the call to prayer, and in a hurry to either come downstairs or to kneel, he tripped over his long robe and tumbled down the stairs. Four days later he died of his injuries, at the age of fifty-one. Look at the star patterns that have been used to decorate this structure. They were probably inspired by the use of the building as an observatory.

Somewhat to the north-west of the Sher Mandal is a **baoli**[5], closed off by a metal railing. A long and rather narrow stepped passageway leads down to the water level. Baolis were designed to allow easy access to the water via steps, though usually there was also a conventional well at the back where water could be drawn up in a bucket.

To the south of the Sher Mandal is a brickwork structure, the **hammam[6] or bath house.** Its ruined state makes it difficult to reconstruct what it must have looked like, but you can see the remains of terracotta pipes, water chutes and brick-work chambers. Nearby, at a somewhat higher level, is a well, which may have supplied water to the hammam.

Further south, at the extreme end of the path that leads from the Talaqi Darwaza, is the **Humayun Darwaza[7]**, the third entrance into the fort. From the inside, broad steps lead down to the lower part of the gate, which, like the other gates, has several chambers arranged at different levels. The decorative part of the gate is actually on the outside, and can only be seen from the Zoological Park. It is similar to the Talaqi Darwaza. One point of difference is that it still has a few sandstone covered merlons, which have disappeared from the other gates. In the panels above the two jharokhas are two finely-carved, small, marble elephants. Though its name suggests that it was built by Humayun, some historians believe—on the basis of an inscription in ink which was found in one of the rooms—that it was built during Sher Shah's reign.

On your way out of the fort, you might like to visit the archaeological museum located near the Bada Darwaza. It has artefacts from different eras in Delhi's history, particularly finds such as pottery and other everyday objects unearthed in excavations in the Purana Qila and elsewhere, for instance at Lal Kot.

Across the road from the Purana Qila are two further buildings of interest. One is the **Lal Darwaza[8]**, an impressive grey quartzite and red sandstone gateway. It can be approached via a broad path on either side of which are arcades that might have contained shops. Attached to either side of the gate are battlemented walls and bastions suggesting that this was the southern limit of a walled city, most certainly the Sher Garh founded by Sher Shah Sur. The northern limit of this city is to be found some 3kms north, at the gateway known as the Khuni Darwaza, located near Firoz Shah Kotla.

The Lal Darwaza is in a ruined state, with a supporting wall added some time ago, but you can still see some remains of ornamentation. There are jharokhas, white and black marble inlay, lotus rosettes, and some tile work. The battlements along the top of the gate and wall consist of arrow/gun-slits and kanguras.

Not far from the Lal Darwaza, just beside the road is the building known as **Khair-ul-Manazil**[9]. This is a mosque and madrasa complex built by Maham Angah, the wet nurse of the emperor Akbar. To be appointed a wet nurse to a prince of the royal family was a great privilege, which was reserved for women of noble families. The wet nurses were still an important influence in Akbar's life and in the court when he became emperor at just thirteen years of age. Maham Angah commissioned this building to house a mosque and an educational institution in 1561-62, the early part of Akbar's reign.

The gateway is fairly plain-looking and inside, the

building is rather the worse for wear. Across the courtyard, facing the gateway is the main part of the mosque. An inscription over the central arch tells us name of the building, the year of its construction and the name of its patron. There are some remains of the attractive tile work and incised plaster that was used in decorating the walls. The rooms arranged around the other sides of the courtyard on two levels would have housed the college or madrasa.

We learn from one of the histories written during Akbar's reign that this was the scene of an attempt on the life of the emperor. One day, in 1564, while returning from a hunting expedition, Akbar was passing through the bazaar of Delhi, presumably the street in front of Lal Darwaza, when a man standing on the roof of the madrasa shot an arrow at him, which luckily only grazed the skin. The would-be assassin was immediately caught and put to death.

7

NIZAMUDDIN

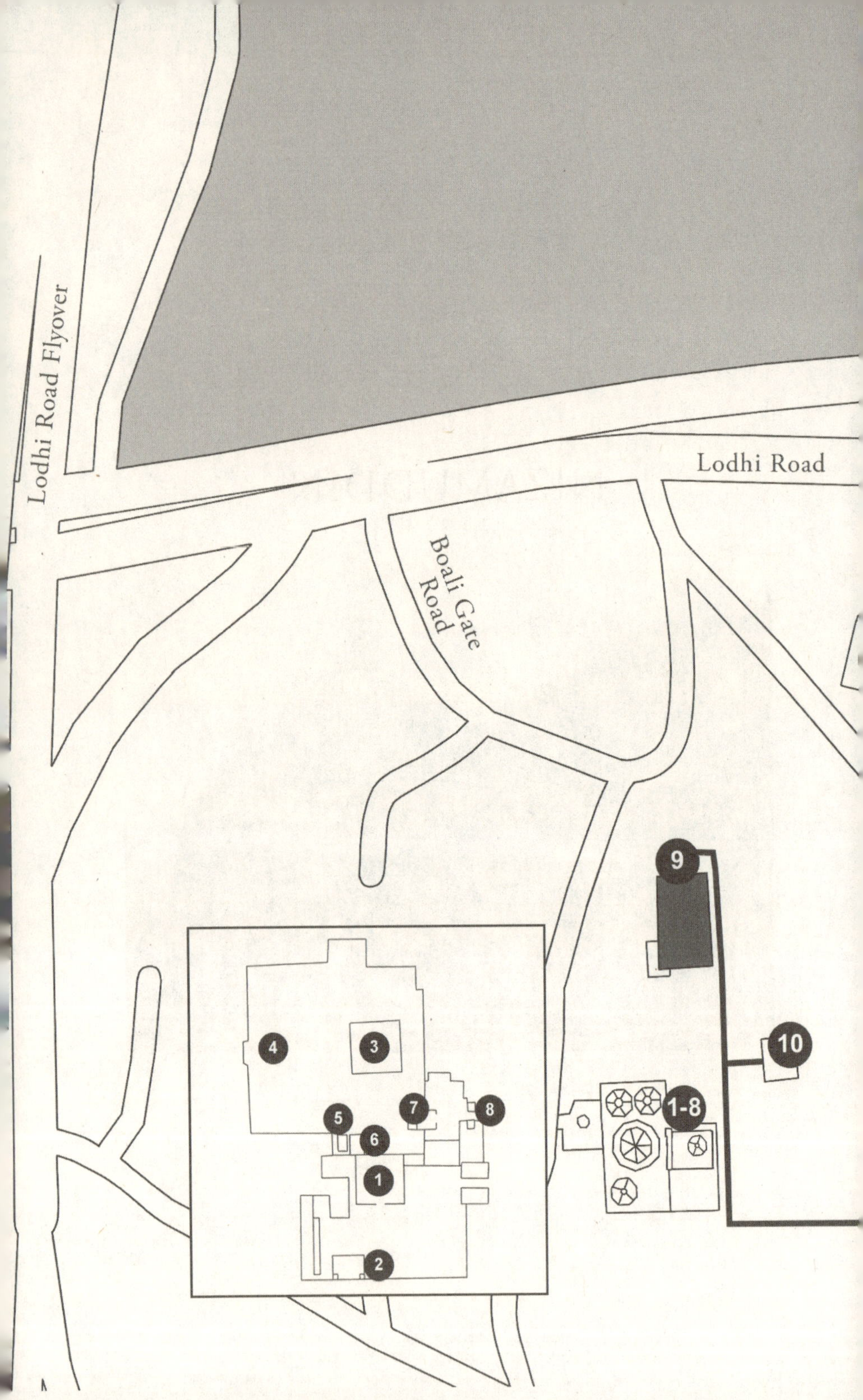

Lodhi Road Flyover
Lodhi Road
Boali Gate Road
1
2
3
4
5
6
7
8
9
10
1-8

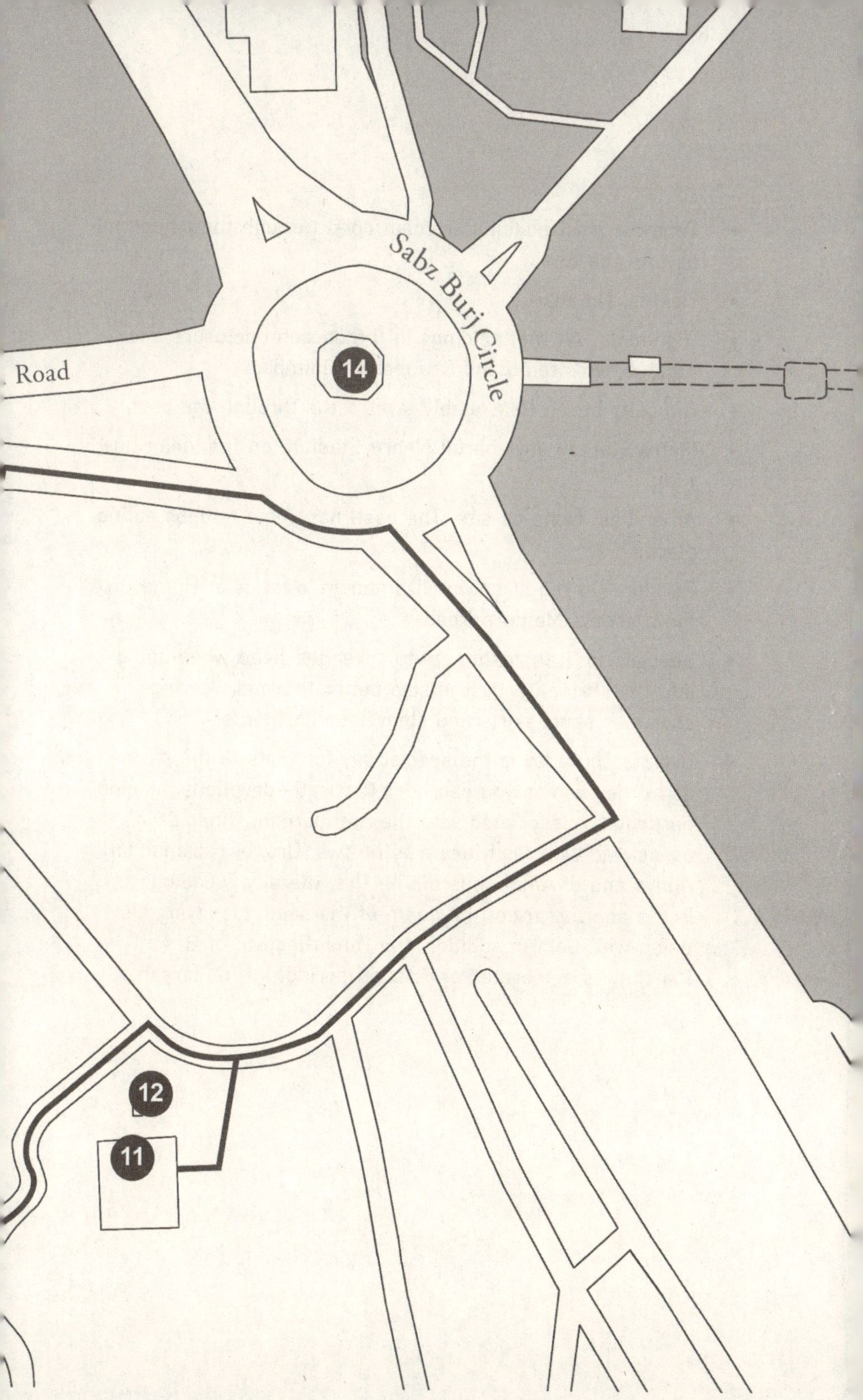
Sabz Burj Circle
Road
14
12
11

- Timings: Most buildings remain open through the day on all days of the week.
- Tickets: No charge.
- Highlights: All the buildings in the dargah enclosure and Atgah Khan's tomb and Chaunsath Khamba.
- Difficulty Level: Reasonably level paths through the basti.
- Metro Station: Jawaharlal Nehru Stadium on the Violet line, 1 km.
- Amenities: None on site. The basti has some famous eating places.
- Parking: On the street in Nizamuddin West or at Humayun's tomb across Mathura Road.
- Special Tip: It is customary to cover the head when going into the shrine itself. It is also better to avoid wearing shorts or short skirts and sleeveless garments.
- Events: Thursday is the special day for visits to the shrine as in the evening you can hear Qawwali—devotional singing particularly associated with the Sufi dargah. Other days associated with festivities are the two 'Urs' of Nizamuddin Auliya and of Amir Khusro. The Urs, literally 'wedding', is the anniversary of the death of the saint, signifying his union with God. In addition, the Hindu festival of Basant Panchmi is celebrated as Basant (spring) in the dargah.

HISTORIC BASTI

NIZAMUDDIN IS A name which many associate simply with a posh residential area in central Delhi, or with the major railway station located there. The locality, in fact, gets its name from one of the major Sufi saints of Delhi, Nizamuddin Auliya, whose burial place is one of the most revered shrines in India and an important centre of pilgrimage.

Mohammad Nizamuddin was born in 1235 in Badaun (in the state of Uttar Pradesh), to a family with a background of learning and piety. He lost his father at a young age and while still a youth, came to Delhi with his mother. His early years in Delhi were spent in scholarly pursuits, but were also marked by the death of his mother. Though his initial ambition was to become a qazi or a jurist, he started spending a lot of time in the company of men who were Sufis, or Islamic mystics. In particular, he found himself being mysteriously drawn to a great Sufi of the time—Fariduddin Ganj-e-Shakar, who lived in Ajodhan (now in Pakistan) and of whom Nizamuddin only knew by reputation. At the age of twenty, Nizamuddin had a mystical experience and his soul was illuminated with the love of God that replaced all worldliness. He set out for Ajodhan to meet Fariduddin Ganj-e-Shakar, who was the direct spiritual successor of the great saint, Qutubuddin Bakhtiyar Kaki. The Sufi received

Nizamuddin and eventually appointed him as his spiritual successor.

Nizamuddin returned to Delhi and began to live in the locality of Ghiyaspur, or present day Nizamuddin. He soon acquired a large following, which included the emperors Alauddin Khalji and Mohammad Tughlaq, and powerful courtiers like Amir Khusro. He was buried close to where he had lived, and his grave became an important place of pilgrimage and the centre of a bustling settlement or 'basti'. Many burials down the centuries have also taken place in the vicinity of the saint's grave, in a wide radius that extends to the tombs of the Mughal emperor, Humayun and the poet and soldier Rahim. As a result, this is an area rich in buildings and stories.

The immediate surroundings of the dargah are a web of narrow lanes. Many of the people living here have done so for many generations and are connected to the shrine. There is also a constant stream of visitors.

The Walk

The lane that runs to the south of the Nizamuddin police station, (located on the roundabout just outside Humayun's tomb) takes you into the basti. Turn right at the end of the lane and you will see signs that you are nearing the shrine—a narrow lane lined with shops selling flowers and other items for offering at the shrine. Follow this lane and after a few turns it will bring you to a gate leading into an enclosure. You can leave your footwear here and enter. There is an 'official' shoe deposit place where you might leave a few rupees as a tip, though it is not strictly required. Alternately if you buy flowers at one of the many stalls, the vendor will also look after your shoes for free.

Immediately as you enter you will see before you an enclosure made of red sandstone screens. Within this is the **tomb of Amir Khusro**[1]. He was born in 1253 in Etah in modern Uttar Pradesh and was a powerful courtier under several reigning emperors within his lifetime. He was also a devoted disciple and close friend of Nizamuddin Auliya. Amir Khusro was a multifaceted genius, who is credited with a major role in the development of the Hindustani music tradition. He is even better known as a poet in Persian and Hindi, his eloquence earning him the sobriquet 'parrot of India'.

Though an influential nobleman, Khusro spent a lot of time in the company of Nizamuddin, and when the latter died, he was heartbroken. He sat mourning beside the saint's grave until, six months later, he too passed away. The tomb building is of marble and is covered with a vaulted roof. It dates from 1605, built by a devotee, probably to replace a simpler structure. Only men may enter the inner grave enclosure.

South of the tomb of Amir Khusro is a 'dalan'—a pillared verandah, now covered with a colour wash. This is the **dalan of Mirdha Ikram**[2]. Ikram, who died in 1801-02, was an army officer under the Mughal emperor Shah Alam. The main point of interest here however are two graves, covered in black granite. One is of the historian

Ziauddin Barani, who lived in the years 1285–1358. The other is that of Shams Siraj Afif, another historian, who lived in the second half of the fourteenth century.

It is customary to proceed to the **tomb of Nizamuddin Auliya**[3] after one has paid one's respects to his disciple Khusro. Nizamuddin's tomb is a marble building, very elaborately gilded and painted. Initially, Nizamuddin's grave was a very plain, but over the centuries many elaborate structures were built over it, and most of the marble structure seen today dates from the first quarter of the nineteenth century. The inner chamber is surrounded by a pillared verandah and topped by a bulbous, striped dome with a gilt finial on top. A distinctive feature is the elaborate parapet around the roof, which is made up of a mini arcade, topped by many small domes, each with a tiny pinnacle. At the four corners are chhatris, and below all this runs a deep chhajja.

It is immediately clear that there is a constant stream of devotees at the shrine of Nizamuddin. This swells into a packed crowd on Thursdays and during the Urs celebrations. Many who come are troubled by personal problems, medical conditions or financial difficulties. They ask the saint to intercede with God on their behalf. Others come back in gratitude when their prayers have been answered. Many come simply because it is a holy place and has a special atmosphere. Those who can afford to, often dispense charity at the dargah. This may take the form of donations with the khadims and pirzadas, who are the functionaries at the shrine. Or it may involve feeding the poor at one of the many eating places just outside the dargah. This keeps alive a tradition of charity that dates from the time of Nizamuddin.

The power of the prayers of Nizamuddin is legendary. Many prodigious feats have been attributed to him over the centuries. In 1303, when the emperor Alauddin Khalji was on the throne, the Mongols attacked and laid siege to Delhi (which at the time was centred at Mehrauli). After two months, they inexplicably retreated. Ziauddin Barani in whose lifetime these events took place, attributed the mysterious withdrawal of the Mongols to the effect of the prayers of Nizamuddin.

It is best to orient yourself through the mosque which faces west. This will make it easier to navigate through the enclosure with the help of the following description.

To the west of the tomb of Nizamuddin is the **Jamat Khana mosque[4]**, the oldest building in the complex. Believed to have been built in the early fourteenth century by Khizr Khan, the son of the emperor Alauddin Khalji, it has distinct similarities to the Alai Darwaza in the Qutub Minar complex. Look carefully for instance at the lotus bud fringe around the inside of the arches, the combination of red sandstone and white marble and the flattish domes. An interesting feature of the mosque is the spikes or spearheaded shapes that edge the roof. It is more usual for Sultanate period buildings to have a parapet of kanguras or merlons.

One story associated with the mosque is that its central chamber was originally built as a tomb for Nizamuddin Auliya during his lifetime. The saint however said that he did not wish to be buried there. Later therefore, a side chamber was added on either side of the central chamber, and it was converted into a mosque. On the other hand, architects have pointed out that the side chambers do not appear to be later additions.

There are several grave enclosures within the dargah complex. To the south-west of Nizamuddin's shrine is the **tomb of Jahanara[5]**. Jahanara was the daughter of the Mughal emperor Shahjahan, who accompanied him when he was deposed by his son Aurangzeb and exiled to Agra. On Shahjahan's death in 1666, she came back to Delhi, where she died in 1681. She was buried in this tomb, which she had had commissioned during her own lifetime. The enclosure is made up of delicately carved marble screens. Inside, there is more than one grave. The central one belongs to the princess. At its head is a slab of marble which has an inscription. Essentially this inscription tells us that this is the grave of Jahanara, who was a devotee of the Chishti saints (the order to which Nizamuddin belonged), and that she wished that her grave be covered only by grass. Her wish was honoured to the extent that the marble gravestone has an open space in the middle. While grass originally grew in it, today it is mostly covered with rose petals strewn by visitors. There are other graves too in Jahanara's tomb enclosure. These belong to members of the Mughal royal family from a later date.

Just east of Jahanara's tomb is the **tomb of Mohammad Shah[6].** He was the Mughal emperor who reigned from 1719-48 and was nicknamed Rangila or literally 'colourful' for his pleasure-loving lifestyle and his special interest in poetry and music. The Mughal Empire was already in decline when he ascended the throne, but he was the last Mughal emperor to rule with a semblance of power. One catastrophic event during his reign was the invasion of the Persian emperor Nadir Shah in 1739. On his return from Delhi, Nadir Shah took away vast treasure, including the famed Peacock Throne of the Mughal emperors.

The tomb of Mohammad Shah stands exactly between Nizamuddin's and Amir Khusro's, and it is said in popular tradition that his coming between the two friends brought a curse upon the Mughal royal family, which never flourished after that. The tomb enclosure truly represents the artistic refinement of the age, as it is exquisitely and elaborately carved from white marble. Even the leaves of the door are of marble, beautifully carved with a floral pattern.

There are several graves inside the enclosure. The largest one is that of the emperor. To the west of him lies his wife, Nawab Sahiba Mahal. At the foot of her grave is that of her daughter who was given in marriage to the son of Nadir Shah. Next to her grave is that of her baby, and it is possible she died in childbirth. The other graves are of lesser-known members of the royal family.

To the east of Mohammad Shah's tomb is the **grave enclosure of Mirza Jahangir**[7], who represents the last phase of the Mughal dynasty. His father, Akbar II, who was on the throne from 1806 to 1837, was a pensioner of the British East India Company and an emperor in less than name. His territories were actually administered by the British. Akbar II wanted his younger son Jahangir, to succeed him on the throne, but the British insisted that his firstborn Zafar was entitled to succeed. Jahangir, who was an impetuous young man, nursed a grudge. Soon after, orders were given for British troops to occupy key positions in the Red Fort, and Jahangir decided that he would oppose this and block their entry. He and his followers took up a position inside the gate and fired on the party of the British Resident (highest administrative official stationed in Delhi) as it entered the gate. Though no one was hurt, Jahangir was arrested and later exiled to Allahabad. He ultimately died there and his body was brought back to Delhi for burial.

This tomb enclosure, like the previous two, is made of elaborately carved marble screens. The grave of Jahangir is the second from the west. The gravestone is beautifully carved with a pattern of leaves and flowers. Curiously, its design is that of a woman's grave, as it has the typically flat, rectangular takhti or slate on it. Clearly then, it belonged to a woman's grave and for reasons unknown, was removed from there to be placed over Jahangir's body. To the west of Jahangir's grave is that of his brother Babur. In this case too, the stone originally belonged to another grave and bears an inscription which dates from 1579-80. Two other graves in the enclosure belong to unknown persons, most certainly from the Mughal royal family.

One doorway leads out of this enclosure to the east, into a space known as the **house of Mirza Jahangir**[8]. The name should not be understood to mean that this is where Mirza Jahangir lived. This is simply where members of the family were buried (for a similar use see 'dalan of Mirdha Ikram' above). Though most of the graves here are unmarked, one has an inscription that tells us that it is the grave of the wife of Mirza Babur.

Go back into the main shrine courtyard and go out through the gateway to the north of Nizamuddin's tomb. A few twists in the narrow passageway will bring you to the **baoli of Nizamuddin**[9], which is a large, open source of groundwater. A wide flight of steps leads down to the water on the northern side. A number of tombs have been built around the baoli, particularly along the western side, but while one has glimpses of intriguing architecture from the baoli, they are otherwise inaccessible to the public.

The baoli dates to the lifetime of the saint and has a few captivating stories attached to it. It is said that at the same time as Nizamuddin was having it built in 1321, the emperor Ghiyasuddin Tughlaq began work on the mammoth fortifications at Tughlaqabad (now in south Delhi). The emperor decreed that all workmen would spend the entire working day at his project, but the workmen continued to work on the baoli at night. The enraged ruler prohibited the sale of oil, so that they would have no lamps to light their work, but through the miraculous powers of the saint, the water of the baoli effectively worked as oil for the lamps. The baoli was completed, Nizamuddin blessed its water, and ever since it has been believed to work wonderful cures.

From the baoli, go back to the shrine courtyard and out through the gateway through which you first entered. Collect your shoes, then follow the path back just a bit until you climb up a few steps and come to a fork in the path. Turn left, and then right, which will shortly bring you into **Atgah Khan's tomb**[10]. Atgah Khan, whose given name was Shamsuddin Mohammad, was an important nobleman at

the court of the emperor Humayun, to whom he displayed a high degree of loyalty when the emperor was defeated by Sher Shah. His wife, Jiji, was given the honour of being the wet nurse of Humayun's son Akbar, with the customary title 'Angah'. Her husband thus got the title 'Atgah' along with his other titles from the court. As Akbar ascended the throne in 1556 at the tender age of thirteen, his wet nurses and their families remained influential at his court for a long time. In particular, the family of another wet nurse, Maham Angah, was engaged in a rivalry with Jiji Angah's family. Maham Angah's son, Adham Khan, murdered Shamsuddin Mohammad, for which Akbar punished him by having him thrown from the ramparts of the fort at Agra, where this incident took place in 1562. The body of Shamsuddin Mohammad was brought to Delhi and buried here. The building was constructed over the remains in 1566-67 by Atgah Khan's son, Mirza Aziz Kokaltash. Kokaltash literally means 'foster brother' in Turk, which was the mother tongue of the Mughals. It was a title received by Mirza Aziz as he was the son of Akbar's wet nurse, Jiji Angah.

The tomb of Atgah Khan is a beautiful example of the architecture of Akbar's reign. The most striking ornamentation on the outside are the beautiful geometric patterns made up of an inlay of mainly red and yellow sandstone, white and black marble, and coloured tiles. Besides this, there is low relief carving, stone screens, and wide bands of calligraphy with verses from the Quran carved in stone. Inside, there are remains of some finely incised and painted plaster. There are three graves inside. The central one is that of Atgah Khan, the one to its east is that of Jiji Angah and the other is unidentified.

To the west of the tomb is a wall mosque, decorated with beautiful coloured tiles that are unfortunately very damaged.

The bright blue, green and yellow pigments, derived from crushed coloured stones, have not faded through the centuries. In the south-western corner is a dalan or pillared hall, which was used as a khanqah for Sufis. The slender pillars and cusped arches of this structure suggest that it dates from the late Mughal period, maybe the eighteenth century.

Once you leave Atgah Khan's tomb, trace your way back through the path leading from the dargah, past the shops until you come out into the open. Keep going straight and you will soon find a Mughal era sandstone gateway to your right. Enter it, and to your right again you will find a doorway leading into an enclosure. This contains the building known as **Chaunsath Khamba**[11], literally 'sixty-four pillars', which is the tomb of Mirza Aziz Kokaltash.

Built during Mirza Aziz's lifetime, the tomb is a large, open pavilion made of marble. It actually has sixty-four pillars, as you will find if you count carefully. There are groups of four closely set pillars at each of the four corners, totalling sixteen. Between the corners, along the four sides there are four double pillars that add up to thirty-two. Within the hall there are sixteen single pillars, making it sixty-four in total.

The ornamentation of the hall is minimal, both inside and out. There is very little carving and it is the overall form and the large expanses of marble that are the principal attractive features. The graves inside the pavilion are made of beautifully carved marble. The large one, second from the west, is that of Mirza Aziz, and the one to its west, is that of his wife. The other graves are presumed to be of other members of the family. There are many other graves in the yard immediately outside the tomb, some of them quite beautifully carved out of sandstone. Some of these are said to belong to the daughters of Bahadur Shah, the last Mughal emperor.

A doorway in the northern wall of the enclosure in which Chaunsath Khamba stands, leads into another enclosure. This contains the **tomb of Mirza Asadullah Khan Ghalib**[12] who lived from 1797-1869 and was a famous poet who wrote in Urdu and Persian. He lived at a time when the Mughal emperor simply lived on a modest allowance given by the British East India Company's government, and therefore could not afford to patronize poets, painters, musicians and builders on the lavish scale customary for his ancestors. The new government had different priorities and represented a different way of life with different tastes. Ghalib therefore spent most of his life in financial difficulty, to which were added the tribulations of the uprising of 1857, which was suppressed very harshly by the British. He died in 1869 and was buried in a very simple grave. Later, in the middle of the twentieth century, a tomb was commissioned by the Ghalib Memorial Society and designed by the Hyderabad architect, Zain Yar Jang. It is a fairly plain but fitting structure. In the twenty-first century, new paving and a screen with a few couplets of Ghalib's poetry was added to the enclosure.

Return to the Mathura Road the way you came, turn left and walk along the road, past the police station, until you come to a park with a stone building in it. This is **Barah Khamba**[13], the tomb of some unknown person, dating from the fifteenth century. The name is purely descriptive—a reference to the twelve pillars that hold up the domed roof.

Now, if you are feeling adventurous, you may cross this very busy road to look at the **Sabz Burj**[14] situated on the roundabout in the middle of the road. Believed to date from the early Mughal period (1530s or 1540s), this is the tomb of a now unknown person, and its name literally means 'green tower'. The distinctive features of this building are Timurid in style, characteristic of the architecture created by Timur or Tamerlane and his immediate descendants in Samarkand and Herat. The Mughals were descendants of Timur and their architecture in India too owes much to this legacy. Similarities with buildings of Central Asia, as in Samarkand, are quite apparent, including the tall drum and high peshtaqs (projecting façades) on the four long sides.

Of the ornamentation that remains today, the painted plaster in the arched niches on the outside is noteworthy. For many years during British rule, the Sabz Burj, was used as a police station. Sometime in the 1920s, the police station was moved out to its present location, beside the road.

8

HUMAYUN'S TOMB COMPLEX

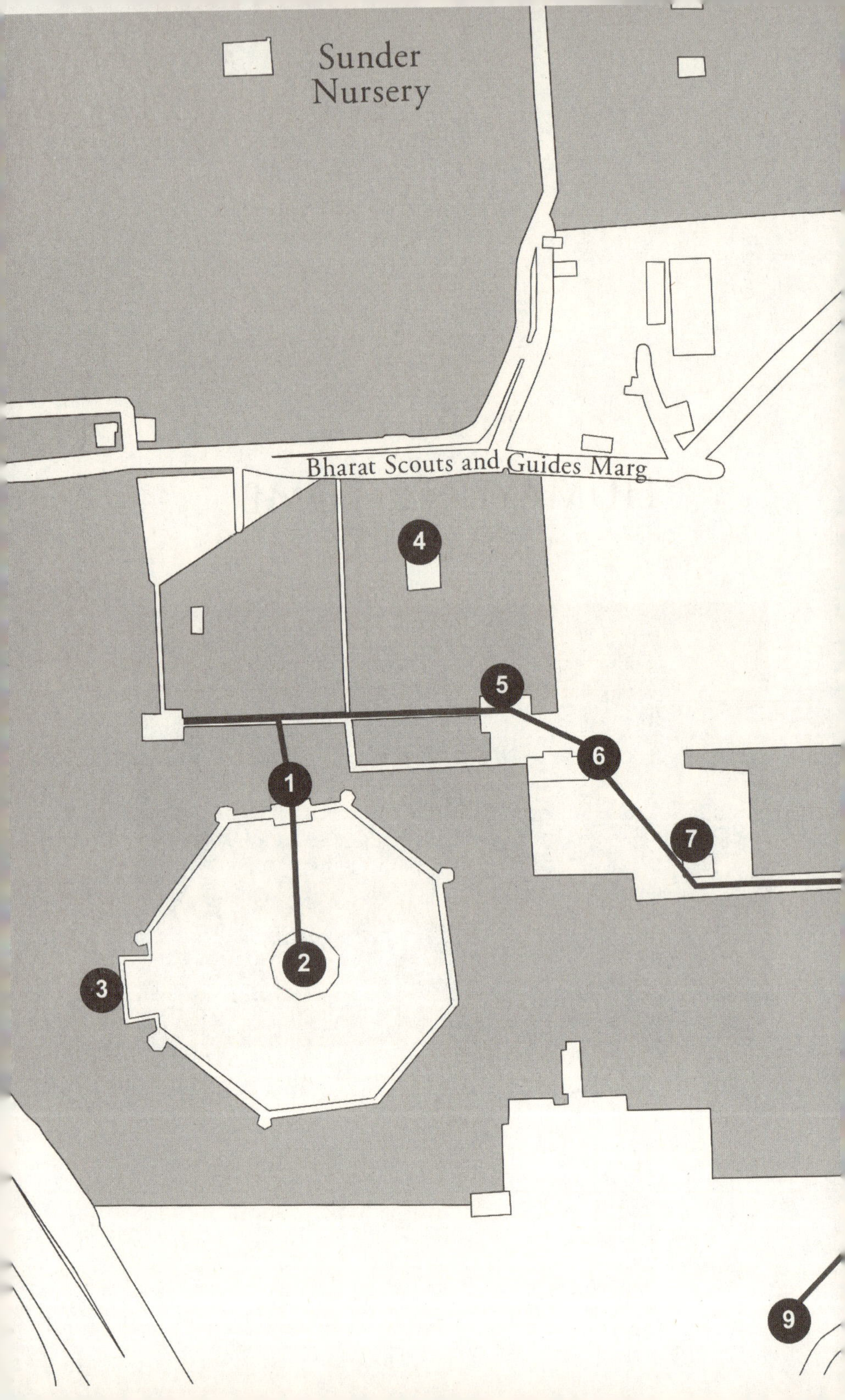
Sunder
Nursery
Bharat Scouts and Guides Marg
1
2
3
4
5
6
7
9

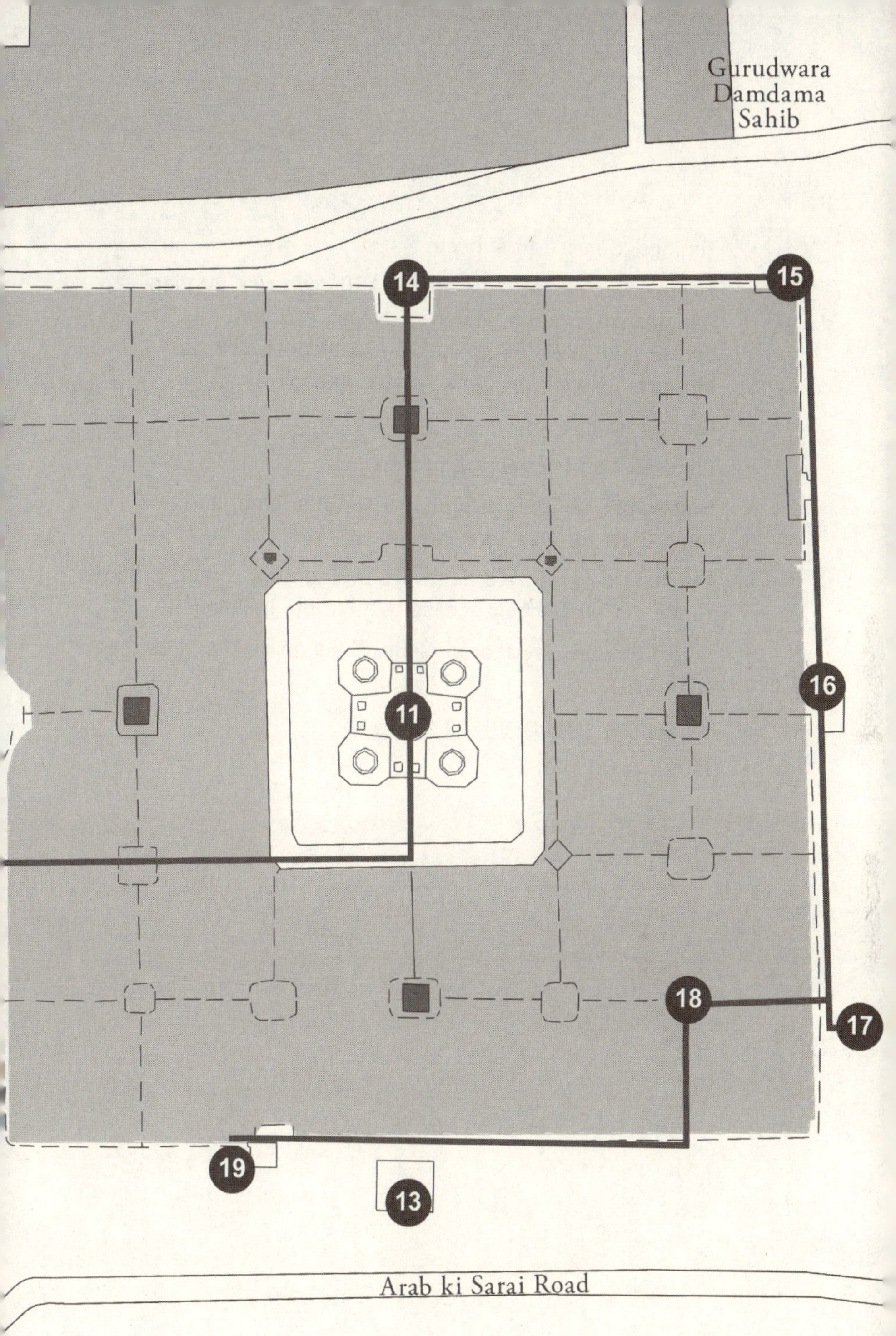

Gurudwara
Damdama
Sahib
14
15
11
16
18
17
19
13
Arab ki Sarai Road

- Timings: Sunrise to sunset.
- Tickets: Citizens of India and SAARC countries (Afghanistan, Bangladesh, Bhutan, Maldives, Nepal, Pakistan and Sri Lanka) and BIMSTEC countries (Bangladesh, Bhutan, Myanmar, Nepal, Sri Lanka and Thailand): Rs 35
- Others: Rs 550
- Children up to 15 years old: free
- Highlights: Isa Khan's tomb, Humayun's tomb, barber's tomb (best for an abbreviated walk).
- Difficulty Level: Paved pathways through the complex. Some ramps for wheelchair access but not into buildings.
- Metro Station: Jawaharlal Nehru Stadium on the Violet line, 1.5 kms.
- Amenities: Washrooms.
- Parking: On site.

MUGHAL MAUSOLEUM

THE MUGHAL EMPEROR Humayun died in January 1556, at the age of fifty-one, in Dinpanah (now called Purana Qila), a fortress he had constructed in Delhi beside the river Yamuna. Upon his death, he left behind an empire that was precariously held together. It had only been a few months since he had regained control of the territories of India, after fifteen years of exile, following his defeat at the hands of Sher Shah Sur in 1540. His son Akbar, who inherited the throne, was only thirteen years old and was, or rather his generals were, immediately faced with the task of dealing with insurrections in many parts of the empire.

The first four or five years of Akbar's reign saw the consolidation of the empire, mainly through the efforts of Bairam Khan, Akbar's tutor and regent. Bairam Khan's power, and some of his policies, had made him unpopular with other influential people at court, including the family of Akbar's wet nurse, Maham Angah. Akbar was soon persuaded to shake himself free of the influence of Bairam Khan, who departed for Mecca, but on the way he was assassinated. Maham Angah's power did not last long either, and she died soon after.

So, by 1562, Akbar had come of age, and this was when he started work on the mausoleum of his father. Humayun's chief wife, Bega Begum or Haji Begam (who was Akbar's step-mother), is often credited with the building of his tomb but in fact, she was away most of the time on pilgrimage, and Akbar merely put her in charge during some of the time that she was in Delhi. The scale of the project and its timing suggests that the young emperor himself was responsible for commissioning it.

The site chosen for the mausoleum was significant. It was just a kilometre and a half south of the fortress built by Humayun. It was picturesquely situated beside the river, though since then the river has moved considerably eastwards. It was also fairly close to the holy shrine of the Sufi saint, Nizamuddin Auliya. The saint's shrine had prompted the practice of many burials in the vicinity, and Humayun's tomb was simply the most monumental among these. Finally, it was located on the road to Agra, where Akbar's capital had shifted in the late 1550s.

The Walk

The area contains many buildings apart from Humayun's tomb, and this walk will take in those that are within the ticketed walled area. The entrance leads into a sunken plaza, to the left of which is a new site museum. Your first destination is past this, where a short path to your right will bring you to the **tomb of Isa Khan Niyazi**[1-3]. He was an Afghan who was one of the most important nobles of Sher Shah Sur and his successor Islam Shah Sur. He built this tomb within his own lifetime, in 1547-48, and clearly intended it to be a sort of family mausoleum as there are a number of graves within it, all uninscribed.

Enter the enclosure through the ruined **gateway**[1]; notice how the carved corbels of grey quartzite frame the top of the doorway. This is a hangover from the typical architecture of the pre-Delhi Sultanate period, when Indian builders spanned space using techniques based on horizontal beams placed on vertical columns. The Sultanate architects introduced the use of the arch to India, but also adopted indigenous Indian forms, which they used frequently, such as in this doorway. The structure around the doorway is in ruins, so you can see the materials out of which the core was constructed. These basically consist of rough stones held together by a mortar that contained limestone, brick powder, and a variety of organic material including cow dung, jaggery, lentils, greens, and the viscous pulp of bel or wood apple. These materials produced a mortar that was durable, but could also breathe. A side effect is that organic growth tends to take place on these buildings, giving them a dark patina, which is harmless, though some might consider it unsightly.

The gateway leads to an octagonal garden within an enclosing wall. In the centre is an octagonal **tomb[2].** It has some characteristic features of late Sultanate octagonal tombs. The verandah is made of double pillars, and the corners have sloping buttresses. Above the verandah is a sloping chhajja, and the roof has an edge made by a pattern of kanguras, which in a fortification are a part of the defensive battlements but here, are simply a decorative motif. Eight chhatris or pillared kiosks on the roof surround the central dome that has a lotus-shaped crest on top.

The stone used in the lower part of the building

It is easier to orient yourself if you remember that the entrance from beside the ticket window, where you first entered, is at the extreme west of the complex.

is quartzite, which is widely available in Delhi, with some details picked out in red sandstone. The upper parts of the structure are covered in limestone plaster. The embellishments are also typical of the late Sultanate period—finely incised plaster and tile work, mostly in brilliant blue and green mineral pigments. Walk around to the back, to the southern side, facing away from the entrance gateway. This is the entrance into the tomb and the façade is decorated slightly more elaborately. Conventionally, in all Islamic burials, the body is placed such that the head is to the north and the feet to the south, and the face is turned towards Mecca, which in India is to the west. Most tomb buildings are entered from the south.

Inside the tomb, there are several cenotaphs, which mark the position of the burial, since the actual burial is deep within the ground. Isa Khan's grave, though uninscribed, is probably the one in the middle, on the northern side. Let your eyes adjust to the darkness inside and then look at the ceiling, which is beautifully decorated with incised and painted plaster.

To the west of the tomb is a **mosque**[3], which was probably built at the same time. Here too notice the beautiful tile work in bright blue, green and yellow. Inside, the west wall is marked out by three red sandstone mihrabs. This enclosure containing the tomb and grave came to be used as homes sometime in the eighteenth century by a large population. It was acquired from them in the early twentieth century by the Archaeological Survey of India, and conserved.

Leave the enclosure and turn right on the main path leading from the main entrance. You will pass through a break in an old wall and find yourself in a garden, at the far end of which is a square platform, which is the **tomb of Bu Halima**[4]. At ground level is the burial chamber in the centre, and it is surrounded by smaller chambers. It is not known who Bu Halima was, but the architectural features of this tomb suggest that it was probably built in the late sixteenth century. The tomb is set in a walled garden, and an attractive feature is the chhatris that top the corners of the enclosure wall on the north side. Bu Halima's garden too was occupied by a resident population until its acquisition in the early twentieth century.

At the eastern end of this garden, directly opposite the ticket window entrance is a plain looking **gateway**[5] finished in white plaster. Walk through it and you will come out towards what was clearly its 'right' side. It is nicely proportioned and shaped, and was apparently designed as the main entrance into Bu Halima's garden. Note the two beautiful tile work medallions in the spandrels of the large arch. This gateway makes it clear that the garden was originally meant to be entered from the eastern side. It was only later, when Humayun's Tomb became a major tourist attraction, that a part of the western wall of the garden was broken to allow through access.

To the south-west of this gate, and set at right angles to it, is the **gate of Arab Sarai**[6]. It is said that when Haji Begam, Humayun's widow, came back from her pilgrimage to Mecca, she brought with her 300 Arabs and built this complex to house them. The gate is an attractive example of early Mughal architecture. During this time, there was a shift away from the limestone plaster decoration that was popular under the Lodi dynasty, to the use of inlay patterns in different coloured stones. This gateway has a base of neatly cut golden-grey quartzite with decorative details in red sandstone inlaid with white marble. Look at the intricate lotus motifs set in the spandrels on either side of the arches, and the fairly simple but beautiful border running across the top. Also notice the jharokhas supported on elaborately carved brackets.

Enter through the gateway and you will notice that not much is left inside. This was in fact a well-populated neighbourhood until the early twentieth century, and in typical Delhi terms, it was a comparatively 'good address', in contrast for instance to the settlement in Isa Khan's tomb. Conservation work by the Archaeological Survey removed the houses within, leaving the older and bigger structures. A little way in, to your left, are two buildings next to each other—the **Afsarwala tomb and mosque**[7]—the name simply means the 'officer's tomb and mosque' and nothing further is known of the patron, or who is buried here.

These buildings too show some typical early Mughal features. The tomb is essentially square, but with the corners cut off, which gives it the shape of an irregular octagon. The dome is placed on a high drum and it is actually a 'double dome'. This means that there is an outer dome in proportion with the outer dimensions of the building, and within it is a smaller dome which is better suited to the proportions of the inner chamber. The Mughals popularized the double dome in India. One of the graves inside has the date 1566-67 on it, so this tomb is at least as old as that.

The mosque next to the tomb was most likely built at the same time. It looks quite plain and rough, because the red plaster that covered it has mostly fallen off. Inside, built against the qibla wall, is a minbar from which the imam or priest led the prayers. On the other side of the mosque is a low chamber which is believed to have been a hammam.

Taking the path that leads south-east of these buildings

you enter another enclosure which is the **Jahangiri mandi**[8]. It is said that this was a wholesale market (mandi) built during the reign of the emperor Jahangir (1605-27) by the chief eunuch, Mihrban Agha. Known as khwajasara, some eunuchs were put in charge of the royal harems and thus became powerful and influential. Walk out through the gate which is at the eastern end of the enclosure to see its façade of cream plaster and tile panels. The inscription in red sandstone on either side at the top of the arch tells us that it was built by Mihrban Agha in the reign of Jahangir.

Inside, the ruined rooms along the long edges of the rectangular enclosure must have been shops, with probably store rooms behind them. At the western end of the enclosure is another gate, quite plain, which led to another part of Arab Sarai. Against the southern wall is a **baoli**[9]. Examine it carefully; you don't want to fall in! In style, it is not like other baolis in Delhi, which usually have a single broad flight of stairs leading down to the water. It is said that it is modelled on baolis found in the Malwa region of central India.

Go back the way you came, on the path that you took from Afsarwala tomb. Continue straight on that path and it will bring you out right beside the **western gate to Humayun's tomb**[10]. Note the six-pointed star on either side of the arched entrance. This kind of star is a cosmic symbol common to several religions including Hinduism and Islam. Also note the chhatris at the corners on top of the gate.

As you pass through the gate you get your first glimpse of the magnificent **Humayun's Tomb**[11]. Stop and take in the large and spectacular tomb from afar. The top of the finial of the dome is some fifty metres above the level of the ground. For comparison, this makes it more than two-thirds the height of the Qutub Minar. Look at some of the distinctive features of the building. It was designed and executed by the architect Mirak Mirza Ghiyas, who was of Iranian descent and had worked in Central Asia as well as India. The building thus combines principles from different building traditions.

In shape, the dome is very typical of Central and West Asian buildings of the time. It bulges slightly above the drum and is pulled up to a point at the top. Unlike most such domes, there is no lotus crest on top, and the finial rises directly from the dome. This finial, which is in the form of a number of copper vessels on top of each other, is itself nearly six metres tall. However, unlike the tile work that was popular in Central and West Asia, this dome is covered in marble, and in fact, the use of stone for decoration was a very Indian tradition. The surface of the building is decorated in a striking way. Bold inlay patterns outline the shapes and planes of the structural form—such as arches and rectangular panels. The stone used is red and yellow sandstone, along with black and white marble. Chhatris of various sizes and at various levels around the dome provide an interesting outline at the roof level—again a very Indian feature, but with the addition of bright blue tiles.

Do not go closer to the building at this point but turn right and walk for a bit along the boundary wall, which will enable you to take in the garden. Humayun's was probably the first char-bagh tomb in India, or a tomb set in a garden that was divided on a four-fold grid pattern by walkways and water channels. The garden today, though beautiful, does not look exactly as it did when the tomb was built. In the climate of north India, expanses of grass were not practical—they soaked up water and provided no shade. The gardens under the Mughals would have consisted of flowering and fruit trees, bushes, and some flower beds. By the second half of the nineteenth century, the garden of the tomb had been destroyed by neglect, and later restorations paid little attention to the original layout of paths and water channels. The new landscaping of the early twentieth century was responsible for the extensive lawns, which were a part of the British colonial idea of an ideal garden. In the early years of this century, a revitalization project was carried out in the gardens which restored the old pattern of water channels and paths. During this time, some low trees were also planted, keeping in mind the varieties that would have been popular in Mughal times. You can see these in clumps, mainly at the edges of the lawns.

Walking along the wall, you will come to a small water feature on the right—**a chute**[12] carved in chevron pattern, down which water, emerging from an opening in the boundary wall, flows. This was one of the points at which water entered the garden, supplied from a well located outside the wall. The carved pattern causes the water to ripple attractively. Water was an important part of Mughal buildings and gardens. In this char bagh, water entered from two points, passed through a system of channels and pools, and finally flowed out to the river.

Turn left from this chute and walk up to Humayun's tomb. Continue until you are squarely facing the southern side of the tomb, and if you look across the garden to your right, you will see the **southern entrance gateway**[13]. Do not walk up to it yet, but notice that it is wider and more elaborate than the western one. Its full size and splendour can best be appreciated from outside the complex, so if you have the time after the walk, you might like to go to the residential area known as Nizamuddin East. Here, from the road that runs around the northern periphery of the houses, you can get a good view of this gate.

Turn back to the tomb, and look at the red sandstone covered platform on which it sits. There are arched recesses that run in a row right around the platform. The entrances set into them lead into a total of 124 chambers. In one of them is the grave of Humayun and the others house the many graves of family members who were buried there over the course of several centuries. Climb up the stairs to the top of the platform. The tomb was designed to be approached from this side, the south, even though most visitors approach it from the west these days.

'It is adorned inside with many paintings and stones of various kinds, and the roof of the dome is gilded...over the tomb a coverlet made of rich brocade. At the sides of this covering are placed the arms of the dead king...his quiver full of arrows, his bow, his sword, his dagger or poignard, lance, musket...'—Niccolao Manucci, *Storia do Mogor* (1653-1708)

The ornamentation on the outer walls mostly consists of large panels of different coloured stones—red, white, yellow. There is a relatively small amount of stone carving. For instance, look at the slender pillars (called engaged pilasters) that are attached to the corners of the entrance arches. Towards the bottom, the red sandstone has been finely carved in a herringbone pattern, with the rounded shape of a kalash below it. The kalash-shaped carving was frequently used in Islamic tombs and even mosques in India, and is clear evidence of the cultural synthesis that developed in the Sultanate and Mughal periods.

As you step into the entrance chamber, the ceiling is worth looking at, as it has some intricately carved and painted limestone plaster. Walk through this chamber into the central tomb chamber. Its large size is emphasized by its emptiness and plainness; but it was not always thus. The seventeenth century British traveller, William Finch, described the floor as being covered in rich carpets, the cenotaph covered in a white sheet with a canopy overhead, and also little tables holding the emperor's Quran, his shoes, turban and sword. The Venetian traveller, Niccolao Manucci, described the walls and ceiling as being decorated with paintings, stones and gilt. So what has happened to the tomb since then?

'It was from these vaults, after Delhi had fallen, in September 1857, that"Hodson, of Hodson's Horse"... dragged out the last of the Moghuls, the puppet king who had been the nominal head of the rebellion. The coffin of his ancestor could not shield the trembling old intriguer.'—Sidney Low, *A Vision of India* (1906)

As long as the successive Mughal emperors lived and ruled, the mausoleum was maintained and many members of the royal family were buried in the crypt below (where there are more than 150 graves). This continued even when, in 1803, the British East India Company became the actual ruler of Delhi. In 1857, during the uprising against British rule, Delhi became a major centre of the revolt. Bahadur Shah II, pen named 'Zafar', was at the time on the throne, as a pensioner of the British with no real sovereign powers of his own. He became a leader of the uprising. When the British re-conquered Delhi, Bahadur Shah and members of his family escaped to Humayun's tomb and took shelter in it. The British finally came to arrest them from here, and presumably it was at that time that the tomb was despoiled. Nothing more was heard of its contents.

Despite being bare, the chamber is atmospheric. Notice how the stone jalis that fill the windows let in a filtered light. The patterns of the jalis vary, generally becoming finer in the smaller windows. The western side, which is the qibla, has an arch-shaped panel set in the screen. The dome rises beautifully in an uninterrupted manner from the sides. The net pattern, which forms the curve between the arches, was typical of Mughal architecture. The dome is a double dome—the inner shell is in proportion with the burial chamber, whereas the much bigger dome which you see from the outside, is in proportion to the dimensions of the entire building.

Leave the central chamber and you can visit some of the side chambers in the building. There are a number of marble cenotaphs in them. Most are unmarked, but according to some recent research, it is now believed that the western-most grave in the north-western chamber may be that of Dara Shukoh, the scholarly and mystically inclined eldest son of Shahjahan, who was put to death by his brother Aurangzeb who then ascended the throne. If you come out and walk around on the large platform on which the tomb is built, you will see more cenotaphs. Most do not bear the names of those who are buried here.

Leave the platform on the northern side and walk down the path to the building set against the wall at the extreme end. This is the **northern pavilion**[14], with a small pool that might have been used as a bath. Outside the boundary wall, at this point, is a well, the water of which is used to feed the channels in the garden. It flows through the building and down a chute.

Walking along the wall, in an easterly direction from this building, will bring you to another building set in the corner of the garden. This is the **north-eastern pavilion**[15], which would have overlooked the river. Notice the open plan and the beautiful, red sandstone pillars. It now overlooks the large white building of the Gurdwara Damdama Sahib. This is a modern structure, but marks a historic spot. This is where prince Muazzam, the son of the Mughal emperor Aurangzeb, met the Sikh Guru Gobind Singh, and asked for his help in his struggle for the throne. The help was given, and the prince ascended the throne as Bahadur Shah, in 1707.

Continue walking along this eastern wall of the garden. See how the ground level falls away from the level at the tomb platform. This was the natural slope of the land towards the river, which was landscaped into a terrace. In the middle of the wall there is the quite elaborate **eastern**

pavilion[16], with a pillared verandah and arcaded rooms. This would have overlooked the river, which flowed at one time just under the wall at this point.

Continue further along the boundary wall of the tomb complex, and a gate in the south-eastern corner leads you into **Nila Gumbad**[17]. There is some uncertainty about this tomb. Though some history books refer to this as the tomb of one Fahim Khan, who died in 1624, the source of this information is not certain. Moreover, the architecture suggests that it was built in the early part of the Mughal period, that is, in the first half of the sixteenth century. The most striking feature of the tomb is its brilliant tiles on part of the façade, and also on the dome, which has a beautiful shape and colour. The inside is decorated with beautifully coloured incised plaster medallions.

Come back to the main tomb garden and a bit to the west you will see a building which is known as the **barber's tomb**[18], though it is not known who exactly is buried here. The popular name by which it is known is most likely not related to any historical fact. If there ever was a barber influential enough to justify a grand tomb within the tomb garden of the emperor himself, he probably would have found mention in the historical record. On the other hand, it is possible that the tomb existed here before Humayun's tomb was built, and the latter's garden simply incorporated it. The tomb building should catch your eye—note the elaborate dome drum, which brings to mind, in a highly stylized manner of course, a battlemented fort wall. It has a border of kanguras punctuated by little turrets. Of the two cenotaphs inside, the one with the takhti (which indicates that it covers the grave of a woman) has a date inscribed on it which corresponds to 1590. The other grave is that of a man, which is apparent from the qalamdan on it.

From here you may proceed to the **southern gate**[13] of Humayun's tomb, which you saw before from a distance. It has a number of rooms, and for quite a while under British rule, it was used as a rest house for visitors. A little to its west is a small **mosque**[19] built, sometime in the eighteenth century, of blue-grey quartzite stone.

9

RED FORT

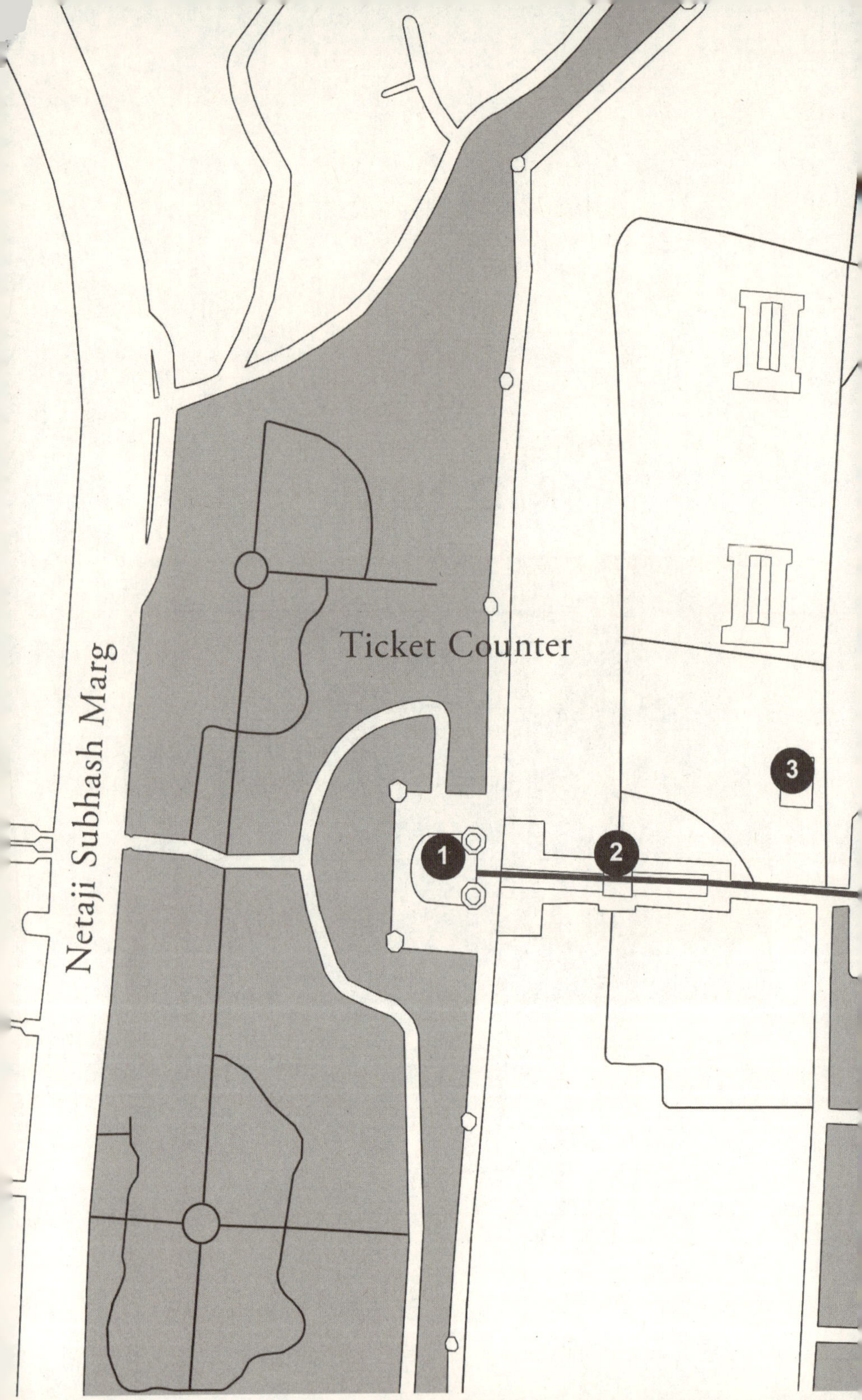
Ticket Counter
Netaji Subhash Marg
1
2
3

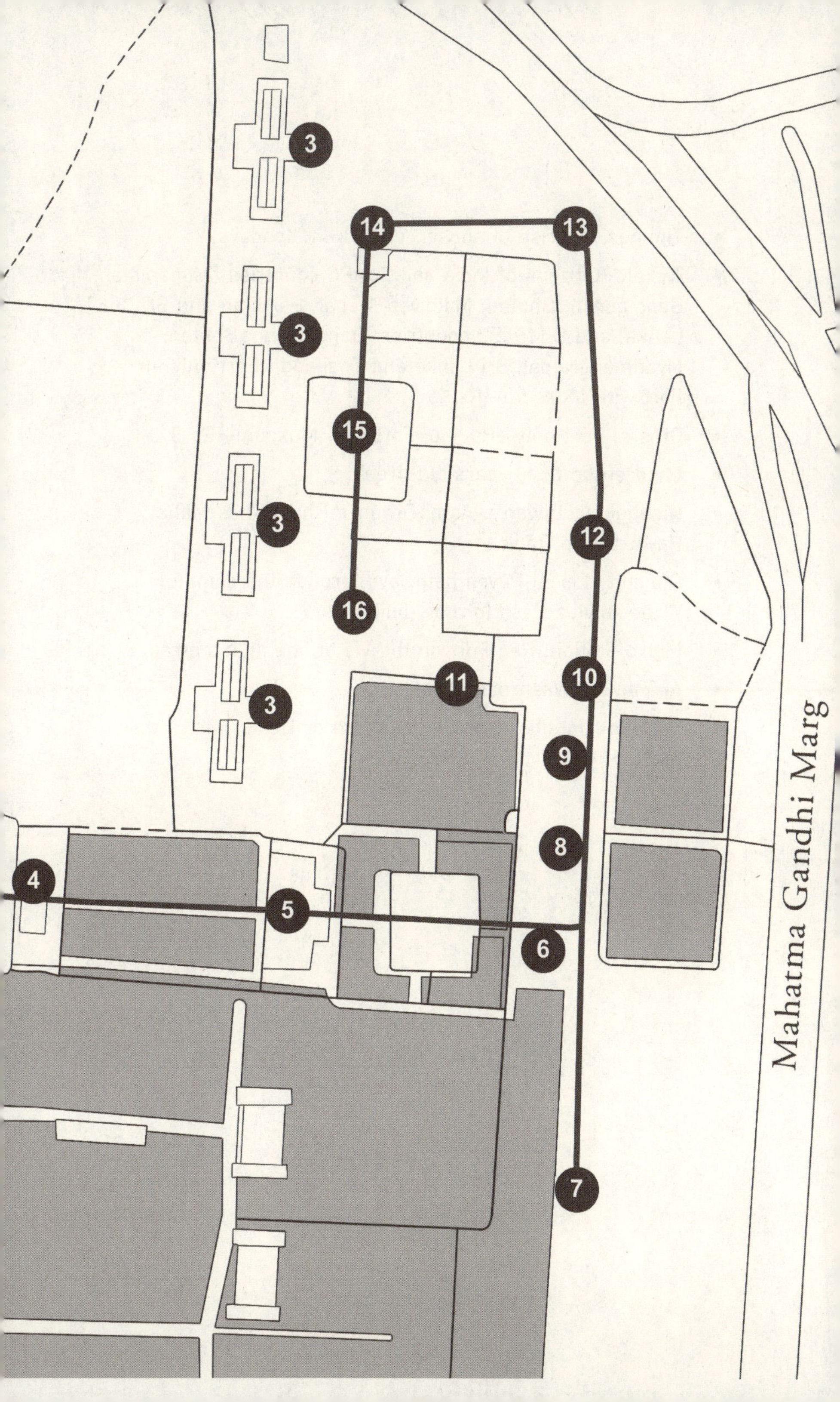
3
3
3
3
14
13
15
12
16
11
10
9
8
4
5
6
7
Mahatma Gandhi Marg

- Timings: Sunrise to sunset; closed on Mondays.
- Tickets: Citizens of India and SAARC countries (Afghanistan, Bangladesh, Bhutan, Maldives, Nepal, Pakistan and Sri Lanka) and BIMSTEC countries (Bangladesh, Bhutan, Myanmar, Nepal, Sri Lanka and Thailand): Fort only—Rs 35; Fort with Museum—Rs 56
- Others: Fort only—Rs 550; Fort with Museum—Rs 870
- Children up to 15 years old: free
- Highlights: Diwan-e-Aam, Diwan-e-Khas, Khas Mahal, Hayat Baksh Bagh.
- Difficulty Level: Paved pathways through the complex. Wheelchair access to most buildings.
- Metro Station: Red Fort on the Violet line, 300 metres.
- Amenities: Washrooms, cafe.
- Parking: On site (near the southern or Delhi Gate of the fort).

ROYAL CITADEL

RED FORT IS the popular colloquial name for this magnificent palace complex. Its name during Mughal times was Qila-e-Mubarak ('auspicious citadel'), Qila-e-Moalla ('exalted fort'), or Qila-e-Shahjahanabad (the 'fort of the city of Shahjahanabad'). It was an important part of the new capital city, Shahjahanabad, that the Mughal emperor Shahjahan established in the middle of the seventeenth century.

It is said that Shahjahan was fed up with Agra (also called Akbarabad), which had been the capital continuously from the time of his grandfather Akbar. It was hot, it was crowded, the fort was small, but probably most of all, it did not afford full scope for Shahjahan to indulge in his passion for building. By the late 1630s, one major project in Agra, the Taj Mahal, was well under way and Shahjahan needed something new to occupy his attention. Delhi had a long history as an imperial capital, under the Turks during the Delhi Sultanate, and in the early part of the Mughal dynasty, when his great-grandfather Humayun had established the city of Dinpanah. It is said that Shahjahan visited Delhi several times, and with the advice of the royal astrologers and doctors, settled on a site on the bank of the Yamuna for the new city and its citadel. It was located further north than all the previous cities of Delhi, just south of a small fort called

Salimgarh that had been constructed in 1546 under orders of Salim Shah, the Sur ruler.

The foundation stone for the fort of Shahjahanabad was laid on 16 April 1639. Two master builders were appointed—Ustad Hamid and Ustad Ahmad; and the overall supervision of construction was entrusted to a series of officials, the last of them being Makramat Khan. Over a hundred lakhs of rupees (Rs 10,000,000) were spent—about half on the walls of the fort and half on the buildings within. Just over nine years later, Shahjahan entered the fort for its inauguration on 17 May 1648. The splendours of the darbar (ceremonial court) that was held on that and other subsequent occasions have been described by historians in detail.

The glory days of the fort did not last very long. In 1658, Shahjahan was deposed by his son Aurangzeb, and lived the rest of his life as a prisoner in Agra. Aurangzeb, busy with campaigns in his extensive and increasingly hard-to-manage empire, did not spend much time in Delhi. In temperament too he was, very unlike his father and most of his ancestors, not in favour of much opulence and ostentation. Over the years there were signs of increasing austerity in court ceremonials. Music in court was discontinued, and so was the practice of celebrating the emperor's birthday by weighing him against gold and silver and distributing the proceeds to charity. The fort must have been a fairly sombre place during his reign.

Aurangzeb's successors were not all like him. In fact, Mohammad Shah 'Rangila', the 'colourful' (1718-48), was very fond of poetry, music and dance. However, after Aurangzeb's death in 1707, the Mughal Empire was often in turmoil and perceptibly in decline. Through the eighteenth century, there were many changes in succession, with many of the emperors being mere puppets of more powerful ministers. Territories and resources too were shrinking. Regional powers were carving up parts of the erstwhile empire between them. To top it all, there were at least two important occasions when the city or the fort was sacked. The first was in 1739, when the Persian ruler Nadir Shah invaded Mughal territories right up to Delhi and went back with a huge tribute. Then in 1788, the Afghan, Rohilla Ghulam Qadir sacked the fort and blinded the emperor Shah Alam II.

By then, the British East India Company was the new power on the scene and began to rule Delhi in 1803. The Mughal emperor became a mere pensioner, living on a small allowance within the fort with hundreds of near and distant relatives to support. Then, in 1857, the then emperor Bahadur Shah II, and some of his close relatives took an active part in the widespread revolt against the British rule. When Delhi was recaptured by the British, Bahadur Shah was exiled to Burma, all the occupants of the fort were turned out and it was occupied by the British Army.

Today the fort is a tourist attraction and one of Delhi's three monuments inscribed by UNESCO on its list of World Heritage Sites.

The Walk

Visitors enter the Red Fort through the west-facing **Lahore Gate**[1]. You may have to approach this from the south, where the parking lot and ticket counters are also located. The actual gateway through which you enter was not there when Shahjahan was emperor. In the original plan, the gateway to the fort directly faced the broad street running down the middle of the city of Shahjahanabad, now known as Chandni Chowk. Sometime during the early part of his reign, Aurangzeb (reigned 1658-1707) had a barbican or outer defence constructed in front of the actual gate, and that is what you today go through first. It is said that when he heard of this construction, Shahjahan wrote to Aurangzeb lamenting the fact that the latter had treated the fort like a bride, putting a veil before her face.

You go through the outer gate to enter a quadrangle formed by the barbican, and what you see to the left is the original gate to the fort, the Lahore Gate—so named because it faces west and in the direction of Lahore, an important Mughal city. This certainly looks more impressive as a gate and has enchanting decorative features typical of the architecture of Shahjahan's reign. Look for instance at the row of small chhatris at the top, and the subtle low relief carving that decorates the surface of the stone. Just below the chhatris is a row of kanguras with a decorative edge. These are to be found all along the fort wall on the outside as well.

Look around you. The top of the barbican wall that encloses this gate is now shorn of its battlements, covered with earth and planted with grass. At one end, encased in sandstone but nevertheless unmistakable, is an elevator shaft. This carries, among other important persons, the prime minister to the top from where he/she addresses the nation every year on 15 August, India's Independence Day.

Walk through the Lahore Gate, and the long covered passage you enter is the **Chhatta Bazaar**[2], literally 'shopping arcade'. The shops on either side, which now sell articles to tourists, once sold high quality goods to inhabitants of the fort and visitors. Notice how halfway down, the arcade opens up into a square open to the sky. Some of the painting on the walls has recently been revealed during restoration.

You emerge from the arcade into a large open space which is the interior of the fort. Here you must begin to exercise your imagination because the fort today looks nothing like it did in Shahjahan's time. As you move around the fort, you essentially perceive it as a large open space dotted with buildings. This is not how a seventeenth century visitor or even one in the first half of the nineteenth century would have experienced it. Coming through the Chhatta Bazaar, he would have instead found himself in a large courtyard surrounded by colonnades. The emperor's guard was stationed here, and the visitor would have to dismount, leaving his horse or carriage in the court before proceeding further.

If that visitor had looked left or right, he would have seen an arcaded street leading in either direction from the square. A channel of water flowed through the middle of these streets, widening into a tank in the middle of the courtyard. The rooms on either side of the arcaded streets were occupied by various officials connected to the fort. The street on the right led eventually to the other main entrance to the fort, the Delhi Gate, so named because it faced the older cities of Delhi as opposed to this, Shahjahanabad. This was probably an entrance reserved for the inhabitants of the fort. It was used for instance by the emperor when he went to the congregational mosque in the city—the Jama Masjid. This was also the entrance where the covered carriages of the ladies passed. They would not have used the main visitors' entrance, which is incidentally the only reason why our imaginary visitor has been given a male identity.

'After passing into the citadel through this gate [Delhi Gate], there is seen a long and spacious street, divided in the midst by a canal of running water. The street has a long divan, or raised way...It is upon this long divan that all the collectors of market dues and other petty officers exercise their functions.'—Francois Bernier, *Travels in the Mogul Empire* (1656-68)

The question that immediately occurs of course is, where

did all these buildings go? They were all there till the late 1850s, and in fact by that time many more had been added and the fort had become quite full. After the uprising of 1857, when the British Army occupied the fort, a vast majority of the buildings were demolished. Part of the space that was freed up was then used in the 1860s to build barracks for the use of the army. These **barracks**[3] can still be seen to your left as you emerge from the Chhatta Bazaar.

'In this place...in the night, particularly, when in bed and afar, on my terrace this music sounds in my ears as solemn, grand and melodious.'—Francois Bernier, *Travels in the Mogul Empire* (1656-68)

Across from the Chhatta Bazaar, at the eastern end of the imaginary courtyard in which you have been standing is the **Naubat Khana** or **Naqqar Khana**[4], the drum house. From here, the visitor to Shahjahan's court would have proceeded on foot. In Shahjahan's time this is where the ceremonial drums would have been housed, and played three to five times a day, depending on whether the emperor was in the fort or not. The musicians would have sat in the large open gallery at the top of the building—the part that is now enclosed with windows. The building of the Naqqar Khana is not overly opulent but it has nice, low relief carving. Particularly see the floral motifs in the many red sandstone panels. The flowers and leaves look realistic but they were to some extent stylized by the artists.

Once through the Naqqar Khana, our seventeenth-century visitor would have found himself in yet another courtyard. This courtyard too was surrounded by an arcade of many rooms, and some of these were occupied by lesser nobles who mounted a guard in rotation in the fort. To the north of this courtyard, not visible to the visitor, was the imperial kitchen. To the south, again out of sight, were the private areas of the fort where most of the members of the extended royal family—women, men and children—lived.

The focus of the visitor however would be on what he saw to the east, in his direct line of vision as he emerged through the Naqqar Khana. Here, still standing, is the **Diwan-e-Aam**[5], the hall of public audience. It is a large and beautiful building. In particular, note the red sandstone pillars, and the typically Shahjahani 'cusped' or 'scalloped' arches. The beauty is not so much in the intricacy of detail but in the clean flowing lines of the stylized foliage that encases the pillar bases and capitals. There are images and descriptions of the Diwan-e-Aam from the early nineteenth century which show all the pillars actually covered in painted and gilded limestone plaster.

At the eastern end of the hall is the white marble throne platform, where the emperor sat, under a canopy with a 'bangla' or curved roof. Bangla was an adjective applied to roofs that were inspired by Bengali huts. In fact the term later came to be used for a number of different kinds of buildings and evolved into the word 'bungalow'. The throne platform and canopy are ornately carved and inlaid with semi-precious stones; behind is one of the most fascinating walls in all of Mughal architecture. It is inlaid with a large number of panels, each painstakingly made up by a technique known as 'pietre dure' or small pieces of hard, coloured stones, cut and inlaid to form complex designs. In this case, these are images of birds and flowers, and even a panel showing the Greek god Orpheus playing the lute surrounded by different animals. Some of these panels were imported from Italy and others created by Mughal artists and craftsmen.

Art historians believe that the ornamentation of this wall bears a strong symbolic significance. It was meant to convey certain values that the Mughal empire aspired to. The message was that the realm ruled over by Shahjahan was a

'Immediately under the throne is an enclosure, surrounded by silver rails, in which are assembled the whole body of Omrahs [nobility], the Rajas, and the Ambassadors, all standing, their eyes bent downward, their hands crossed...the whole courtyard, is filled with persons of all ranks, high and low, rich and poor.'—Francois Bernier, *Travels in the Mogul Empire* (1656-68)

paradise—the concept of paradise as a garden being reinforced by the foliage on the pillars, and by the flowers, birds and animals depicted in the inlays. Even more specifically, the reign of Shahjahan was like the reign of Solomon, the Islamic ideal of the just king, whose throne is often thus depicted in paintings. The imagery of Orpheus playing to the beasts was intended to depict the peaceful reign of the emperor, where predator and prey were reconciled, and all were safe from oppression. The status of the emperor was further emphasized by the name given to the throne platform—Nasheman-e-Zill-e-llahi or 'the seat of the shadow of God'.

We do not know how much of this our seventeenth century visitor understood or even got close enough to see. The emperor sat on a seat placed under the canopy, with his sons standing on either side of him. On the large marble platform at the lower level stood his wazir, who passed on the petitions received in court to his majesty. A wider area around this core was demarcated by railings, within which stood noblemen, feudatories of the empire and ambassadors, but all had their eyes downcast. The rest of the hall was occupied by officials of a fairly high order. Outside the Diwan-e-Aam proper, in the space just in front of it, was an area enclosed with red sandstone railings known as the Gulal Bari or red enclosure, where the minor officials stood. Outside this stood those of the general populace who got the opportunity to enter the darbar at all.

The business of court over, the emperor would have left the Diwan-e-Aam through a door set in the wall behind the throne. This took him, through the rooms behind, into an enclosed private courtyard, with a beautiful pool in the middle. To see this, you will have to go around the Diwan-e-Aam. The courtyard, like the others, is now missing but you can see the pool and a large white building beyond it. The pool is considerably altered from its original level, which was lower. Look at the large marble basin in the centre, which is carved out of one large slab of stone. This too originally would have sat lower, probably level with the surface of the water. Water flowed into this pool via a channel leading from the building beyond. This was the emperor's own palace—the **Imtiyaz Mahal** or 'palace of distinction', now more popularly known as the **Rang Mahal**[6]—'palace of colour'. This building, like the Diwan-e-Aam, is essentially a large pillared hall, with smaller, partly enclosed rooms at the northern and southern ends. This open pavilion design was quite flexible and practical. Heavy drapes could be hung to give privacy or protection from the cold and wind. Split bamboo screens, called chik, could provide shade against the sun without completely blocking out the air and light. And

screens of khas (a kind of fine grass), when sprayed with water, would cool the air passing through them.

Of course, when the days became unbearably hot, there was the option of retreating to the basement, which runs along the length of the building—you can see the ventilation apertures of its upper part on the western side, and a flight of stairs leading down to it on either end of the building. Basements such as this were built precisely for this purpose as they were cooler than the rooms above, which were exposed to the sun.

The Rang Mahal is beautifully decorated. The plastered surface of the upper walls and pillars was covered with moulded, painted and gilded patterns. Some of it has survived in the undersides of the arches. The ceiling of the main hall was originally made of silver, but was removed during the reign of the emperor Farrukhsiyar (1713-19) to be converted into much-needed ready cash. Mirror mosaic, another technique that was popularized by the Mughals, is visible in the rooms at either end of the building. Hundreds of tiny pieces of mirror are set in the plaster of the walls to produce an enchanting effect in the light. Rooms with this kind of decoration came to be known as Shish Mahal—'mirror palace'.

An immediately obvious feature of this palace is the water channel running through its length, and forming a beautiful pool in the middle. Water was an important design element in Mughal architecture, and found a place within its buildings as well as in the gardens. A stream of water, an offshoot of a canal that was cut from the Yamuna river somewhat north of Delhi, ran through the gardens and buildings, and was known as the Nahar-e-Bahisht or 'the stream of paradise'. Inside the buildings, its effects were ornamental, cooling, and from the sound of the gentle rippling of water, soothing.

The pool in the Rang Mahal is now hard to see because one cannot walk into the hall. It is also damaged, because many of the semi-precious stones used in the floral decoration have been gouged out long ago. We do have descriptions of it which tell us that the rippling water made the inlaid flowers and leaves which adorned the bottom of the shallow pool appear to be gently waving in the breeze. Some of the water flowed in a channel to the front of the building, where it cascaded down a section of wall set with many small arched niches. At night these niches held small lamps, and the water flowing in front of them in a thin sheet produced an effect that has been described as 'a quick fall of stars'. You can see this feature at the front of the building.

'The young prince led me through different parts of the palace, and I was taken into a superb hall: formerly fountains had played there; the ceiling was painted and inlaid with gold. In this hall were three old women on charpais (native beds), looking like hags...From a verandah, the young prince pointed out a bastion in which the king was then asleep.'—Fanny Parks, *Wanderings of a Pilgrim in Search of the Picturesque* (1838)

From the level of the Rang Mahal, one notable feature of the fort becomes clear: the main buildings are arranged in a row above the eastern wall. This was the side that overlooked the river, and the buildings with their open windows were designed to catch the cooling breeze. The river has now changed its course considerably eastwards, but even in Shahjahan's time there was a wide sandy bank where people of the city would frequently gather for recreation. Royally sponsored elephant fights and kite flying contests also took place here, with the members of the royal family getting a ringside view from their overlooking palaces.

The Rang Mahal is generally described as the palace

of the emperor's harem or seraglio—where his wives and/ or concubines lived. Some historians however speculate that this was actually the emperor's own private palace. Apart from being conveniently situated just behind the main court of audience, it is also located at an important focal point of the fort—roughly at the midpoint of the eastern wall. It is moreover at one end of the axis that leads to the main entrance of the fort and through the main street of the city beyond. Another important clue is the fact that it was frequently described by visitors who, being male, would not have penetrated this far into a building that was primarily occupied by women.

What was definitely a palace for women was the building that is now to the south of the Rang Mahal. This is the **Mumtaz Mahal**[7] or 'eminent palace', also known as the **Chhota Rang Mahal,** or 'small Rang Mahal'. Originally similar in its style of decoration to the Rang Mahal, it has been through many incarnations since 1857—a military prison, a sergeants' mess, and a museum. The museum has now been moved out of the building and you can appreciate the structure better, including the walls that still bear some traces of the original decoration.

Much of the area to the south and west of the Mumtaz Mahal, making up about a quarter of the entire area of the fort, was a complex that was the living quarters of the royal family and its attendants. The buildings, courtyards, and gardens are now gone. These have been partly replaced by colonial architecture dating from the British occupation of the mid-nineteenth century.

Go back past the Rang Mahal to the building just north of it, known as the **Khas Mahal**[8] or 'royal palace'. It has various chambers inside—**Baithak** or 'sitting room', **Khwabgah** or 'bedroom', **Tasbih Khana** or a 'room for telling of beads'. In the covered verandah facing the Rang Mahal, note the beautifully painted marble surfaces, in particular the subtle colours used. Also note the finely carved filigree of the marble screens and the translucent, carved, marble slabs set in the walls.

Go around to the northern side, and on the way you will see a doorway at the ground level. This led to the riverside, and was the route by which Shahjahan ceremonially entered the fort when it was first inaugurated.

Climb up to the plinth of the building on the northern side if it is open for access, and on your right you get a different view of the Khas Mahal. You can see the covered verandah that served as a royal seat. Here the emperor would sit, on furnishings of red and gold, and above him was the carved marble panel depicting the scales of justice. At the eastern end of the rooms, jutting out of the line of the fort wall is an octagonal turret, which is known by its

'On passing a screen of Indian connaughts we proceeded to the front of the Tusbeah Khana, and being arrived in the presence of the King, each of us made three obeisances in turn, by throwing down the right hand pretty low, and afterwards raising it to the forehead.' —W. Franklin, *An Account of the Present State of Delhi* (1801)

Persian term—Mussamman Burj. Set in this is a jharokha which looks out over what would have been the river bank. This is the Jharokha-e-Darshan, where the emperor showed himself to his subjects every morning so they could reassure themselves that he was alive and well, and be blessed by the vision.

Names and functions have changed over the course of the centuries as it was occupied by various Mughal emperors, but this certainly seems to have been a more formal building than is suggested by the appellations usually given to it—sitting room, bedroom, prayer room. From their size, location and design these rooms appear to be a sort of private office for the emperor. This was the heart of the empire, where the business of the realm was conducted. Decorative features such as the scales of justice symbolize the ideology of Mughal rule. Long inscriptions over the arches in the inner rooms record the important dates in the history of the fort, including the laying of the foundation, and the inauguration.

'In front about forty yards was the Dewan khass, or throne-room, in which the King was already seated....a long lunged crier proclaimed that we came to see the "King of the World".—A description of the British Commander-in-Chief's visit to Akbar II in 1828; from Major Archer, *Tours in Upper India*

To the north of the Khas Mahal is one of the most magnificent buildings of the fort, the **Diwan-e-Khas**[9], or the 'hall of private audience'. This is where the emperor held a more exclusive court with important ambassadors, courtiers and officials of the realm. This pavilion building too, like the Diwan-e-Aam, was set in a courtyard of its own that was demarcated by a row of arcaded buildings. While the emperor entered the Diwan-e-Khas through the Khas Mahal, most of those who attended the court came from the western side. Our visitor would come past the Diwan-e-Aam, through a passage that connected it to the courtyard of the Diwan-e-Khas, without even a glimpse of the Rang Mahal and the Khas Mahal. He would enter the Diwan-e-Khas courtyard through the door in western wall, which was hung with a red curtain, literally 'lal parda', and from this point he would have to bow and make salutations to the throne as he approached it. He would see, as much as his respectfully lowered eyes would allow, a marvellous spectacle.

Though much despoiled and damaged over the centuries, the Diwan-e-Khas is still a beautiful building. The clean lines of the silhouette and the beautifully curving arches and the light chhatris on the corners of the roof give it an overall sense of simple balance. In decorative detail it manages to be opulent and restrained at the same time. In each of the panels inlaid with coloured stones, which cover the pillars, look at the unfussy flowering plant set amidst the floral border. Particularly observe the very Chinese

stylized cloud motifs on either side of the plant. These were influences that had come into the art of the Mughals through their Central Asian heritage. The upper part of the pillars and the ceiling are beautifully painted. On a section of one pillar capital in the south-western part of the building, the gilding has been restored to show what it all must originally have looked like. The floor of this building was in its heyday covered with rich carpets, and a bright red awning provided additional shade on all sides of the building.

The opulence of this court was crowned by the famed peacock throne that was placed on a marble platform in the eastern part of the hall. Made of precious metals and studded with an incredible number of precious stones, this was a legendary piece of furniture. It was only too likely to excite avarice and unsurprisingly formed part of the treasure taken away by the Persian ruler Nadir Shah when he extracted a tribute from the prostrate empire in 1739. Nadir Shah had it dismantled and the jewels re-used. While it was still in Delhi and in use, it helped to underline the reputation of the emperor, in the words of contemporary Europeans, as 'The Great Mogul'. This epithet was used for instance, by John Dryden as the title of his largely fictional play about Aurangzeb.

A well-known Persian verse incorrectly attributed to the fourteenth-century Delhi poet Amir Khusro is inscribed over the arches on the inside of the southern and northern walls of the Diwan-e-Khas. In translation it reads: 'If there is paradise on the face of the earth, it is this, it is this, it is this.'

These strong statements of Mughal majesty had to be symbolically countered by the British when they occupied the fort. It was to strike at the very heart of the aura of Mughal sovereignty when the British captured the fort in September 1857, after suppressing the rebellion in Delhi, that the health of Queen Victoria was toasted in this room. Soon after, it was again in this room that the last emperor Bahadur Shah II was tried and sentenced to exile in Rangoon, in what was then Burma.

Next to the Diwan-e-Khas, but sadly out of bounds for visitors, is the **Hammam**[10] or bath house. It is a complex building with pools, provision for hot and cold water, steam rooms, and some particularly interesting features such as a basin for a perfumed water spray. The rooms are lavishly decorated with stone inlay. Take a peek through the window, and you should be able to see some of this. Particularly note the floor. Since this was one building that did not have carpets, the floor was decorated to practically look like one. The hammam was more than a utilitarian area for washing the body. The emperor relaxed here and often conferred with close courtiers too.

West of the hammam is another building that is kept locked up. This is the mosque known as the **Moti Masjid**[11], or 'pearl mosque'. Built by Shahjahan's son Aurangzeb, it is made entirely of marble. What you see on the outside however are rather plain, plastered white walls. Look closely at the slender minarets and you will realize two things. The actual mosque, of which the minarets are a part, sits inside a box formed by the plastered walls. You will also notice that the minarets do not line up evenly with the sides of the enclosing box. In fact, the sides of the mosque are out of alignment with the walls of the enclosure. The most probable explanation for this is that when the mosque was built, several years after the fort itself, it was realised that aligning it to Mecca, which was required, would put it out of alignment with the symmetry of the other buildings of the fort. Since this was anathema to the strong sense of symmetry that was a part of Mughal aesthetic sensibilities, it was put inside a box which was in symmetry even if the mosque couldn't be. Incidentally, if you are interested, a satellite map view is a good way of understanding the mosque-in-a-box.

You can get a glimpse of the interior through a window if you go around to the northern side of the mosque. There is a fair amount of lavish carving. The floor is marked out in individual panels, each in the shape and size of a mosalla or prayer carpet. The mosque was for private everyday use within the fort, with the emperor going occasionally to the large congregational mosque, the Jama Masjid, in the city. The Moti Masjid originally had copper domes, which were badly damaged by shelling during the British attack on the fort in 1857. They were later rebuilt in marble.

North of the Hammam is a small marble pavilion known as **Hira Mahal**[12] or the 'diamond palace'. This was built during the time of Bahadur Shah II and its modest size is proof of the meagre resources of the last in line to an illustrious dynasty. There were other buildings in this line along the wall but they were demolished after 1857.

Keep walking past Hira Mahal, and at the extreme northern end of the terrace is a beautiful marble pavilion, the main feature of which is a water chute, the head of the Nahar-e-Bahisht—the water channel that ran through the buildings of the fort. This pavilion takes its name from the structure behind it, the **Shah Burj**[13], or literally the 'royal tower'. This tower, located at the junction of the eastern and northern walls of the fort, was originally three-storeys tall. The upper part was much damaged in 1857 and never fully rebuilt. Originally this tower contained an elaborate hydraulic system which controlled the circulation of water within the fort buildings through a complex system of valves. Some water may at one time have been pumped up from the river in the days when the river was closer. For the most part however, it came from a channel that entered the fort from an opening in its north-western side. Before entering the fort this channel flowed through the city of Shahjahanabad. Notice the vaulted roof of the pavilion. This too is a bangla roof, such as the one over the throne inside the Diwan-e-Aam. The broad carved chute is where the water would have emerged and flowed down into the channel.

The garden to the west of these northern buildings is known as Hayat Baksh Bagh—'life-giving garden'. It is now very unlike a traditional Mughal garden. In Shahjahan's times, a garden implied shade-giving fruit and flowering trees and bushes. Expanses of lawn, which soak up water and give little in return are not practical in the north Indian climate. The present sensibilities, as reflected in the layout of the garden today, can be dated to British colonial times, when the administrators sought to recreate the grassy look of their own homeland.

The marble pavilion which you see at the northern end of the garden is called **Sawan**[14]. There is a large pool in the middle of the floor of the building, though it is hard to see since you cannot climb up to it. This would have held water which would then have flowed into the channel and fallen in a sheet in front of the rows of small niches, which contained flower vases during the day and lamps at night. This was the part of the Nahar-e-Bahisht that flowed through the garden. Walk along its length to the large tank with a red sandstone building in its middle. This is **Zafar Mahal**[15] constructed on the orders of Bahadur Shah II, who used the pen name 'Zafar'. It is not a particularly attractive specimen of architecture, testament to the reduced circumstances of the last Mughal emperor. Its construction moreover was particularly unfortunate, because it ruined one important feature of the garden. As per the original design, the Sawan pavilion was meant to face a mirror image across the garden, on the other side of the pool. This is **Bhadon**[16], visible once you come around the Zafar Mahal. The names Sawan and Bhadon are those of the two rainy months of the monsoon season, very appropriate for two garden pavilions with water features.

10

SHAHJAHANABAD

Mahatma Gandhi Park
Khari Baoli
Katra Neel
Shanti Desai Marg
16
12
15
14
11
Chandni
Katra Bariyan
Gali Qasim Jan
13
Nai Sarak
Charkhewalan Gali
Laalkuan Bazaar Road

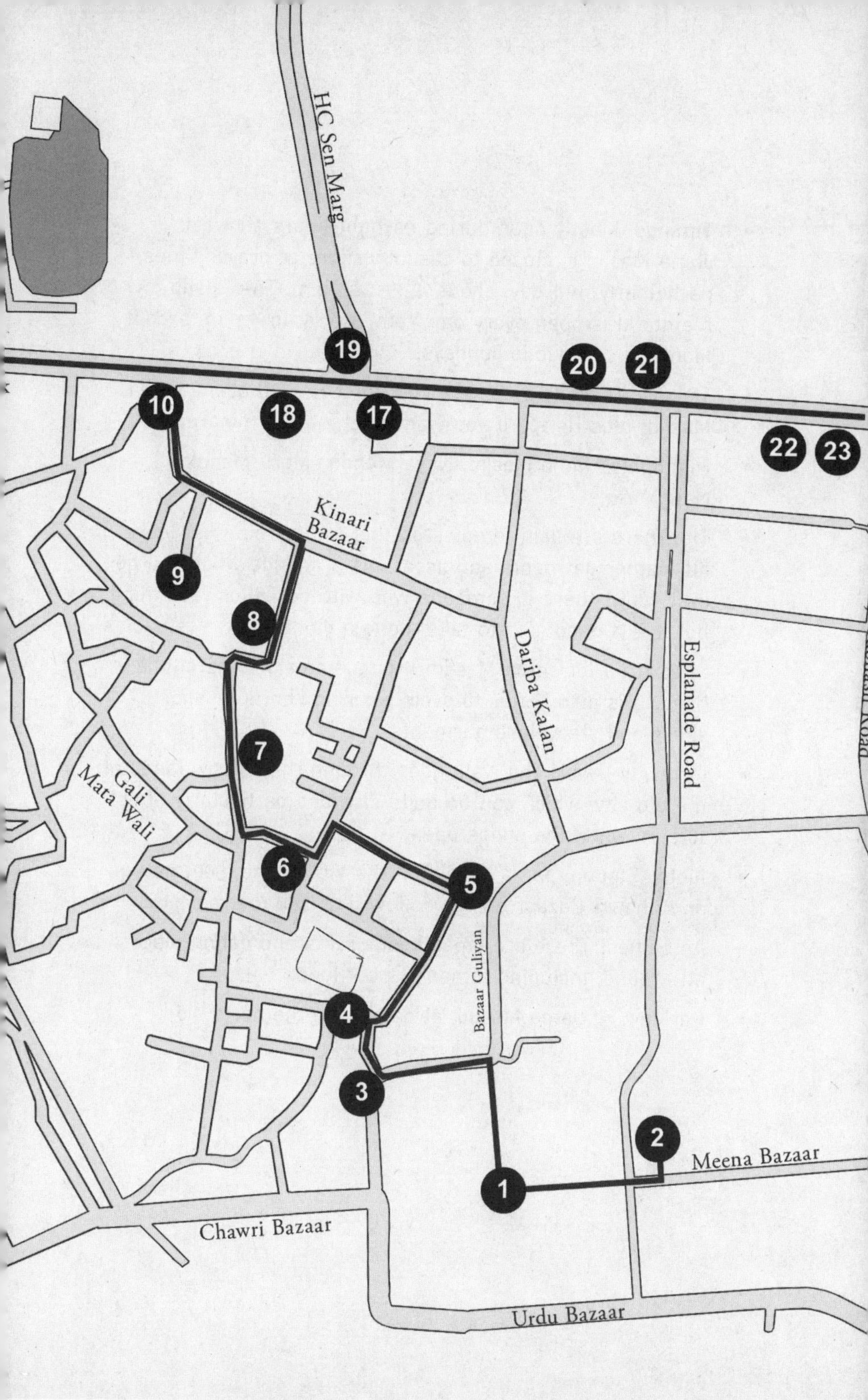
HC Sen Marg
19
20
21
10
18
17
22
23
Kinari Bazaar
9
8
Dariba Kalan
Esplanade Road
7
Gali Mata Wali
6
5
Bazaar Guliyan
4
3
2
Meena Bazaar
1
Chawri Bazaar
Urdu Bazaar

- Timings: Mostly open during daylight hours all week. Jama Masjid is closed to casual visitors at prayer times, particularly mid-day, about 12.15-1.45 p.m. The Ghalib memorial is open every day from 11 a.m. to 5 p.m. except Mondays and public holidays.
- Tickets: There is a camera charge of Rs 300 at the Jama Masjid, plus Rs 100 if you want to climb the minaret.
- Highlights: Jama Masjid, Naya Mandir, Meru Mandir, Naughara.
- Tip: There are Jain temples on this route. You must leave all leather garments and accessories outside when you go in. Usually there is someone who will look after your things but it is a good idea to take along a cloth bag for valuables.
- Special tip for Jama Masjid: It is customary to cover the head. It is also better to avoid wearing shorts or short skirts and sleeveless garments.
- Difficulty Level: The walk goes through the narrow lanes of the old city, which can be quite crowded particularly after 10 a.m. when the shops open.
- Metro Station: Jama Masjid on the Violet Line, 300 metres, and Chawri Bazaar on the Yellow line, 750 metres.
- Amenities: There are small restaurants and eating places all around, including famous street food.
- Parking: At Jama Masjid, at gate 3, on the north side.

IMPERIAL CITY

In the year 1639, the Mughal emperor Shahjahan decided to build a new capital at Delhi—Shahjahanabad ('founded by Shahjahan'). Over the next few years, attention and resources were completely focused on the palace complex that would be built within it—what we today know as the Red Fort. It was only as the citadel was nearing completion that the city began to be built. In shape, it was roughly semicircular, or bow-shaped, with the straight or 'string' side towards the river on the east. Its perimeter wall was more than 6 kms in length, and punctuated by thirteen gates and numerous small wicket gates.

The middle half of the river front was occupied by the fort, and around the fort, on the remaining sides, lay the city. One broad street stretched from the western or the Lahore gate of the fort right through the city. This is what we today call Chandni Chowk. Another street, known as the Faiz Bazaar, led from the southern or the Delhi gate of the fort to the Delhi Gate of the city through Daryaganj, and north to Kashmiri Gate. Finally, one shorter street led from the southern gate of the fort to the main congregational mosque of the city—the Jama Masjid ('jama' being congregation).

Imperial planning went no further than the fort, the city wall, some of the main streets, and landmarks like the Jama Masjid. The remaining spaces were filled in through individual enterprise. Some of these were by the members of the royal family—three of the emperor's wives built mosques; his favourite daughter, Jahanara, laid out a large garden and a sarai. The rich set up estates which housed their own mansions and gardens, their considerable domestic staff and often small manufacturing units for the needs of the household. There were entrepreneurs who built markets; many built places of worship, and finally the mass of the population built their own more modest houses.

The city has changed considerably in the more than 350 years since it was first established. The change started quite early. One of the first signs of decline in the Mughal empire, which set in by the middle of the eighteenth century, was the fading fortunes of the noble families. Over time, the large estates were sold and/or partitioned, and denser neighbourhoods grew up in their place. These were not exactly poor settlements, as the eighteenth century was by no means a time of unmitigated decline. Mercantile groups still flourished and in fact there was a flurry of building activity, particularly of temples and mosques, but also of markets and houses.

A major change came after 1857. The Revolt and its brutal suppression by the British armed forces was a traumatic episode in the history of the city. In its aftermath came a deliberate destruction of many buildings. Some of it was an ostensibly defensive measure—to clear a 500-yard swathe of land around the Red Fort, which was now occupied by British troops. Some of it was the confiscation and replacement of Mughal structures with British colonial ones—like the Town Hall and Clock tower. And finally, the railway was driven through the heart of the city, destroying many buildings in the northern half of Shahjahanabad.

Today Shahjahanabad is a bustling place. Its narrow streets

are crowded with people going about their business—and a lot of this is commercial activity in wholesale markets and small workshops. But despite the crowds and the less-than-clean lanes, it has its charm—in the unexpectedly beautiful building façades and balconies, the colourful markets, and the street food. In the age of isolated and climate-controlled shopping malls, daily life here still goes on at street level.

The Walk

Begin at the major landmark of Shahjahanabad—the **Jama Masjid**[1]. Tourists usually enter through Gate 3, which lies to the north and has a parking lot beside it. But, you may enter from one of the other two gates too. In case you do that, it is best to carry your footwear with you, as you will exit at Gate 3. It is customary to carry footwear with the soles held together.

The Jama Masjid was the congregational mosque of the city of Shahjahanabad, and was built on a natural rise in the ground, called Bhojla Pahar. The foundation was laid on 6 October 1650 and it took six years to build at a cost of Rs 1,000,000 at the time. It represents a high point in Mughal architecture. The shape and proportions of the gateways, the western façade, domes and minarets attain a perfection that spawned many copies, but was never entirely successfully replicated.

All three entrances into the mosque are reached by broad steps, and this was a busy social space through much of the city's past. The steps were crowded with hawkers and street food vendors, jugglers and storytellers. Particularly in the evenings, this was the place to be. The famous eighteenth-century Delhi poet, Mir Taqi Mir, is believed to have said that to understand his poetry it was essential to be familiar with the steps of the Jama Masjid! Today the steps are generally emptier, but particularly on festivals, the congregation in the mosque spills over onto them. The markings in white paint demarcate standing and kneeling space for each person. Whichever gate you enter through, begin the walk at the eastern entrance. This faces the Delhi gate of the Red Fort and was the royal entrance, through which the emperor would have entered. The broad street between the fort and the mosque, just under a kilometre long, was lined by shops that made up the Khas Bazaar.

At the bottom of the steps outside the eastern gate, is the **shrine of Sarmad Shaheed**[2]. Sarmad was an intriguing personality—a Jew from Armenia (some say Iran). He was a successful trader but while on trip to Sindh, he converted to Islam and also became attracted to mysticism. He distanced himself from worldly concerns, his asceticism even leading him to discard his clothes. After travelling around for a while he came to Delhi, where Shahjahan's son, Dara Shukoh, himself interested in mysticism and with an unorthodox approach to religion in general, became his disciple. Dara Shukoh, however, was put to death on the orders of his brother Aurangzeb in a tussle over succession, and Sarmad wound up on the wrong side of the political divide. His unorthodox ways gave Aurangzeb ample ammunition against him. Sarmad's nudity was one charge against him. The other was that when asked to recite the Islamic creed—'There is no God but God, and Mohammad is his Prophet', he stopped short at 'There is no God', saying that in his attempt to understand the mysteries of God, he had so far only got to this stage.

Sarmad was found guilty of heresy and beheaded at the orders of the emperor. The story of his death itself is fascinating and has two versions. One is that as soon as his head hit the ground, his mouth spoke the entire kalima, and the head rolled the distance from the palace to the Jama Masjid reciting praises of God. The other version is that the headless body picked up the head and started to walk towards the mosque in anger. As the body reached the foot of the steps, the voice of Sarmad's spiritual master, Syed Hare Bhare Shah, who was buried there, could be heard asking 'where are you going?' When Sarmad replied that he was going to lay his case before God, Hare Bhare Shah persuaded him to give up his anger, as he had reached his destination. Sarmad's body collapsed right there, and he was buried at that spot. The interior of the shrine is painted red. Next to it is the shrine of Hare Bhare Shah.

Now climb up the steps, and enter the large courtyard of the mosque. The inside of each entranceway is beautifully made of red sandstone. The eastern or 'royal' gateway has a beautiful jharokha above the central arch. Along the top is a row of kanguras. The other gates are also alluring; look at the row of miniature chhatris along the top. The arched, open verandahs that run along three sides of the courtyard are a perfect design element—they are open so they give a view out over the city and the fort, at the same time they provide a covered space that can be used for various purposes, especially as a resting place. Notice the large chhatris that add a neat finish to the corners of the courtyard.

The pool of water in the courtyard is the traditional wuzu tank. This provides water for the ritual ablutions that precede prayer. Now of course water is also provided via taps set up elsewhere. In the north-western corner of the tank is a small spot that has been marked off with a low marble railing. Mohammad Khan Tahsin, an important eunuch in charge of the royal harem, saw the Prophet Mohammad standing at this spot in a dream. This took place in the year 1180 of the Hijri calendar, corresponding to 1766-67. He decided to put up this small enclosure to mark the spot.

In front of the pool is a small, beige sandstone kiosk. This was put up in 1928 to serve as a raised pulpit for the mukabbir, who calls out praises of God during prayer, for the benefit of those in the courtyard who cannot see or hear the imam himself.

'If you want to know what the vault and cupola of its prayer chamber are like, nothing can be said except [that they resemble] the Milky Way and sky. The dome would have been matchless had the firmament not been its equal, the vault would have been unique had the Milky Way not been its pair.'—Inscription on one of the arches of the façade of the Jama Masjid.

On the western side of the courtyard is a façade of arches, behind which is a covered area. This shape of arch—with little scallops coming to a point at the top, is a particular feature of Mughal architecture from Shahjahan onwards. The inscriptions in black marble inlaid on the white marble panels above the arches, talk in hyperbolic terms of Shahjahan and the building of the mosque. The central arch simply has two circular medallions on which, written in Arabic, is 'O Guide!'—one of the ninety-nine names of Allah.

At the foot of the central arch is another kiosk built about 1829 by Mirza Salim, the son of the emperor Akbar II. Climb on to the covered area of the mosque. Notice that the floor is divided by lines of inlaid black marble into rectangles that mimic the shape of the mosalla, or prayer rug. There are 899 of these. The minbar beside the central mihrab is carved out of a single piece of marble.

The Jama Masjid, being the main congregational mosque of the city, was under the direct management of the Mughal emperor, who appointed its important functionaries such as the imam. After quelling the uprising of 1857 and capturing Delhi, the British confiscated the mosque and quartered soldiers there. For a while there was also the talk of destroying the mosque altogether as a punishment for the people of Delhi. There were others who were opposed to this and so the mosque survived. Another royal mosque close by—Akbarabadi masjid, built by a wife of Shahjahan—was not so fortunate. It was only in 1862, after much negotiation, that the Jama Masjid was handed back to the Muslims of Delhi. Shockingly, one of the conditions was that Europeans would be allowed to enter it without taking off their shoes!

It is easy to recognize heritage buildings in Shahjahanabad from the iron sign boards that stand before most, proclaiming them as such.

Leave the mosque by the northern gateway. Cross the street outside and go a little way to the left, to the corner formed by a row of buildings that line the large square surrounding the mosque. In the corner is the **Indraprastha Girls School**[3], founded in 1904. This was also the first premises of the Indraprastha College for Women, one of the leading colleges of Delhi. The college eventually moved closer to the North Campus of Delhi University, but the school continued here. The haveli, or mansion that houses the school already existed here when the school was founded. It is a well-kept building as is obvious even

from the outside. The inside is equally interesting, though it is usually not possible to visit it.

Come back from the school and take the first turning to the left, into a narrow passageway. This is bounded by a high old wall and as you emerge into the open, on your left is what remains of the **Chah Rahat**[4], or the 'well with the Persian wheel', which supplied water to the Jama Masjid. A Persian inscription written on a stone slab set in the wall tells you just that. Behind a door that is usually kept closed, the well survives, but is not in use.

The lanes of Shahjahanabad can be confusing. Shops however, often have names of streets written on them, and you can ask to verify that you are on the right track.

Take the lane going north (also known as Chah Rahat) and you will find crumbling old buildings, particularly on the left. This area is all that remains of one of the original large estates of Shahjahanabad. It belonged to Ustad Hamid, a master builder, who was responsible for the construction of the Red Fort. In time, the estate broke up and the plot was divided up to hold independently owned buildings. At its end, you will pass through a gateway, which is probably all that remains of the original structures of the estate. This is called the gateway of **Kucha Ustad Hamid**[5]. Kucha means lane; so the name of Ustad Hamid still survives in the name of the street.

From the gateway of Kucha Ustad Hamid turn left and proceed a little way down. This street is known as Bazaar Gulian. Go past the first lane to the left and turn left into the second. You are now in an area called Dharampura. Walk a little way down this lane until you come to a lane to your right. At the corner of these two lanes, at the first floor level you will see an ornately carved building.

This is the **Digambar Jain Naya Mandir**[6]. The Jains have been an important religious sect in Delhi for many centuries. The Digambars are one of the two main divisions of the Jains (the Swetambars being the other). In the times of the Mughals, the Jains were important merchants and bankers who played a crucial role in provisioning the royal armies and otherwise financing the business of the empire. A part of their wealth went towards financing many temples in the city. This is particularly true of Dharampura.

The temple is called Naya Mandir, which means 'new temple' but it was actually built in 1807. People at the time called it 'the new temple' and the name stuck. It has lovely carving on the outside, in beige sandstone. Look at the curving brackets that support the kiosk on top of the doorway. It is worth going inside and up to the first floor, if just to see the beautifully painted ceilings. The room adjoining the courtyard is done in attractive colours and is reminiscent of the style used in the Red Fort. The inner shrine is extremely rich and ornate.

Come back to the street after you leave the temple, and turn right into it. You will have to turn right at the end of the street, and then right again. This will bring you out to a street known as Gali Masjid Khajur. It has a few captivating doorways, finely carved in sandstone. A little further on this street, on your right, you will notice an elaborate doorway with a projecting balcony over it. This is the **Digambar Jain Meru Mandir**[7]. Built in the mid-eighteenth century, this is a temple worth a visit. It is less touristy than some other Jain temples, and there has been relatively less alteration and painting-over. There are interesting images and paintings inside, particularly a room which has a number of pedestals with little idols on top.

Continue up the street and it will come to an end; turn left and soon after, right. This lane is Katra Khushal Rai. Walk along this lane and soon, on your left, will be the haveli or house known as **Shish Mahal**[8]. This is a modestly-sized haveli and you can peek inside. The rooms are arranged around a central courtyard, originally only on two storeys. This building has an interesting association. This is where St Stephen's College, one of the better-known colleges of the country, had its humble beginnings in 1881.

Katra Khushal Rai ends up in the busy Kinari Bazaar.

This is a street specializing in gilt laces and other similar accessories and raw materials suitable for weddings and festivals. It is bright and colourful and often full of tourists in rickshaws.

Turn left into the bazaar, and then shortly after, left again, into a cul de sac called **Naughara**[9] or literally, 'nine houses'. This is a surprisingly tranquil residential street, with a row of house fronts on the right. Most of them are now painted in a variety of colours, but the base is the same sandstone you see on haveli façades throughout the city. On the left, behind an old doorway with a pointed arch is the common open area that was shared by these households. At the end of the cul de sac is a Jain temple called Jauhri mandir, literally 'jewellers' temple', named after its patrons. It is said that this temple existed here even during the time of Shahjahan, though the visible parts of it have obviously been rebuilt. It is quite opulent and also very well visited by tourists. Much of the ornamentation is recent.

Kinari Bazaar continues in a north-westerly direction until it meets up with two other lanes, forming a tiraha or tri-junction. On the right is **Parathe wali gali**[10]. This is famous for its roadside eateries serving deep fried parathas with an unusual variety of fillings. This short street has two sharp turns, right and then left, which brings you on to a broad street. This street, now known as Chandni Chowk, was the main avenue of Shahjahanabad, leading from the Red Fort to one of the major mosques of the city. In its heyday, it was even wider than it is today, had a channel of water running down its middle, and shady trees on either side. Shops, with the fronts shaded by awnings, lined either side. The water channel was supplied by an offshoot from what is known as the Western Yamuna Canal, a major irrigation canal. An uneven supply in the canal led to the drying up of this channel from time to time, particularly, if nothing was actively done to keep it open. Finally, in late nineteenth century, it was decided to close up the channel completely and in the early twentieth century, a tramline was started in the middle of the road. This was discontinued in 1963.

Turn left onto Chandni Chowk. As you walk, you will see several interesting buildings on either side of the road. On your left is the **Allahabad Bank building**[11]. This and other early twentieth century bank buildings on this stretch of road have delightfully flamboyant and eclectic façades—look particularly at the fussy but charming grill-work. Some of the best buildings on this street are actually bank buildings.

A little further on, to the right, is the wide frontage of a two-storeyed building with a verandah running its length on the first floor. The ground floor is occupied by shops. This is the **haveli of Chunna Mal**[12], a rich merchant of the nineteenth century. Chunna Mal speculated in the fluid property market in the years after 1857, and did very well out of it. This enabled him to build this grand building with this unusually broad frontage on the main street.

Across from Chunna Mal's haveli, but on the left, is the entrance to a street called Ballimaran. There is some controversy about the name. Most say it refers to the makers of 'ballis' or oars. One source from the nineteenth century (a letter from the poet Ghalib) suggests that the word might actually have been 'Billi-maran', referring to the killers of cats! More than cats or oars however, Ballimaran has been known historically for its hakims or doctors of the system of medicine called Yunani. Yunani literally means Greek and it was an ancient system picked up by the Arabs from the Greek tradition and then disseminated further around the world.

The best-known family of hakims in Ballimaran is the Sharif Khani family, whose members were physicians to the

Mughal emperors. One member of the family—Hakim Ajmal Khan, was a noted nationalist leader. As you make your way down Ballimaran, you will find the lane, Gali Qasim Jan, on your right. One of the first important buildings in this lane, to the left, is the **haveli of Mirza Ghalib**[13]. It is entered through a semicircular arch made out of brick, and there is a small memorial inside it. Acknowledged as one of India's greatest Persian and Urdu poets, Ghalib lived in Delhi from his early teens, or about 1810 onwards, to his death in 1869. In the nineteenth century, the Mughal emperor was an impecunious pensioner of the British, and the traditional nobility was also in decline. Ghalib therefore was perennially short of patrons and funds to support his modestly lavish lifestyle, which was dictated by his inherited noble status. He never owned a house, and moved several times, from one rented place to another. This house belonged to one of the hakims, and he lived here towards the end of his life. Only a small part of the house—much modified, is the memorial.

After this detour to see Ghalib's house, you can come back to Ballimaran and thence to Chandni Chowk. Turn left and walk till you come to the end, at which you will find **Fatehpuri Masjid**[14].

Enter it, keeping your footwear, held with the soles together, with you. This mosque was built in 1650 by one of the wives of Shahjahan, Fatehpuri Begum or 'the lady from Fatehpur'—the polite way of referring to royal consorts. It is smaller but in some essentials similar to the Jama Masjid. It has a particularly tranquil atmosphere. The several graves in the courtyard belong to people who have been associated with the mosque. If you go outside the southern gateway of the mosque, you can see the Mughal building of a library on the first floor, and the adjoining British colonial style building of a school.

This mosque too was confiscated by the British government after the uprising of 1857. The surrounding arcade, which had shops on the outside, was sold to Lala Chunna Mal, whose haveli we saw earlier. This decision was reversed many years later, in 1877, when Chunna Mal was compensated with land elsewhere and the mosque was returned in its entirety to the Muslims of the city.

Leave the mosque by the northern gate (remember, the domed area across the courtyard denotes west). You are now in Khari Baoli, named after a now non-existent brackish well. This is a fascinating wholesale spice market. Turn left and you will soon come to a broad gateway to your left, which leads into the **Gadodia market building**[15]. Built in the early twentieth century, this three-storeyed building has rooms arranged around a large courtyard, which unfortunately has now been built on. The best way to see the architecture of the building is to go to the top via the stairs to the left, a little inside the entrance. The architecture of the building is of a mixed Indian and colonial style, known as Indo-Saracenic. The rooftop also gives you a good view of the Fatehpuri Masjid, which is immediately to the east; and beyond it down the length of Chandni Chowk, the street that leads to the Red Fort. A bit to the right, you can find the domes and minarets of the Jama Masjid in your view too.

'...the narrow counters, so gorgeous with silks and brocades and heavy embroideries, so tempting and so costly... the broad avenue, with its umbrageous trees...the glaring lights, the masses of colour, the noise and the hubbub, the raucous conversation in stentorian tones.'—Lovat Fraser, *At Delhi*, 1902

Descend and go back to the front of the Fatehpuri Masjid. Now if you are really tired, you can take a rickshaw, and head up Chandni Chowk towards Red Fort at its other end.

Or you might feel energetic enough to walk, which will give you the most leisurely view of the street.

On the way, you will again pass Chunna Mal's haveli, and a bit later, the road opens up into a square, which is the original 'chandni chowk' or 'moonlit square'. During Shahjahan's time, this square had a pool of water in the middle, which prettily reflected the moonlight, hence the name. To the south (now to your right) was a hammam. To the north (now on your left) was the entrance to a large garden laid out by Shahjahan's daughter Jahanara, and called Begum ka Bagh or the 'garden of the lady'. The garden contained several buildings too, including a sarai. In 1857, this was also confiscated by the British government like all the other royal properties. The gardens were re-laid in a colonial style and named Queen's Gardens. The buildings were demolished and a new building, which soon became the **Town Hall**[16], was built. You can still see this on your left, though the statue of Queen Victoria has been replaced by that of Swami Shraddhanand, the noted nationalist and Arya Samaj leader.

The pool of water in the middle of the chowk was replaced by a typically Victorian clock tower, which stood there until 1951, when one morning, it came crashing down and was never rebuilt. The bathhouses at the southern end of the chowk were also demolished and a new road was built through this area. The road was named Egerton Road, after a colonial official, but popularly came to be known as Nai Sadak—'new road'.

The next busy square on this street is called the Bhai Mati Das Chowk, but was originally called Kotwali Chowk or 'the square of the police station'. The southern end of this square was occupied by a building housing the main police authority of Shahjahanabad during the time of the

Mughals. Certain important events took place here. One was the execution of Guru Tegh Bahadur in 1675, by orders of emperor Aurangzeb. Tegh Bahadur was the ninth Guru or leader of the Sikhs, who carried on a persistent armed movement against the Mughal empire. However, later in the eighteenth century, the Sikhs were allowed to build a memorial to the Guru near the spot. The **Gurudwara Sis Ganj**[17] has grown and has acquired the buildings all around, finally pushing out the kotwali itself, the last buildings of which were demolished some decades ago.

To the right of the gurudwara is a mosque that is rather dwarfed by it—**Sunehri Masjid**[18] or the golden mosque, so named because of its gilt domes. Built by a nobleman around 1721-22, it has a rather bloody incident associated with its name. In 1739, the Persian invader, Nadir Shah, entered Delhi and the city. Although the then emperor submitted fairly quietly to him, there was one incident when some of Nadir Shah's soldiers were killed in the streets of the city. This prompted him to order a massacre of the city's population until the Mughal emperor, Mohammad Shah, literally begged him to stop. It is said that Nadir Shah watched the massacre from the steps of this mosque.

In the north of the square is a sandstone

fountain, nowadays painted white and blue. This is the **Northbrook Fountain**[19], named after Lord Northbrook, the Viceroy of India (1872-76). This was added to the streetscape of Chandni Chowk as a colonial 'improvement', to commemorate the visit of the Viceroy. The paint, as well as the finial, is a later addition.

A little further down, to the left, is the **Central Baptist Church**[20], built in 1858. It is a rather plain and uninteresting building but is one of the oldest churches in Delhi. Soon after, on the same side of the road, is the imposing structure of the **State Bank of India**[21], an early twentieth century building.

After this, on the other side of the road are two temples—first, the **Gauri Shankar temple**[22], with its tall white shikhar or spires, and second, the only slightly shorter **Jain Lal Mandir**[23]. The Gauri Shankar temple was originally a family shrine inside the haveli of a Maratha administrator from the late eighteenth century, when the Marathas ruled Delhi. The present structure, much enlarged, dates from the twentieth century. The Jain Lal Mandir is the most important of the Jain temples of the city. A Jain shrine existed here even in the time of Shahjahan, though this building dates mostly from the nineteenth and twentieth centuries. Attached to it is a bird hospital run as a charity by the Jains who have a special reverence for the sacredness of all life.

11

MEHRAULI VILLAGE

Ambience Tower Lane

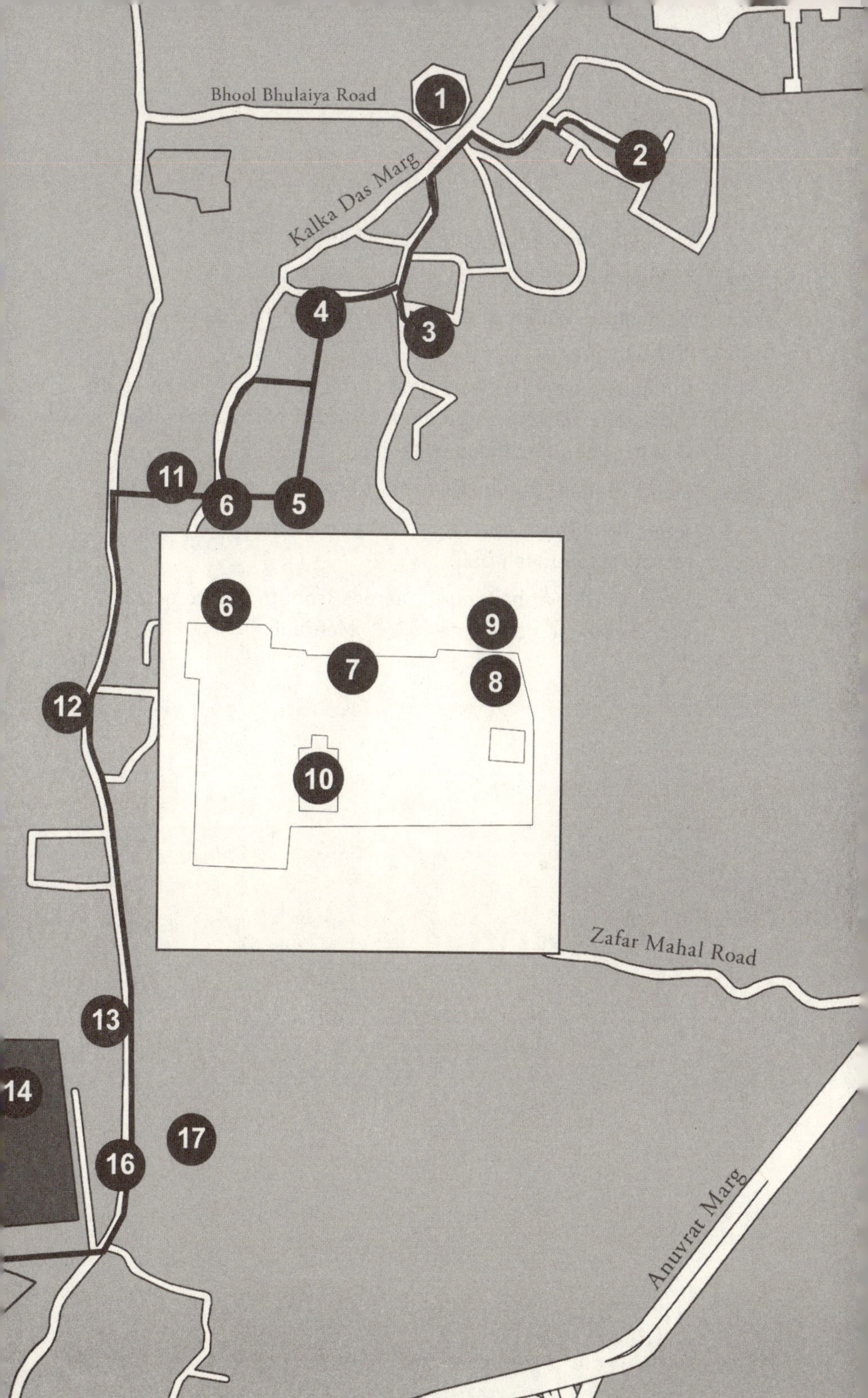
Bhool Bhulaiya Road
Kalka Das Marg
Zafar Mahal Road
Anuvrat Marg
1
2
3
4
5
6
11
6
9
7
8
12
10
13
14
17
16

- Timings: Open all day during daylight hours.
- Tickets: Free.
- Highlights: Adham Khan's tomb, Zafar Mahal, Jahaz Mahal, Jharna.
- Difficulty Level: The walk goes through the narrow lanes of the village, which can be quite crowded particularly after 10 a.m. when the shops open.
- Metro Station: Qutub Minar on the Yellow line, 2 kms.
- Amenities: There are shops and even some quite fancy restaurants in Mehrauli.
- Parking: Official parking lot across from the office of the Sub Divisional Magistrate (SDM), Mehrauli.

HISTORIC VILLAGE

LOCATED BESIDE THE World Heritage Site of the Qutub Minar, this historic 'urban village' is densely populated with beautiful old buildings, each with fascinating stories and contemporary beliefs and practices attached to it. In the early thirteenth century, this settlement began to spread out to the south of Lal Kot, the fortification in which the Qutub Minar is situated. Lal Kot had been established by the Tomar Rajput dynasty in the eleventh century. The late twelfth century saw the founding of the Delhi Sultanate—the empire founded by the Turks. They conquered this fortified city from the Chauhans and made it their capital for the next more than 100 years.

As the population grew to the south of Lal Kot, material and cultural infrastructure grew with it—houses, wells, tombs, the seat of a revered Sufi saint, a large water reservoir. Even after the capital of the Sultanate moved away from here, and newer cities were established, Mehrauli continued to be populated and thrived reasonably well. The shrine of the saint Qutubuddin Bakhtiyar Kaki continued to receive visitors from near and far, as did the nearby Hindu temple of the goddess Jog Maya and an important Jain site in the Dadabari Jain Mandir. The belief in the sacred aura of Qutubuddin encouraged burials in the vicinity. There were other spots associated with the early history of Islam in India located here too, and mosques and shrines, big and small, grew around them.

The topography of the area, with its picturesque hilly terrain, the streams, and the reservoir, made it a popular recreational area too. There was game in the surrounding area for the city folk to go hunting. Finally, the micro-climate here was believed to be healthier than in the newer cities such as Shahjahanabad in the north. These factors led the rich to build picturesque country retreats here—homes and gardens. A climax in this trend was reached in the early nineteenth century when the last two Mughal emperors built a palace complex here and began to regularly spend time in it.

Today, the Mehrauli village is a bustling part of the city; a fascinating mix of traditional and modern ways of life.

The Walk

The walk begins at the **tomb of Adham Khan**[1], situated prominently on a height near the busy bus terminal. It is also popularly known as Bhulbhulaiyan or maze. Adham Khan was the son of Maham Angah, the wet nurse of the Mughal emperor Akbar. There was some amount of rivalry between the family of Maham Angah and that of Jiji Angah, another wet nurse of the emperor. One day in 1862, Adham Khan and a few of his associates stabbed Jiji Angah's husband—who went by the title of Atgah Khan—to death. As punishment, Akbar had Adham Khan thrown from the ramparts of the fort at Agra, which was at the time the capital of the Mughal empire and where these events took place. Adham Khan's body was brought to Delhi to be buried near the shrine of the revered saint Qutubuddin Bakhtiyar Kaki. Akbar had this grand mausoleum constructed, and when Maham Angah died soon after, she was buried here too.

This eight-sided tomb is built mainly of grey quartzite, widely available in and around Delhi. The upper part of the building is covered with limestone plaster—sparsely decorated with carved or incised motifs. The upper part of the building has a passageway of connected rooms that runs around the central room. The arrangement is confusing as it is not easy to spot the entrance to the steps leading down. This is the reason for the building's popular name—Bhulbhulaiyan. The enclosure in which the tomb is placed is located on a bastion in the thick wall of the ancient city of Lal Kot or 'red fort', so called because of the bricks from which the upper part of it was originally constructed.

The village of Mehrauli spreads out to the south of Adham Khan's tomb. Upon emerging from the tomb, the steps lead down on to a busy space and a broad road leading to the bus terminal. Do not go towards the terminal, but take a narrow road to the left of this road, which will bring you to **St John's Church**[2]. The architecture of the church is quite striking. It combines a number of Indian features—the entrance is through a pointed arch between stone turrets, and the spire is shaped like the shikhar of a temple. Even the name of the church is written in Urdu over the entrance: 'Muqaddas Yohanna ka Girja'. The architect of this church, which was completed in 1928, was a priest, Reverend

Alfred Coore, and the design of the church consciously draws on the multicultural setting of Mehrauli.

Come back to the road in front of Adham Khan's tomb, and turn left. Again ignore the road leading to the terminal, and take the one after it, turning left on to it. Once you are on it, take the first turning left. This street leads to the **Gandhak ki baoli**[3], which you will find within a fenced enclosure on your left. This was a well that was fed by a natural sulphur spring, hence the name 'gandhak', which means sulphur.

This is an old well, dating to the time when Iltutmish, one of the Turk 'slave sultans' was on the throne (1210-35). The slave sultans are so called because they were technically slaves, purchased when young and raised to be very competent soldiers and administrators. During the early years of the Delhi Sultanate, usually it was a slave who was the successor to the throne of his master. Hence Qutubuddin Aibak followed Mohammad Ghori, and Iltutmish followed Aibak. Anyhow, this makes it one of the oldest surviving step-wells in Delhi.

Turn back from the baoli and go a short way back up the street via which you came. Take the first turning to the left. It is a path winding between various buildings. Ignore the first turning to the left, and take the next. Continue southwards on this and you will soon come to two tallish piers of an old gateway known as the **Naubat Khana**[4]. This gateway was built as an entranceway to the shrine of Qutubuddin, also known as Qutub Sahab, during the reign of Sher Shah Sur (1540-45).

The gateway is in a sad and dilapidated condition now. The gallery which once connected the top of the two piers, has disappeared. The eastern pier has been taken over by a gurudwara and whitewashed. The western pier at least has signs of its original ornamentation and colour. Look at the beautifully carved brackets that supported the jharokha. This pier too has recently been converted into a shrine for Banda Bahadur, a Sikh warrior who took on the might of the Mughal empire, for which he was executed in 1716, in Mehrauli.

The location of the Naubat Khana tells you that the dargah or shrine must be close, and soon you will come to a busy junction of narrow lanes, on one side of which is the entrance to the shrine. Though this is the more popular way in, it is better for the purposes of this walk to enter through the western entrance further on. So turn right at this point into a very narrow lane and take the first turning to the left. This will climb for a bit before coming into a somewhat open space. Before you is an imposing gateway, the entrance to Zafar Mahal, but ignore this for now and instead walk through the smaller doorway set to the left. This is the **western gateway to the shrine of Qutub Sahab**[5]. You will have to take off your shoes at some point but it should be possible to carry them with you as long as they are held with the soles against each other.

The shrine complex is a maze of enclosures, mostly occupied by graves. You could spend some time exploring these if you have time, but the focus of the place is the shrine of a saint who has great spiritual and historic significance.

Women are not permitted to enter the enclosure which contains the grave of the saint. They may look in through the screen windows set into the enclosing wall.

Khwaja Qutubuddin Bakhtiyar was born in Osh (now in Kyrgyzstan), but came to India at the time when the Turks first founded the Delhi Sultanate, in the late twelfth century. He became a disciple of Muinuddin Chishti, who founded the Chishtiya Sufi order in India and had his seat in Ajmer.

Muinuddin Chishti nominated Qutubuddin as his spiritual successor, and ordered him to go to Delhi. The latter came to Delhi during the reign of Iltutmish. Delhi, under the protection of the Sultanate had become a major centre of Islamic learning, culture and spirituality after the destruction of the Central Asian centres by the Mongols under Genghis Khan.

The work and popularity of the saint extended to non-Muslims too, and he and other Sufis won over many Hindu followers. Qutubuddin's popularity meant that he received large donations from the rich, which were then expended in charity. The traveller, Ibn Batuta, who visited Delhi about a century after the death of the saint, tells us the story behind the nickname of the saint—'Kaki'. According to Batuta, the saint was frequently visited by those in financial need, and he helped them out by giving them a biscuit or kaka of gold or silver and thus came to be known as 'Kaki'. After his death in 1235, his shrine continued to be a popular place of pilgrimage. It still is, and is visited by many, including, non-Muslims, particularly during the annual celebration of the urs. The urs of a saint, literally 'wedding', is the date of his death, the imagery of a wedding symbolizing the union with God.

You can leave the dargah the way you entered, and then visit the complex on the left, which is **Zafar Mahal**[6-10]. It is named after the last Mughal emperor Bahadur Shah 'Zafar', who built the imposing gate, but his father Akbar II had already built substantial portions of the palace.

There were good reasons for building a palace in Mehrauli. The later Mughals were devotees of Qutub Sahab, and several members of the family were buried around the shrine. The practice of visiting Mehrauli was also well established, particularly during the monsoon, when the nearby tank and streams were full of water and there was plenty of greenery around.

In the year 1811, a new tradition was instituted, which strengthened the tie between the Mughal royal family and the shrine. In 1809, Mirza Jahangir, the son of Akbar II, was exiled to Allahabad by the British. His mother, Mumtaz Mahal, took a vow that she would offer a canopy and coverlet of flowers at the shrine of Qutubuddin Bakhtiyar Kaki if her son returned to Delhi. When he returned, this was done with great pomp. The flower sellers of the city, who were commissioned to prepare the floral offerings, added floral pankhas or fans to the procession on their own accord, to be presented at the dargah and at the temple of the goddess Jog Maya, north of Adham Khan's tomb. This was such a popular event that it immediately became an annual fair sponsored by the palace, and was continued under Bahadur Shah II as well. The fair was celebrated each year sometime in the monsoon, the date being fixed by the emperor at the request of the flower sellers. It is still held each year, though now just before winter sets in. It is called the 'Phoolwalon ki sair' or more formally in Persian—'Sair-e-Gulfaroshan'.

'The fair at Mehrauli especially is a favourite resort for the Delhi people...It is called the "Pankha Mela", because "Pankhas" are carried in procession on Wednesday to the Hindu temple, "Jog Maya" and on Thursday to the Kutbdin.'—Oswald Wood, *Final report on the settlement of land revenue in the Delhi district* (1872-77)

The entrance to Zafar Mahal is through a **large doorway**[6], said to have been constructed by Bahadur Shah II (Zafar) to allow elephants to enter. The inscription on the marble slab over the doorway gives the date of its construction as 1264 Hijri, or 1847-48. On either side of the doorway, note the jharokhas with curved 'bangla' roofs, very much a late Mughal feature.

Once inside, the passageway leading straight from the doorway has some intriguing painted ornamentation. In style, some of this looks quite European, and we know that a couple of Bahadur Shah's brothers were quite interested in Western architecture. The rooms beyond are in a rather ruined condition. Another passage goes off to the left of the entrance and this will take you into an open space with more or less ruined rooms ranged around.

A series of rooms on your left here have lost their roofs, which were presumably made of wood and have perished. You can see what was once a **double-storeyed section**[7]. It has a border running along the top of the roof which has paintings and a balustrade of a distinctly European style. One of the rooms on the upper floor has a Western-style fireplace.

An opening in the wall across from this building takes you into a courtyard that is very distinctly in the traditional late Mughal style. Note the cusped or scalloped arches placed on delicate pillars. In the north-eastern part of this courtyard is a **grave enclosure**[8] made of marble lattice screens. This houses four Mughal graves. The most central one is that of the Mughal emperor Bahadur Shah I (reigned 1707-12). Immediately to the west of it lies the grave of the emperor Shah Alam II (reigned 1759-1806). To the west of Shah Alam II's grave is that of Akbar II, who was Shah Alam II's son and the father of Bahadur Shah 'Zafar'. To the east of the grave of Bahadur Shah I is the grave of Mirza Fakhru, son of Zafar.

Between the graves of Bahadur Shah I and that of Shah Alam II is an empty place which is frequently pointed out as the space left vacant for the emperor Bahadur Shah Zafar. The last Mughal emperor, Zafar was exiled to Rangoon, Burma for his part in the Revolt of 1857, and died there some years later. This is actually a curious backward projection because the place could not have been 'left vacant' in the time of either Bahadur Shah I or even Shah Alam II. The floor of the enclosure was always paved, and part of it was dug up for each subsequent burial. It is not conceivable that the floor was dug up in preparation for Zafar's body when it was clearly not there.

Kitna hai bad-naseeb 'Zafar' dafan ke liye
Do gaz zameen bhi na mili ku-e-yaar mein

(How luckless is Zafar, that he could not get two yards of land to be buried in his beloved's lane)—A curiously prophetic couplet by Zafar

There are some more graves outside the enclosure, which belong to other members of the Mughal royal family.

A doorway set in the wall immediately to the east of the grave enclosure leads to a small white marble mosque, known as the **Moti Masjid**[9] or 'pearl mosque'. Built by the emperor Bahadur Shah I in 1709, it is reasonably attractive, though not breathtaking. On the western side is the covered portion of the mosque with the qibla wall. Notice that on the eastern side of this mosque, across the high wall, you can see the dome of the shrine of Qutub Sahab. Probably, the mosque was originally much more integrated with the shrine. In 1857, after Bahadur Shah Zafar was exiled, the royal properties were appropriated by the British government. It is likely that the strict division between the shrine and this complex dates from that time.

Return to the courtyard with the grave enclosure. Through the dalan on the west, you can see some structures that are very different in style—heavily built stone pavilions. Note the solid grey quartzite columns and the heavy striped dome. This is the **oldest part of the complex**[10]. It is said that a nephew of the emperor Iltutmish, and a disciple of Qutub Sahab are buried in the square pavilion tomb just north of the domed pavilion. Clearly, the Mughal palace was built around these older structures.

To the north of these is a broad staircase that leads to a higher level, in fact to rooms built over the grand gateway of Zafar through which you first entered. This kind of staircase also betrays a European influence. In Indian architecture, staircases were seen as necessary but ugly things that broke up a nice façade. They were therefore to be made as inconspicuous as possible, preferably hidden in the thickness of a wall. In most traditional Indian buildings, you will find that the staircases are steep and narrow, often entered through low doorways. So this was a major innovation.

Climb up the stairs, and to the right you will come across more stairs (this time more like the ones you expect in an old Indian building). These will lead you to the top of the gateway. This is essentially an open pillared verandah overlooking the main street at the foot of the palace. The pillars are slender late-Mughal ones. There is one interesting detail. The pillars in the outer row, facing the street, are made of marble. The pillars to the inside are simply covered with limestone plaster. The resources of the last emperor were straitened but he still wanted to make a show. So the pillars that were in view of the public were marble, but those farther in could get away with mimicking it!

Leave Zafar Mahal the way you came and take the lane on your left from in front of the gate. It is a short lane and on it you will see two rectangular **Mughal tombs**[11] from the sixteenth century. They are now in a sad condition—hemmed in with construction and inappropriately altered. The one to the west has almost completely disappeared under a house.

The lane soon intersects with a broader, busy street, which is the main bazaar of the Mehrauli village. This was once the main road to Gurgaon, and in fact till the mid-nineteenth century it went past Zafar Mahal. This had been a cause for inconvenience to passers-by, who had to respectfully dismount every time they went past the gate. Thus, Bahadur Shah Zafar arranged to have it realigned so it would not pass directly under the gate of his palace.

Turn left into this road. It is very busy, but particularly if you are there at a quiet time of day you might be able to concentrate on some interesting architecture along the way. After you have walked a bit, you will see a doorway on your right that leads to **Hijron ka khanqah**[12]. This khanqah, or hospice, is named after hijras, a category of transgender people with a distinct historical sub-culture. Though not much can be found in written histories, the hijras of Delhi believe that this place contains the graves of hijras from many centuries ago, and therefore contribute to its upkeep. There is also a popular belief that a visit to this place to seek the blessings of those buried here will answer prayers of the childless or for those wanting to get married.

Continue down the street and after a while the view opens up a bit, and on your right, set back from the street level, is an old stone building with chhatris on top. This is known as **Jahaz Mahal**[13], or 'ship palace'. From its architecture, it seems to be a Lodi period structure, dating to the late fifteenth or early sixteenth century. Inside, there are arcaded rooms. There is interesting stonework around the courtyard—quartzite blocks in variegated colours arranged in imaginative patterns. If you climb to the roof you will get a closer look at the chhatris, which are of different shapes and sizes. Look at the nicely carved sandstone pillars and the roofs which have some remnants of the original tile work.

From the roof you can also appreciate the location of the building, as it is on the edge of a water body, hence the imagery of a 'ship' palace in the name. This tank, though now considerably shrunk, is the **Hauz-e-Shamsi**[14]. An interesting story is attached to it. In the early days of the Delhi Sultanate, the population of Mehrauli was growing and the emperor Iltutmish wanted to build a water reservoir for the city. It is said that one day the Prophet Mohammad came to him in a dream, riding a horse, and told the ruler to build the tank at the spot he had appeared in. The next morning, Iltutmish went with Qutub Sahab to inspect the area and together they found the spot, with the mark of a horse's hoof on it. The tank was dug in that location, around the year 1229-30.

The reservoir was an ambitious enterprise, occupying a large area, and fed by underground springs as well as streams. The **pavilion**[15] you see across the tank from the Jahaz Mahal once stood in the middle of the water. It covered a stone slab with the mark of a hoof print, believed to have been made by the horse the Prophet was riding. The tank had a tendency of silting up and required repeated excavation—first by Alauddin Khalji and then by Firoz Shah Tughlaq.

According to some sources, it was the former who had the pavilion built, but the building now standing there is distinctly of the Lodi period in its style.

On the same side of the road as Jahaz Mahal, a little further down, is an easy-to-miss modern mosque. The current building is however located at the site of one of the first mosques to be built in India—the **Auliya Masjid**[16], or the 'saints' mosque'. This is believed to be a spot where the saints, Muinuddin Chishti and Qutubuddin Bakhtiyar Kaki, offered prayers. The original mosque is said to have been built by Iltutmish.

On the other side of the bazaar road from Jahaz Mahal, down a slope, is the last destination on this walk—**Jharna**[17] or a 'waterfall', now dry. It was an overflow from the reservoir during the rainy season, which was diverted to this spot by way of an attractive cascade. This waterfall was developed as a recreational area around the year 1700 by an important Mughal nobleman of the time of Aurangzeb,

Nawab Ghaziuddin Khan. The Nawab incidentally was the father of Nizam-ul-Mulk, prime minister of the Mughal Empire and founder of the independent state of Hyderabad.

Ghaziuddin Khan built the small pavilion through which the water flowed into the garden, and the tank in front of it. In time, other structures were added to the garden. Akbar II added the pavilion to the north, and Bahadur Shah Zafar added the pavilion in the middle. The later Mughals used to come to this place to picnic on a regular basis in the rainy season, and it became one of the venues for the Phoolwalon ki Sair.

12

MEHRAULI ARCHAEOLOGICAL PARK

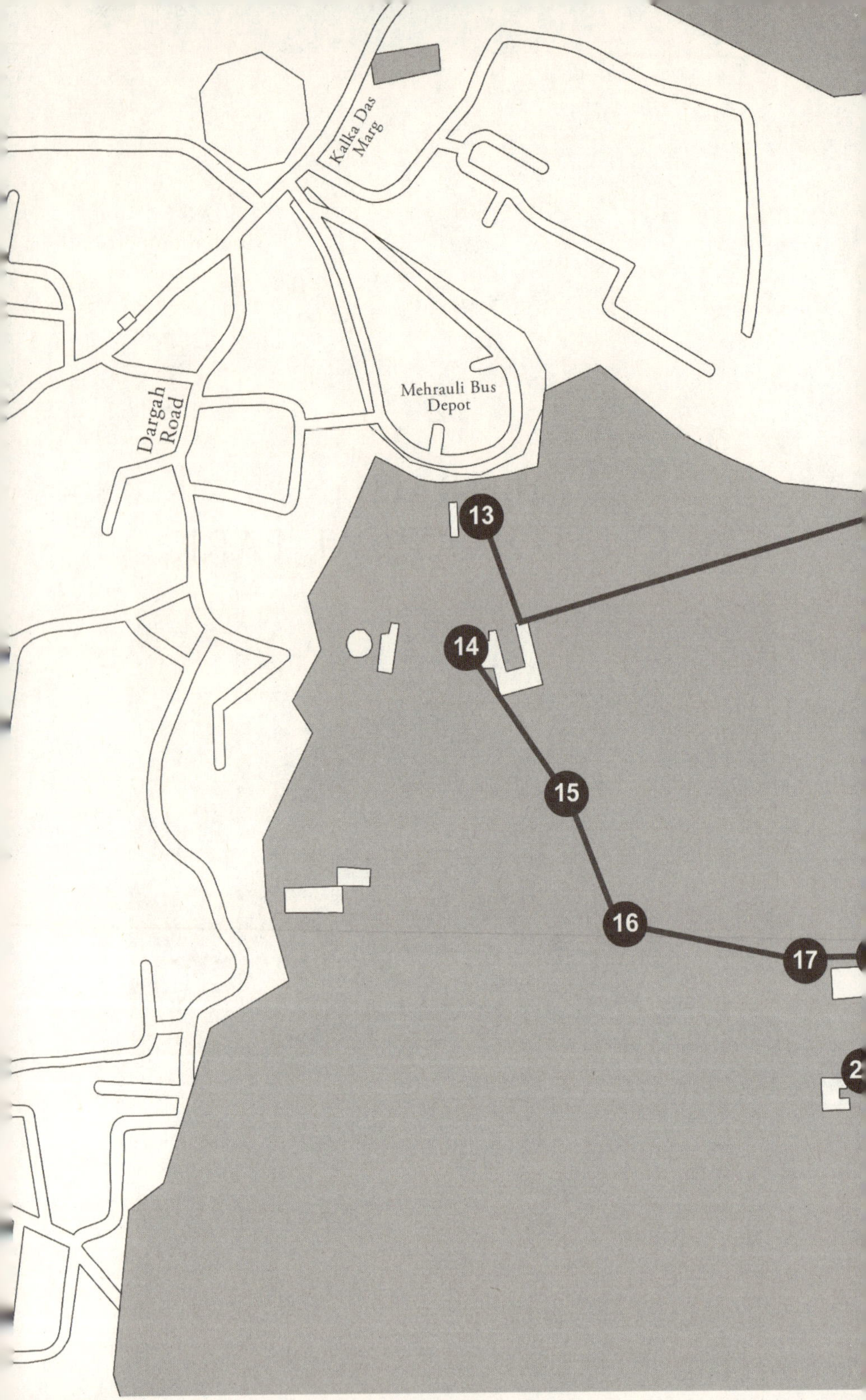
Kalka Das Marg
Mehrauli Bus Depot
Dargah Road
13
14
15
16
17

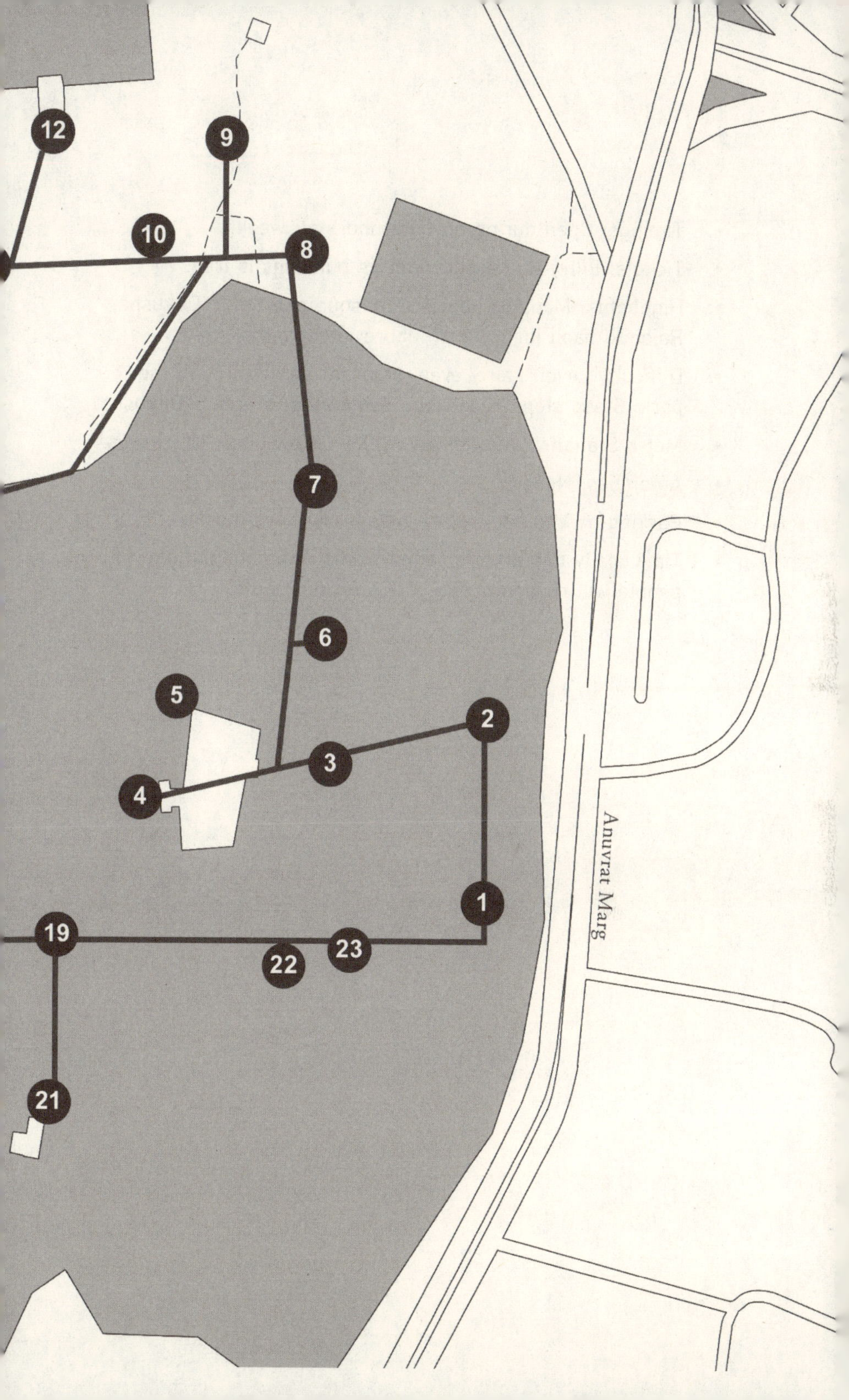
12
9
10
8
7
6
5
2
3
4
1
19
23
22
21
Anuvrat Marg

- Timings: Open during daylight hours all week.
- Tickets: Entry to the park and its buildings is free.
- Highlights: Maulana Jamali's mosque and tomb, Dilkusha, Rajon ki baoli (best for an abbreviated walk).
- Difficulty Level: Fairly even, pleasant paths through the park. Steep steps have to be negotiated to access Dilkusha.
- Metro Station: Qutub Minar on the Yellow line, 500 metres.
- Amenities: None.
- Parking: At the site, near Maulana Jamali's mosque.
- Tip: Locally this area is called 'Jamali-Kamali' and few people will recognize the park's formal name.

SYLVAN RETREAT

Mehrauli is probably the oldest continuously inhabited area of Delhi, and the archaeological park lies adjacent to it. It has some fascinating buildings set in a pleasant parkland, some of it landscaped. This park lies alongside the southern edges of the now barely discernable fort walls of Lal Kot. When Lal Kot was the fortified centre of the capital city of the Delhi Sultanate, some buildings, such as the tomb of emperor Balban, had begun to be located just outside the southern walls. Slowly the population grew in this area and habitation spread along the valley which sloped down from the higher ground on which Lal Kot was situated. The population flourished even after the capital shifted away from Mehrauli in the fourteenth century. More buildings came up here—mosques, tombs, baolis, gardens and houses.

In the nineteenth century, when the British administered Delhi, Mehrauli was a popular location for second 'country homes'. The British as well as the prosperous local residents of Delhi, which was then centred in Shahjahanabad (now called 'old Delhi') spent some time here as it was believed to have a healthier air than the city.

A considerable stream drained this area, collecting water from the catchment areas on the ridge on which Mehrauli is located. Over the centuries this stream also carried down silt into the valley, covering up lower layers of construction.

In fact, many of the structures of the archaeological park have been fully unearthed only quite recently, some still lie half-buried.

The Walk

A convenient place to begin the walk is **Balban's Tomb[2] and its accompanying gateway[1]** which lies close to the main gate into the park, located on the Mehrauli-Gurgaon road. Just within the main gate, you will see a fenced area to the right. Walk into it through the gate. If the gate is locked, you will have to continue further up the main motorable path, which will curve to the right. Then you will have to enter the Balban's tomb complex from across Maulana Jamali's mosque (see below), and climb down to the tomb itself. Whichever way you get to it, the walk begins at the ruined stone entrance way that lies to the south of Balban's tomb.

This gateway has some distinctive features of early Sultanate architecture. It is made of the locally available, hard quartzite stone. The doorway is corbelled, a construction technique that was prevalent before the Turks popularized the knowledge of the arch in India. The dome is a curious pyramidal-shape, because the arch-making principles have not been used in its construction.

The gateway leads into a paved courtyard, at the other end of which lies a large square building, which is the tomb of emperor Balban. He was originally the slave of emperor Iltutmish, and after the failed reigns of several of the latter's children, Balban became Sultan, or ruler. He ruled from 1266-87.

The building appears quite plain and its basic construction material is exposed. Some remains of red sandstone on the outside, particularly the doorway north, however suggest that it might have been used as an ornamental facing. There is no cenotaph in the room, probably because it might have been made of a valuable stone, like marble, that was stolen. In an adjoining room however there is a large cenotaph covered with red sandstone. This is believed to mark the grave of the son of Balban, who was given the title 'Khan Shahid' or 'martyr prince', after he died in battle with the Mongols during Balban's lifetime.

From beside this tomb chamber, a small flight of stone steps leads to an area at a higher level, which is covered by ruins. All that survives are walls, mostly low, which are the remains of a dense **residential settlement**[3], dating to the Mughal period. Walk through this area in the direction leading away from Balban's tomb, and you will soon come to substantial gateposts, which are nineteenth century British additions to the area. Opposite these, across the narrow motorable track, lies the **mosque of Maulana Jamali**[4].

The courtyard you enter is a quiet, shady place with a pool that is now empty but would have originally contained water for wuzu. The person who commissioned this mosque was a Sufi saint and poet called Shaikh Fazlullah, alias Jalal

Khan, who is better known by his takhallus or pen name of Jamali. He lived under the Lodi and Mughal dynasties and was equally respected by emperors of both. The mosque, built in 1528, is of a style that reflects the transition between Lodi and Mughal architecture. The western side, as in all mosques denotes the direction of prayer or qibla. Note that the arched doorway is set in the large central arch. Above this, is a small, arched opening, with a base supported on carved, stone brackets—an architectural feature that is very typical of this period. On either side of the large, middle arch there are red sandstone pilasters, which mimic the Qutub Minar, in style. Inside the covered part of the mosque, the western wall has the mihrabs which indicate the direction of prayer.

From within the courtyard of the mosque an opening to the north, (you can orient yourself if you remember which is the western side of the mosque), leads you into an enclosure within which stands the **tomb of Maulana Jamali**[5]. He died in 1536 in Gujarat where he had gone with the emperor Humayun, who was engaged in the conquest of that province. It is said that Maulana Jamali's body was brought back to Delhi and he was buried 'in the room in which he had lived'. If so, the heavily ornamented room within which his grave is located makes fairly improbable living quarters.

'By one shower from the cloud of beneficence you wash away the dust of crime from our ashamed face.'

'Cast your eyes upon Jamali with kindness and do not look at his idleness and shortcoming.'

—Two couplets by Jamali, inscribed within the tomb.

Nevertheless, it is an exquisite piece of work and easily the star attraction of the park. The inside is covered with intricately incised and painted plaster, combined with brilliantly coloured tiles. Along the top of the walls, there are panels inscribed with the Persian verses of Maulana Jamali. The western side of the room has a marble mihrab, at the base of which is the pattern of a kalash with mango leaves, and 'Allah' written on it. The combination of these symbols powerfully supports the theory of religious and cultural syncretism and tolerance represented by the Sufi saints.

The grave in the centre of the room is that of Jamali. To the east of that is the grave of an unknown person. Like the grave of Maulana Jamali, this too has the qalamdan which signifies that it is the grave of a man. This was obviously a close associate of the saint to have been entitled to a spot in the same room. We do not know who he was, but popular lore has given him the name 'Kamali', probably just to rhyme with Jamali rather than for any historical reasons. The mosque, tomb and often the whole surrounding area is popularly known as 'Jamali-Kamali'. Outside, in the courtyard and in another enclosure to the east of it, there are many other graves. One of them is under a chhatri, and is clearly the grave of a woman because it has a takhti made on it.

Go back through the mosque and when you leave the courtyard, turn left. The area before you is landscaped and covered with grass. On a high grassy mound on the right is a **domed, stone canopy**[6]. Though it looks older, it was actually built in the 1840s by Thomas Metcalfe, who was the highest British administrative official in Delhi. It is in the tradition of British 'follies' of that period—structures that were meant to look old or exotic and add picturesque appeal to the landscape.

Continue along the path for just a bit and then go straight up the next rise in the ground, which has a **well**[7] on top. On the other side, the ground slopes away again and you will see a broad carriageway, with a low parapet wall on either side. Go up the carriage way and it will bring you to a shady clearing surrounded by buildings. This area formed part of Thomas Metcalfe's estate in Mehrauli, where he built or modified several buildings to make for himself a comfortable and beautiful retreat from the city, which at that time was in Shahjahanabad to the north.

To your right will be a structure known as the **Kabutar Khana**[8] or 'pigeon house' or boathouse. This was a Mughal building that was modified by Metcalfe to form a landing stage for boats. On the other side is the depression in the ground, now covered with vegetation, which was filled with water to create a lake. There are small niches on the roof of the building, which would have held the pigeons that were also kept here.

Going back into the clearing, go up the broad flight of steps and at the top, turn right and walk up to a **circular building**[9]. This was constructed from scratch in the time of Metcalfe and seems to have been a sitting or dining room. The circular inner room has a small decorative fireplace, and spacious shelves. The outer gallery has ledges that might have facilitated the service of food. The roof, of which nothing remains, was probably supported on wooden beams as the slots where they would have fitted can still be seen.

Return to the top of the steps you had ascended, and go

further up the short flight of steps on your right. This leads you to **Quli Khan's tomb**[10], also known as **Dilkusha.** Quli Khan was the son of Maham Angah, emperor Akbar's wet nurse. Quli Khan died in the early seventeenth century and was buried at this spot, not far from the Qutub Minar. The octagonal tomb has beautifully painted and incised plaster decoration. There is no cenotaph marking the place of burial. It has obviously disappeared, though the body was buried in the ground, far below. On one side of the building there are the remains of some attached walls, in a style very different from that of the tomb. This is a clue to what happened to the building in the mid-nineteenth century. Thomas Metcalfe converted it into a house by adding rooms on all sides, and named it Dilkusha, which means 'delightful'. He surrounded it with a garden, landscaped with terraces, pavilions and watercourses. The family of Metcalfe appears not to have used the building after the Revolt of 1857. Probably at some later date, the archaeology department dismantled most of Metcalfe's additions, leaving just a portion by way of a sample.

In the grounds behind Dilkusha is another one of **Metcalfe's canopies**[11]. Painted in red, on the ceiling, is a circular pattern of fishes. Not far, in the direction of the Qutub Minar, which at this point dominates the skyline, is another building modified by Metcalfe. This is likely to have been a Mughal period gateway that connected the Qutub Minar precincts with the grounds of Quli Khan's tomb. Metcalfe added rooms to it to create an **annexe**[12] to the main house. The first section that you enter has a row of curious, somewhat narrow, pointed arches. The next wall has circular arches. These walls were added in the nineteenth century. The inner room also has a fireplace. Beyond that is the original Mughal gate, with a broad, pointed arch. Its

Mughal character is also evident in the net-vaulting pattern in the area where the arch meets the wall. Another British addition is the small plunge pool constructed behind this wall. If you look carefully to the left, you can see the opening from where the water once entered the pool. On the other side of the wall, (not visible from here) is the well which supplied the water.

It is worth climbing up the steps that lead to the roof of this building for the breathtaking view it gives of the Qutub Minar. It is quite clear why Thomas Metcalfe picked this spot!

On the way back to Quli Khan's tomb, look for signs of the old water channels that were a decorative element of the garden. From the tomb, go back down the steps. Proceed back along the carriageway and at the end of it, turn right, to join a path that proceeds further along in the same direction. A moderate walk of a few minutes will bring you to some ruins clustered among trees. These are mainly tombs and grave platforms from the fifteenth century. On a raised area on the right side, there is a large platform with a canopy and several graves. This is a typical **burial site**[13] of that period. Though there is no historical evidence of who exactly is buried here, it is likely that all of these were members of the same family, buried in a family graveyard.

Across this enclosure, on the left of the path, there is another significant group of buildings, the **Rajon ki Bain/ Baoli**[14] and an adjacent mosque and tomb. The baoli dates from the Lodi period and is a large one. The steps would have given access to the water, which would be spread out in a pool at the bottom. There is also a more conventional well opening at the far end. People would have come here from the neighbouring settlement, maybe with bundles of clothes or dishes to wash. Once the clothes had been washed (probably away from the pool itself) and left out to dry, one could relax for a few hours in the shade of the rooms surrounding the well. These rooms might also have been used by travellers. The name 'raj' means 'mason', thus 'baoli of masons'. Maybe this name was given because at some time the baoli was used by a group of masons.

A doorway and some steps take you to a higher level where there is a **tomb and a mosque.** The tomb, which is in the form of a chhatri or pavilion over a grave, has an inscription on the southern side. The language is somewhat ambiguous, but it suggests that it was built in 1506, during the reign of Sikandar Lodi by Daulat Khan, possibly over the remains of one Khwaja Mohammad. It is likely that this tomb was constructed about the same time as the baoli, in which case we have a date for the latter. On the ceiling of the chhatri there is a circular pattern made of red paint, which suggests that this was the inspiration for Metcalfe's canopy ceiling.

Close to the tomb is a mosque, presumably built at the same time. It is fairly small but has the fine incised plaster that is characteristic of the Lodi period. It appears that the mosque was occupied as a home for quite some time, as the plaster inside is blackened with soot. A decorative doorway leads from the platform on which the mosque and chhatri are located, down some steps to the other side of the baoli. By following this somewhat overgrown route, you can get a view of the back of the well, which has quite a nice, round shape and is decorated with plaster.

Through the scrub at this point, you will be able to see some buildings fairly close by. One is a wall mosque, now whitewashed and in use. Closer in there is an enclosure which might have been a sarai (a medieval inn) or a residence. Beside this is a path that leads in a south-easterly direction back through the park. If the area behind the baoli is very overgrown, you might like to go back the way you entered the baoli complex, and join this path from the other side.

Beside the path, you will see a large sunken area containing a group of buildings from different periods. The largest, and by architectural style datable to the Mughal period, consists of a **dalan**[15], or **pillared hall** at one end of an enclosure. The path goes over a bridge and parallel to what was the old channel of the major stream that once drained the area. Now it is a noxious drain, mainly directed through a large underground pipe.

As you go along, you will see various buildings beside the path. On the left are two identical box-like structures, probably **gatehouses**[16] from the Metcalfe era. A little further on, also on your left you will see a **building with jharokhas**[17]. The style and positioning of the jharokhas suggests that this building might have been a fifteenth century gateway.

Next to this building is a **tomb**[18] located right behind a **wall mosque,** both probably from the early Mughal period. Beyond this is a long arcaded building believed to be **Mughal-era stables**[19]. On the other side of the path is a compound that contains the **mosque of Maulana Majduddin**[20] with an attached graveyard.

Proceeding a little further down the path, on the right, there is a barred stone gateway leading into a garden, now in private ownership and out of bounds for the public. This is the **Bagh-e-Nazir**[21], a large garden laid out in 1748 by Roz Afzun Nazir, the Khwajasara or chief eunuch in charge of the household of the Mughal emperor Mohammad Shah.

Next, again to your right, is a slightly raised **walled enclosure**[22] for the last few years occupied by a madrasa. This is evidently a tomb set within a garden. You can particularly see the remains of the water features. The tomb building is very ruined, though you can see some remaining walls with pretty plasterwork. The ornamentation clearly indicates that it is of the Mughal period.

Adjacent to this enclosure and entered through it, is a space that contains an attractive rectangular **pavilion**[23]. A local tradition developed here at some point, held that this was the tomb of Khan Shahid, the son of Balban. This is highly improbable, firstly because Khan Shahid is believed to be buried in the chamber next to his father's. Secondly, the style of this building, with its shallow relief incised plasterwork, is quite certainly Mughal. The ceiling is particularly beautiful, with Quranic verses inscribed in an unusual pattern. This brings you nearly to the gate where you entered the archaeological park, and the end of the walk.

13

KASHMIRI GATE

22
23
Sham Nath Marg
21
GT Karnal Road
1
2
3
5
4
6
Nicholson Road
Hamilton Road

Yudhister Setu
Lothian Road
4
20
18
19
17
16
14
5
13
7
12
9
8
10
8
11

- Timings: Such buildings as you can enter are open through the day all week, except the Partition Museum which is only open from 10 a.m. to 5 p.m. Tuesday to Sunday.
- Tickets: Free
- Highlights: St James' Church, Nicholson Cemetery, Qudsia Bagh, Dara Shukoh Library.
- Difficulty Level: The walk is mostly on the pavements along busy roads. Watch out for traffic.
- Metro Station: Kashmiri Gate on the Red, Yellow, and Violet lines, 50 metres.
- Amenities: None in particular.
- Parking: Official parking lot next to the Metro station, or on the street next to St James' Church.

NORTHERN SHAHJAHANABAD

THE AREA COVERED in this walk is the north-eastern corner of the city of Shahjahanabad, built by the Mughal emperor Shahjahan in the mid-seventeenth century as a planned imperial capital. Kashmiri Gate, so named because it faced the north, towards Kashmir, was one of the gates in the city wall. This was a part of the city that was just north of the Red Fort or the palace complex where the emperor himself lived. At the same time it also overlooked the river Yamuna. These factors made it prime real estate, and it was therefore the site of the mansions of some very important people. Shahjahan's favourite son Dara Shukoh had his estate here, as did the nobleman Ali Mardan Khan.

In the eighteenth century, there was a decline in the fortunes of some of these grandees and a decline of the Mughal empire itself. The estates fell into disrepair, but did not get built up as was the case with many other areas of the city. In the early nineteenth century there was a revival. The British East India Company was the new power in the region, with an administration in Delhi on a reasonably significant scale. This establishment came to be housed in the area around Kashmiri Gate, still a relatively sought-after prime property. Some of the old buildings were taken over and transformed into 'colonial' buildings by the clever addition of façades. Others were built from scratch.

Soon, apart from houses and offices, this area had a church, a cemetery, a college, and a powder magazine where ammunition was manufactured and stored. Then came the uprising of 1857 and Delhi became a major centre of the revolt against British rule. From May to September, the city ran an independent administration and by the time it was recaptured by the British, some things had changed—the magazine buildings had been blown up and the gate itself was badly damaged. A new cemetery had to be built just outside the gate to accommodate those who died in the fighting.

Soon after, the railway line was driven through the centre of the city, cutting the Kashmiri Gate area off from the rest of Shahjahanabad. It still continued to be a fashionable place to live—until New Delhi overtook it by the middle of the twentieth century. Kashmiri Gate today is quieter and less crowded than other parts of Shahjahanabad like Chandni Chowk, and there is a lot to see.

The Walk

Kashmiri Gate[1] is one of the original gates of the city of Shahjahanabad. It is unusually placed in relation to the city wall. If you look at the line of the wall that stretches on either side, the gate is placed at a sharp angle in the wall. It is mainly built of the thin strong bricks characteristic of Mughal architecture, with some use of sandstone. The severe damage that is still evident was caused by the storming of this gate which allowed the British forces to enter the city on 14 September 1857.

Leave the gate and walk on to the pavement on the right. You will first pass the **Bengali Club**[2] building. Bengalis were an important component of the British administrative staff, and their numbers increased with the shift of the capital of the British Raj from Calcutta to Delhi in 1912. Many of them lived around Kashmiri Gate, and with them came their social and cultural institutions. The Kashmiri Gate Durga Puja, the oldest community Durga Puja festival in Delhi, began here in 1910, and is still an annual event, though located elsewhere. The Bengali Club building was constructed in 1925. Sadly, the club lost its premises some years back, and the building is now occupied by a guest house.

If you turn into the street which lies to the right immediately after the club, you can walk along the **city wall**[3]. To your left lies the area that was a popular residential area till the mid-twentieth century. It still has some old colonial buildings. Turn into the first arched gateway to the left and walk to the end of that short street.

Turn right, and a short way down you will see on your right the red-painted **Sultan Singh building**[4], which was built in the 1890s by Lala Sultan Singh, a rich industrialist of Delhi. It is of an exuberantly eclectic style, combining several Western and Indian elements.

Turn back from here and take the street going straight. It curves to the left and presently you will come to a narrow lane leading off it to the right. The lane will bring you to a building just south of the Bengali Club. This is the **Kashmiri Gate Market**[5] building, also constructed in the 1890s by Sultan Singh. Note the wrought iron pillars and ornamentation.

Walk southwards from here and on the same side of the street you will come across the **Fakhr-ul-Masajid**[6] or the 'pride of mosques'. The main body of the mosque is on the upper floor. This was a common arrangement, as the lower floor was usually occupied by shops, the rent from which was allocated for the upkeep of the mosque.

You can enter the mosque. An inscription over the central arch tells us that it was built in the year 1728-29 by a lady called Kaniz Fatima, in memory of her husband Shujat Khan, a nobleman. The bulbous striped domes and the minarets topped by lanterns are typical of the late Mughal architectural style.

In the early nineteenth century this mosque as well as a large tract of land behind and on both sides of it belonged to Colonel James Skinner, one of the colourful characters of early colonial Delhi. He was the son of an English father and an Indian mother, and began his career as a mercenary soldier under the Marathas. During the Anglo-Maratha wars, he was expelled by the French generals of the Maratha army, and came over to the British side with the troops under his command. The troops under him formed an 'irregular' regiment (so called because it was not formally a part of the British Indian Army), known as Skinner's Horse, which is in fact still a part of the Indian Army, and now called the 1st Horse Regiment.

For James Skinner, crossing over from the Maratha side to the British also ultimately led to a conscious desire to emphasize the British side of his ancestry. He sent his sons to England to be educated. He sold his house which was near Chandni Chowk, and instead bought a large estate in the Kashmiri Gate area where the British used to live. Fakhr-ul-Masajid was on his estate, and Skinner had the mosque repaired so his retainers could use it. The popular story that he had vowed to build a mosque and a church when lying injured on a battlefield, is unsubstantiated.

After the mosque, turn into the broad street to the left, and on your right you will see a large grey stone building. This now houses the offices of the Election Commission, but was built in 1890 for the **St Stephen's College**[7]. The College, which began functioning in 1881 out of a modest haveli near Kinari Bazaar, soon shifted to this imposing building, more in keeping with its status as the premier Western-style institution of its time. The building is an eclectic mix of Mughal and Western forms and motifs. The former include chhatris, the chhajja, and the patterned border over it. Western influences are evident in the square porch and balustrade over it. The architect was Swinton Jacob, a proponent of the 'Indo-Saracenic' style of architecture which sought to incorporate features of Indian 'Islamic' architecture into Classical and Gothic revivalist styles.

Turn right on the main road in front of the St Stephen's College building and somewhat further down you should see, in an island in the middle of the road, what remains of the **Magazine**[8]. The magazine was a large compound with several buildings, where ammunition was manufactured and stored for the British Army. In 1857, when Indian rebel troops took over the city, the British officials in charge of the magazine decided to blow it up rather than allow it to fall into rebel hands. Only these gateposts remain.

To the north of the Magazine gates is the **Telegraph Memorial**[9], a granite column put up in 1901 to honour personnel from the postal department who died in the uprising of 1857. Cross over to the other side of the road and you will see the grand **General Post Office**[10] building dating from 1885. This was obviously built on the site of the old magazine.

A little further down the road, to the left is one of the oldest Christian cemeteries in Delhi—the **Lothian Cemetery**[11], established in 1808. It is in a pitiable condition, as for many years it was encroached upon by people who had built their homes here. Here and there you may still see some interesting tombstones and plaques.

Turn back from this point and travel northwards on the same side of the road. You will come to a gate on the right that leads into the campus of the Ambedkar University. You need to enter this to see the building known as the **Dara Shukoh Library**[12], within which, is the newly opened Partition Museum. The outside of the building has a rather plain neoclassical façade, but it is a delightfully complex structure. This is because it was actually a converted Mughal mansion. This building was part of the estate of Dara Shukoh, the scholarly son of Shahjahan, who was killed on orders of his brother Aurangzeb in 1659. For some time, in the eighteenth century, the mansion was in the possession of a Portuguese lady called Juliana, and then it was sold to Safdarjang, the prime minister.

In the early nineteenth century, it was bought by David Ochterlony, the first British 'Resident' in Delhi after the British East India Company took over the administration in 1803. The title of Resident harked back to the time when the Resident was simply a sort of ambassador to the court of the Mughal emperor. After 1803, the Resident became the head of the British administration in Delhi as well as a mediator of British relations with the several neighbouring independent and semi-independent states in the region. Ochterlony bought this building to serve as an office, and when Ochterlony left, it was bought by the British government as a permanent 'Residency' for the Resident.

Considerable pains and expense were taken to turn the Mughal mansion into a suitably British-looking structure. A façade of Ionic columns was tagged on, and the original façade of Mughal arches was covered over with solid masonry. If you go inside, you can see some of the original features that have been revealed in recent years. If you go around to the back of the building, you can see a lower floor of red sandstone arches and ornamental baluster columns inside, which are part of the original structure. On the side of the building, set high in the wall, is a simple plaque—'Once the Residency'.

In 1844, for various reasons, the Residency was moved to Ludlow Castle, a building outside Kashmiri Gate, and the Delhi College was moved into this building. The Delhi College was the first European-style college in Delhi, where Western sciences were taught through the medium of the Urdu language. Prominent alumni included the Mathematician Master Ramchandra and educationist Munshi Zakaullah. During the uprising of 1857, the college was attacked and its library and laboratory were destroyed. Later in the century, a school was housed in this building, and in a new block which was built to the south east of it. In the mid-twentieth century these buildings came to house the Delhi College of Engineering, and then since the 2000s, it has served as a campus for Ambedkar University.

Return to the gate of the university campus and carry on further northwards on the same pavement. To your right, across from the St Stephen's College building, you can see a block of buildings similar in style to the college. These were the St Stephen's College **hostel buildings**[13].

After you pass the St Stephen's College buildings, you will see **St James' Church**[14] on your right. This church was built by Colonel James Skinner, whom we met earlier. Skinner had been raised as a Muslim and converted to Christianity rather late in life. He wished to move in British social circles, and the building of the church helped establish him within the local British community. He was baptized in the church with his sons when it was consecrated in 1836.

The neoclassical church building has the dome positioned in the centre—an unusual shape for a church. In the garden in front of the building there is a memorial in the shape of a large cross, to those Christians who were killed in the uprising of 1857. Next to that is a sandstone platform that once had a beautiful marble memorial on it. It was a **memorial to William Fraser**[15], a British official who eventually rose to be Resident. Fraser was a somewhat controversial figure who had made himself unpopular in some quarters. His murder, one night in 1835, was traced back to Nawab Shamsuddin Khan, an important nobleman of Delhi. Shamsuddin was charged with having engaged an assassin to kill Fraser, he was held guilty and hanged. The trial was controversial as many of the citizens of Delhi protested that it had not been conducted fairly. The circumstances of his death and its aftermath made Fraser disliked even in death. Fraser was a close friend of James Skinner, who had a memorial constructed in a prominent place within the yard of the church, which was then under construction. When the uprising broke out in 1857, this tomb was savagely attacked and broken up. Interestingly, other graves in the churchyard were unharmed. You can walk around and see some of these.

On one side of the church an enclosure surrounded by an iron railing contains the **graves of the Skinner family**[16]. Look at the inscriptions in Persian, which was the lingua franca in north India till well into the nineteenth century, till English replaced it as the language of higher learning and communication, and of the upper rungs of the administration and law courts. At the back of the church there is also the grave of Thomas Metcalfe, who was Resident and Commissioner of Delhi for many years before his death in 1853.

Skinner died in 1841 and is buried within the church itself, so this is a good time to see the inside of the building. Look at the beautiful stained glass inside the church. This was restored early in the twenty-first century. As you approach the altar, there are two panels in the floor. The first has a colourful pattern of a tree and is a fragment from the tomb of William Fraser. Between this and the altar is the stone under which Skinner is buried.

Look at the many plaques within the church. They give details about the worshippers in this church down the years. Notice the long relationship between the church, the Skinner family and the Skinner's Horse regiment.

As you leave the church gate, turn right and then right again. Walk along this street, which ends at a building belonging to the **Northern Railways**[17]. This is another Mughal mansion that was transformed into an English building—and a rather ornate one! Look at the fussy turrets and arches. Unfortunately it is not normally possible to go inside the building. It has a capacious taikhana or a series of underground chambers which were much cooler than ground-level rooms and so were used as living rooms in the summer.

Beyond the railways' building, to its north, is another old government building, now occupied by the office of the **National Cadet Corp**[18]. It is an unpretentious structure, on the site where the British administration's criminal court was originally located. Behind it lies a curiosity—the **Gallows Bastion**[19]. When you walk around to the area behind the building, you will be on top of the city wall. You will see a well-like hole in the ground. This is where the bodies of those who were hanged were lowered, so that their relations could pick them up from the area outside and below the wall.

Beyond this compound, further to the north, is a row of buildings that make up the **Old Court**[20]. The main court house was situated here during the early part of British rule. Now it is a Sub-registrar's office, or a court at a fairly basic administrative level.

Walk back to Kashmiri Gate from here. On the other side of the metro station is a smallish patch of green known as Maharaja Agrasen Park. North of this park, on the pavement is gate 3 of the metro station. This also serves as a subway pedestrian crossing to the other side of the road. Take it, and get out at gate 4. This will bring you up close to **Nicholson Cemetery**[21].

Brigadier John Nicholson led the British forces that blew open Kashmiri Gate on 14 September 1857 to enter Delhi. He was severely wounded and died a few days later. He became a popular hero to the British, and the new cemetery where he was buried was named after him. His grave lies near the entrance, surrounded by a railing. There are many other graves here, from 1857 and after. Read the inscriptions, which incidentally, reveal the low life expectancy of those times.

One of the graves here, on your right as you walk up the main path, is that of Master Ramchandra—a mathematician who started his teaching career in the Delhi College. He was an original thinker who got some amount of international recognition. He was also very committed to the spread of scientific education in India. He ran a couple of newspapers which aimed at bringing scientific and other useful news to readers. He supported British rule and lived through the uprising of 1857, but was later very disillusioned with the racial discrimination faced by Indians.

If you walk along the road going north, along the east of Nicholson Cemetery, across the road you will see a gate that leads into a garden. This is **Qudsia Bagh**[22-24], or 'the garden of Qudsia'. Qudsia Begum was a dancing girl who rose to be the wife of the Mughal emperor Mohammad Shah 'Rangila', who reigned from 1719-48. She became even more powerful when her son, Ahmad Shah, succeeded to the throne after her husband's death. It was then that she had this garden laid just outside the city walls.

The path that leads into the garden leads straight to a ruined **gateway**[22]. This is almost all that remains of a large, almost palace-like building, which is depicted in some old paintings. The buildings in this garden were severely damaged during the summer of 1857 when they fell in the line of fire that was exchanged between the Indian troops who were holding the city, and the British troops who held the high ground on the ridge. The gateway displays some typical features of late Mughal architecture, such as the heavily applied stucco work decoration. There is some attractively carved red sandstone around the main arch too.

A little past the gateway, on the right is a **baradari**[23] or the garden pavilion. It is located on the edge of a slope that led down to a substantial stream that fed into the Yamuna. Now it is a drain with rather dirty water in it. The building is interesting because it was significantly modified, probably in the early twentieth century. Solid stone walls have been added to close up the arches and create additional rooms; and a sweeping staircase has also been installed in front. You can clearly make out the original features, which are executed in decorative stucco. The modification was probably carried out in 1902, to accommodate an exhibition of Indian handcrafts that was held here as part of the Durbar celebrations, marking the coronation of the British monarch Edward VII, as the 'Emperor of India'.

Further along the garden is the **mosque**[24]. Built at the same time as the garden, this too was badly damaged in 1857. You can see the huge craters that were gouged out when mortar hit the walls. The building is built of brick, covered in limestone plaster, which has been decoratively carved and moulded.

14

CENTRAL VISTA

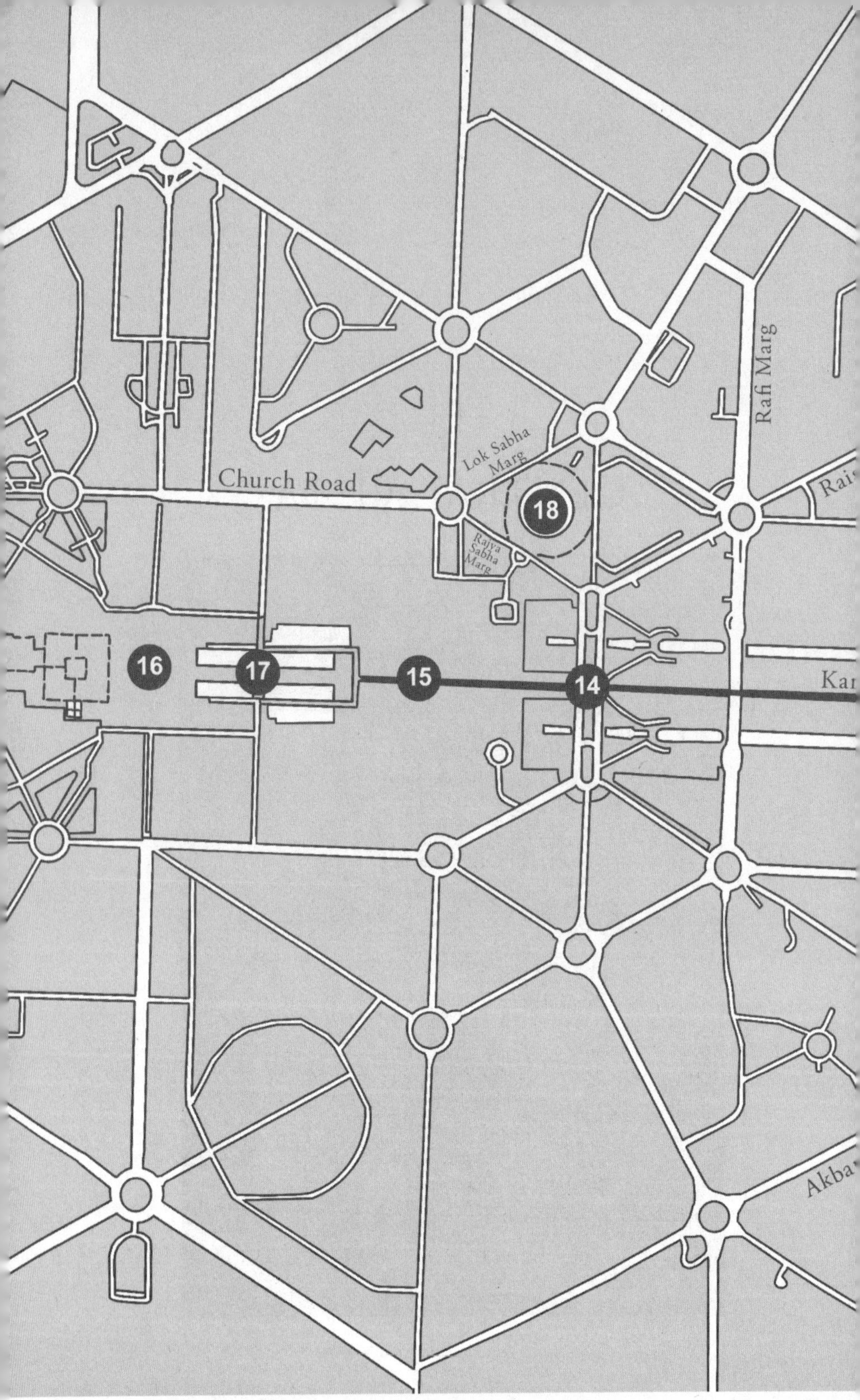

Church Road
Lok Sabha Marg
Rajya Sabha Marg
Rafi Marg
Rai
Kar
Akba
14
15
16
17
18

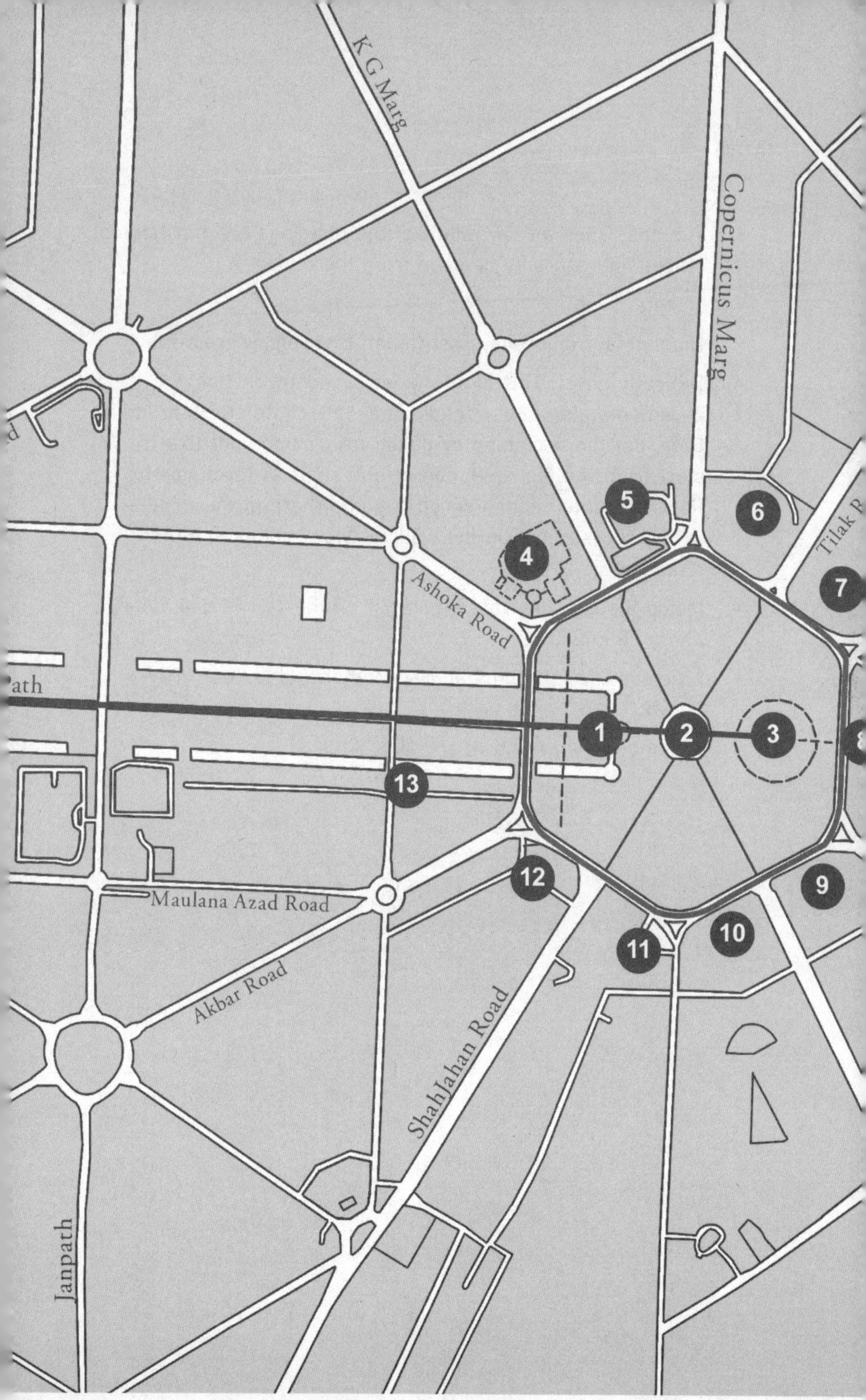

K G Marg
Copernicus Marg
Tilak R
Ashoka Road
Path
Maulana Azad Road
Akbar Road
ShahJahan Road
Janpath
1
2
3
4
5
6
7
9
10
11
12
13

- Timings: Open all day. Many of the buildings are functioning offices and can only be seen from the outside.
- Tickets: Free
- Highlights: India Gate, Rashtrapati Bhawan, Secretariat.
- Difficulty Level: This is a long walk, mostly on the pavements along busy roads. The walk route starts at India Gate, but those coming by public transport might like to start from the Metro station or bus stops at the Rajpath/ Rafi Marg intersection which is somewhere in the middle; in which case, just do the walk in two sections in either direction.
- Metro Station: Central Secretariat on the Yellow and Violet lines, 1.8 kms.
- Amenities: Washrooms at War Memorial and near Vijay Chowk.
- Parking: At Vijay Chowk and Boat Club.

NEW DELHI

Over many centuries, several cities had existed in the area we today know as Delhi. Incidentally, there were more than 'seven cities of Delhi', a number that appears to have been arrived at out of a sense of romance rather than any factual basis. Each of them had occupied a distinct site, and gone by a distinct name—Lal Kot, Kilugarhi, Siri, Tughlaqabad, Jahanpanah, Firozabad, Mubarakabad, Dinpanah and Shahjahanabad.

The last episode in this saga took place in the second and third decades of the twentieth century, with the building of New Delhi. Since the decline of the Mughal empire, Delhi had ceased to be a capital city in any real sense. From the early nineteenth century, it was the British who controlled anything like an all-India empire, and their capital was at Calcutta. A turn in Delhi's fortunes came when the British monarch, George V, announced on 12 December 1911 that the capital of the empire was to be shifted to Delhi. The announcement was made in Delhi, which George V was visiting, to preside over the Coronation Durbar. This was a public spectacle designed to emphasize the position of the British Crown as the sovereign of the people of India, whether they lived in territories directly administered by the British or in the numerous 'princely states', whose rulers were feudatories of the British Crown.

There were various political reasons for the decision to shift the capital away from Calcutta. The choice of Delhi as the alternative location was equally political. It was dictated largely by a desire to make a gesture that would, as the highest authorities in Britain and India believed, be popular through much of India. Popular belief associated the site of Delhi with Indraprastha of the Mahabharata; and for many centuries, before the establishment of British rule, the capital of the empire had been in Delhi. The British government wanted to draw upon these symbolic associations to put forth their claim as legitimate successors to the great Indian empires.

An important part of this gesture of imperial authority was the decision to build a suitably impressive capital city. In fact, the foundation stone was laid in the area where the Durbar was then in progress—north of Shahjahanabad where the British administrative presence was then centred. This was also right next to the Ridge, which had sentimental value for the British for it was here that British forces had hung on during the months after the outbreak of the uprising in 1857, and it was from here that they had launched their attack to retake the city.

The New Delhi Town Planning Committee decided that the site selected was not suitable. Instead, a site to the south of the seventeenth-century Mughal city of Shahjahanabad was chosen. Plans were drawn up for an imperial city to be built on a grand scale. Two noted architects were chosen to design the major public buildings. One of them, Edwin Lutyens, had been a part of the Town Planning Committee. The other, Herbert Baker, had made his reputation as the architect of the government buildings in Pretoria.

There were many different influences that dictated the shape that the new city would take. The idea of the Garden

City was a new urban planning movement that had just caught on in Britain. Lutyens himself had been involved in the design of an early garden city, the Hampstead Garden Suburb in London. It was decided that New Delhi would also be designed as essentially a garden city, with residential houses set in large areas of green. There were also the examples of prominent capital cities around the world. The layout of Washington DC was a popular model, with the Capitol building at one end of a broad ceremonial avenue, the Mall. And then there was Paris, with the Arc De Triomphe at one end of the broad tree-lined Avenue de Champs Elysees, and the Palace of the Louvre, at the other. New Delhi's main avenue, the Central Vista, would borrow heavily from these.

The other question was that of architectural style. Neither Lutyens nor Baker had a good opinion of Indian architecture, and felt that it was European Classicism that could best represent the British Raj. On the other hand, Lord Hardinge, who was the Viceroy of India at the time, as also George V himself, were more in favour of giving the buildings a distinctly Indian stamp. Hardinge, in particular, prevailed upon the architects at several points to put Indian features on the structures they designed.

New Delhi took much longer to execute than had originally been planned, mainly because the First World War intervened and necessitated a diversion of resources. The new capital was finally inaugurated on 10 February 1931. By then, it was increasingly clear that the days of British rule over India were numbered. When India became independent on 15 August 1947, it was only logical and practical that New Delhi, though designed as a city for an imperial power, should be its capital.

The Walk

All of New Delhi is of course impossible to cover in a single walk, but it is possible to take in the stretch known as the Central Vista. Though it is a long walk, it takes you through the major focal points of the city. The Central Vista stretches the length of Rajpath—which has recently been renamed Kartavyapath, but many still refer to it by its older name. At one end of this lies the Rashtrapati Bhavan and the Secretariat Buildings, and at the other, the India Gate. The walk begins at the latter.

India Gate[1] is the popular name for the War Memorial Arch, located off-centre in a large hexagonal space (called 'C-Hexagon' after an early town-planning nomenclature), with roads radiating from it. The arch was designed by Lutyens, and is similar to European memorial arches, notably the Arc de Triomphe in Paris. Finished in 1931, the arch commemorates Indian soldiers killed in the First World War and the Afghan wars. Look at the long lists of names inscribed on it. Within the side arches are set large stone urns with pine cones in them. These have symbolized death and regeneration in Western culture since ancient Roman times.

In 1972, after the Indo-Pakistan war, a memorial called the 'Amar Jawan Jyoti' was set up below the arch. It was removed in 2022, and the eternal flame that burnt here merged with another at the War Memorial.

East of the arch is the chhatri, or **canopy**[2], which is placed in the centre of the hexagon. It was designed by Lutyens as a memorial to George V, who died in 1936. It held a statue of that monarch till 1968, when it was removed to Coronation Park in north Delhi. The primary inspiration for this concept are the baldachins that cover statues in European architecture. But, it also has prototypes in India. The large shells set at the corners of the base symbolize Britain ruling over the oceans. Recently, the statue of a national hero, Subhash Chandra Bose, popularly known as Netaji, has been placed under it.

Beyond the chhatri, is the **National War Memorial**[3], inaugurated in 2019. It is an emotive monument, memorializing the soldiers who have died in the service of the nation since Independence, in India and abroad. The design of the memorial is expansive—consisting of four concentric circles with an obelisk in the centre, containing an eternal flame at its core. The names of over twenty-five thousand soldiers are inscribed on its walls.

The original name for the area around India Gate is Princes' Park. The reference to 'princes' here is to the rulers of semi-independent principalities that existed in India during British rule. Many of these rulers were allotted land in the new capital to build 'houses'. The princes used to spend time in Delhi every year, usually during the winter months, when the higher echelons of the government of India used to shift to Delhi from Simla, which was the summer capital. In these winter

'Here is the site where the palace of the Maharaja of Patiala is being built. There the palace of the Maharaja of Bikaner. Farther on the splendid residence of the Nizam of Hyderabad. The millionaires of Fifth Avenue are beaten by ten lengths.'—Maurice Dekobra, *Perfumed Tigers: Adventures in the Lands of the Maharajas* (1931)

months, Delhi was a lively place. There were many parties and events—balls, polo matches, horse shows, flower shows, etc. There used to be a lull in the summer months, as the government went to Simla and the princes too left Delhi. This cycle was interrupted during the Second World War, when many of the princely houses were requisitioned for wartime needs. Then, after Independence in 1947, the princely states were merged with the new nation and the princely houses became government property.

Some of the most important princes built their palatial residences along the road that runs around the India Gate hexagon. You might like to see some of these more closely, in which case you will have to cross the road encircling the hexagon. The description that follows, proceeds clockwise from Rajpath, west of India Gate, but the order in which you see the buildings is not important, and will depend on where you exit from the War Museum. As you make your way around, you will have to cross several radial roads; do so with care.

The radial road that is next to Rajpath is Ashoka Road, and crossing it brings you to the grand and well-kept **Hyderabad House**[4], designed by Lutyens and completed in 1928. Recent alterations have detracted somewhat from its appearance. The now enclosed but originally open balconies and verandahs would have broken the façade up with deep shadows, making it more interesting. Do note its distinctive architecture, similar in many respects to the Rashtrapati Bhavan, which you will see later. In fact most of the princely houses were made in a 'Lutyenesque' style. There was a reason for this. One condition for the allotting of plots to the princes was that the designs of the houses had to be in harmony with the architecture of the government buildings, and had to be approved by the government architects—

Lutyens and Baker. Most princes therefore chose to actually employ the architects who had worked on the government buildings. Some of the distinctive features of the Hyderabad House include a dome flattened on the top, and slim obelisks on the corners of the roof. Since Independence, Hyderabad House has been a venue where visiting state dignitaries are hosted by the Indian government.

The next radial road is the Kasturba Gandhi Marg, crossing which, you'll arrive at the **Baroda House**[5]. Also designed by Lutyens, and built between 1921 and 1936, this building too has some distinctive hallmarks of Lutyens' style. Notice the dome, which is very similar to the Hyderabad House, and the urns on the parapet, very much like the giant urns at India Gate. The house is now the headquarters of the Northern Railways.

Cross the next road—Copernicus Marg—and you will find yourself in front of an **empty plot**[6] on which no princely palace was ever built. It had originally been allotted to the state of Mysore, which eventually chose to surrender it in 1935. It was then allotted to the Gwalior state, but the ruler of that too eventually did not build a palace, and the plot was surrendered. Then, during the Second World War, the site was used to build temporary buildings for the Royal Air Force. After the end of the war, the site remained in the possession of the army.

Moving on, across Tilak Marg, you will reach **Patiala House**[7]. This plot had originally been allotted for a girls' school to be built by the Begum, or ruler, of Bhopal. She however, surrendered it, and then it was allotted to the ruler of Patiala. The house was built on it only in 1938. The Maharaja, however, soon found himself having to share his palace, as the bulk of the accommodation was first used for wartime purposes, then in 1947 for the accommodation of

Partition refugees, and soon after, for various institutional offices. The royal family vacated the house entirely in 1963, and the Delhi High Court moved into it, prior to moving into its permanent home close by. Once the High Court moved out, the District Court moved in, in 1978.

After Patiala House, across Purana Qila Road, you will find yourself in front of the **Dhyan Chand Stadium**[8] named after India's legendary hockey player of the 1920s-40s. In the original conception of the Central Vista, the view on the eastern side was to end in the Purana Qila, the sixteenth-century fortress, reflected in a lake that would be created at the foot of its tall ramparts. In fact, what can be seen today is just the chhatris at the top of the fort's gates. This is because in 1933, what was then called the Irwin Amphitheatre (after Lord Irwin, the viceroy in the years 1926-31) was built, between the fort and India Gate. This stadium was designed and built by the Public Works Department (PWD), which was actually responsible for many of the buildings in New Delhi, including Connaught Place and most of the bungalows. This building too follows the style of other buildings around the hexagon—note the chhatris on the roof.

The radial road after this is the Sher Shah Road, and beyond it is the **National Gallery of Modern Art**[9]. Also known as Jaipur House, it was built between 1936 and '38. The architects were the brothers Charles and Francis Blomfield. Charles began his career in India as an architect with the PWD in 1913. He was closely involved in the construction of the Secretariat and the Rashtrapati Bhavan. After resigning from the PWD, Charles set up his own practice, and continued to practice in India, with his younger brother, Francis, till 1951. Critically acclaimed, Jaipur House shows the influence of the Lutyens style, but with individual flair. After Independence, Jaipur House came to be occupied by the Lalit Kala Academy, which moved out in 1961 to make room for the National Gallery of Modern Art. The complex now has a new wing, added in 2009. Its design is contemporary, yet beautifully pays tribute to the older structure next to it without in any way dominating it.

Cross Dr Zakir Hussain Marg on the other side of Jaipur House, and you will find yourself before another plot which does not have a princely house. This had been allotted to the Jodhpur state, which relinquished the plot after many years of not having embarked on construction. During the Second World War era, some army accommodation were built here, and has remained ever since. The name curiously, is **Jodhpur Officers' Hostel**[10], a nod to the original intent of this space.

Across Pandara Road from this, lies the **Bikaner House**[11]. The initials plans for this were prepared by Lutyens in 1921, but financial difficulties forced the state to not only suspend further work on the house, but dispense with the architect's services. Some years later, the project was resumed, with Charles Blomfield, as the architect. The house was completed in 1929, on a fairly modest scale. For many years after Independence this accommodated the Rajasthan state tourism offices, but a restoration project in 2014-15 has transformed it into a beautiful place with a gallery and event space, restaurants and a boutique.

Cross Shahjahan Road and you will find yourself at the **Jamnagar House site**[12]. This was allotted to the Jamsaheb of Nawanagar, who engaged Lutyens to design a house. However, even after the passage of many years, the work was not undertaken, and finally in 1939, the site was surrendered by the state. Soon after, it was used for the construction of wartime office buildings. Interestingly, the name 'Jamnagar House' has stuck, despite the absence of a palace.

After this, you cross Akbar Road and your circle is

complete. You will find yourself on the wide strip of green that lines the central ceremonial road leading from the India Gate westwards. Its original name was Kingsway, but after Independence it was renamed, Rajpath—'avenue of the state'. It has recently been renamed 'Kartavyapath'—'the path of duty'. Channels of water flow through the middle of the green strip along either side of the road.

In the green area to the left you can see a whitewashed building. This is an **eighteenth-century mosque**[13]. It should be remembered that the land on which New Delhi was built was part of the older 'cities' of Delhi or their suburbs, dotted with houses, places of worship, and tombs. When the building of the new capital began, only the most important of these were left, the others were swept away. This particular area went by the name of Zabitaganj, named after Nawab Zabita Khan, a Rohilla chieftain.

Carry on beyond the crossroad, and the crossroad after that is Janpath, or 'the avenue of the people', originally called the Queensway. On the north, it leads to Connaught Place, the shopping complex built as part of New Delhi. Just south of its junction with Rajpath is the National Museum. Continue on your way along Rajpath, and you can see the big block of buildings straight ahead. As you approach you will also notice that the central, domed building is slowly sinking from view.

After the next crossroad, Rafi Ahmed Kidwai Marg, you approach **Vijay Chowk**[14] or 'Victory square', originally called 'The Great Place'. This was designed as an open space with large fountains, somewhat reminiscent of the Place de la Concorde on the Champs Elysees in Paris. Notice the stone railing that encloses it. It is on a pattern to be found at the ancient Buddhist site of Sanchi in Central India.

Ahead of you lie the twin blocks of the **Secretariat**[15], popularly known as North Block and South Block. These buildings were designed by Herbert Baker, and constructed between 1914 and 1927. Baker had scant regard for Indian traditions of architecture, but said that he aspired to a 'style of architecture which would satisfy Indian sentiment, but would embody the high ideals of our rule in India.' What was left unstated here was the considerable pressure from Viceroy Hardinge to incorporate Indian features.

'The principle underlying the designs of the architects has been to weave into the fabric of the more elemental and universal forms of architecture the threads of such Indian traditional shapes and features as were compatible with the nature and use of the buildings.'—Herbert Baker, *India* (The reprint of a special India number of *The Times*, 1930)

So Indian features were in a sense tacked on, and the result is an interesting hybrid. Classical columns and domes coexist with chhatris, jharokhas, jalis, carved stone elephant heads, and pillars carved as if surrounded by bells hung on chains. The last was a feature of Hindu temples that was also borrowed by the Mughal emperor Akbar. As you walk up the ramp and into the space between the blocks, look at the central arch in the middle of each block. In proportions and features it is very similar, say, to the Arab Sarai gateway at Humayun's tomb. One major difference is the shape of the arch itself,

which is not pointed (as Indian arches invariably were) but circular. This was a point on which both Lutyens and Baker were adamant, despite the remonstrance of Hardinge.

Four slender pillars, the Columns of the Dominions of Empire, stand in the lawns in front of the two buildings. These were gifts from Canada, South Africa, New Zealand and Australia; territories of the empire with Dominion status. They are all alike, with a bronze sailing ship on top, signifying the maritime history of the empire. Immediately beneath the ship is a replica of the pillar capitals of Ashoka, the famous Buddhist emperor of India in the third century BC.

'Whatever one's opinion may be of the aesthetic value of these palaces, one cannot help trying to discover the significance of this monumental display. One ends up by finding it in the necessity to impress upon the Indians, from the millionaire potentate to the starving sweeper, a respect for British power.'—Maurice Dekobra, *Perfumed Tigers: Adventures in the Lands of the Maharajas* (1931)

At the other end of the quadrangle stands **Rashtrapati Bhawan**[16] or the 'President's House', originally called Government House or Viceroy's House. It was built between 1914 and 1929. This large, handsome building is almost exactly the same size as Buckingham Palace, the residence of the British monarch, and has 340 rooms. Rashtrapati Bhawan and the Secretariat are located on top of a natural rise in the ground called Raisina Hill. In the original plan, only the Viceroy's House was to be placed on top of the hill, and thus it would be the most prominent building, visible from a long distance. Soon after, it was decided that the two Secretariat buildings would also be placed on the hill, at the same level as Viceroy's House. It was a symbolic move, to elevate the whole machinery of empire, and not just the Viceroy.

This modification in plan was accepted by all concerned, but later Lutyens, who designed Viceroy's House, opposed it. This was when it became clear that when all the buildings were placed on the hill, it would cause Viceroy's House, which was set back from the Secretariat, to sink from view as one approached the hill. By then it was too late to rework the plan and that was how it went through. The controversy however caused a serious rift in the relationship between Lutyens and Baker, whose buildings, the Secretariat block, were seen as having stolen the stage, so to speak, over Lutyens' masterpiece, Viceroy's House.

Visits to Rashtrapati Bhawan can be booked through their website, but on this walk you will see the building through its beautiful iron gates and fence. Notice the elephants on the stone posts that support the fencing. The large dome of the building has a flattened top and a projecting drum around its base, based on the Buddhist stupa at Sanchi. Much of the dome is covered in bronze which now has a dark patina of age. Below the drum on either side of the façade are two chhatris. They are placed close against the main building and don't stand out in the typical silhouette of Sultanate and Mughal buildings. Lutyens personally thought chhatris were 'stupid useless things', but as Hardinge insisted on them, he tried to design and place them so as to cause the least interference with the outline of the building. One interesting feature of the building are the fountains on the roof that are visible, at a little distance, on either side of the dome. The introduction of water as a functional and decorative element within a building was a very Mughal tradition.

In front of Rashtrapati Bhawan you will notice a tall, slender column—the **Jaipur Column**[17]. The Maharaja of Jaipur had gifted the column as a reminder of Jaipur's long association with Delhi. His ancestors had been given land in

Delhi by the Mughals, and this, comprising the settlements of Madhoganj and Jaisinghpura, had been acquired by the British as part of the new capital. The column was designed by Lutyens and is based closely on the pattern of the famous pillars in Europe, for instance the Trajan's Column in Rome and the Obelisk in the Place de la Concorde in Paris. It did have some distinctive features though, such as the bronze lotus on top crowned with a star. Lutyens designed this as a consciously Indian symbol.

If you turn back and walk towards Vijay Chowk, on your left is a circular building, **Parliament House**[18], originally called the Council House. In 1912-13, when New Delhi was being planned, it was thought that the very limited legislative council would sit in one of the rooms in Viceroy's House. In

1919 however, Indian representation in the legislative council was expanded and it was realized that a bigger council house would be needed. Therefore this building was designed by Baker and built between 1919 and 1928.

Inside there are large chambers where the houses of Parliament meet, and of course many smaller chambers/ offices. What you can see on the outside is a broad, pillared verandah. The dome is low and therefore all but invisible, particularly as it was decided to add another storey on top. Next to this is the large site where a new parliament building stands.

You are now back in Vijay Chowk. Before you leave, look at the large red sandstone fountains and the beautiful gardens that line the space.

ACKNOWLEDGMENTS

It's been more than two decades since I started leading walks in Delhi, and more than a decade since the first edition of this book was published. Neither the walks nor this book would have been possible without the help of a large number of people. Many years ago it was Arshiya Sethi who first suggested that I could lead walks around historic sites in Delhi and invited me to conduct walks through the India Habitat Centre (IHC). Prof. Narayani Gupta, apart from being a guide and mentor, introduced me to the Delhi Chapter of the Indian National Trust for Art and Cultural Heritage (INTACH) and its walks program. I have had a long association with both IHC and INTACH, and am thankful for all those who over the years have organized the walks, and fellow walk leaders, from whom I have learnt much. I must also thank the hundreds of people who have joined me for walks—they are the reason to keep doing walks, and are frequently the source of new pieces of information.

The initial suggestion for the book had come from Renuka Chatterjee, who also agreed to this new edition being published by Speaking Tiger. Several of Madhulika Liddle's photographs from the original edition have been included. Completely new maps drawn by Devashish Verma, editing by Dyuti Roy, layout by Rajinder Ganju and the cover by Maithili Doshi make this edition a distinct improvement over the old.

GLOSSARY

Arcuate: in construction, that which uses arch-making principles

Bagh: garden

Bangla roof: a vaulted roof in the style of reed huts commonly found in Bengal

Baoli: a well with steps leading down to the level of the water

Bastion: a projecting part of a fort wall, aimed at providing an increased angle of fire

Batter: a backwards slope in a wall, so that the wall tapers on top—a feature typical of Tughlaq architecture

Battlements: top of a fort wall, containing arrow slits and/or merlons

Cenotaph: a gravestone at floor level, where the actual grave is at a considerable depth immediately below

Chaitya window pattern:

Charbagh: a garden divided into quarters in a grid pattern of walkways and water channels

Chhajja: projecting eaves, usually supported on decoratively carved brackets

Chhatri: domed kiosk, supported on pillars, usually placed on a roof

Chowk: square

Corbel: projection from a wall, supporting a structure above

Cusped arch: also called a scalloped or engrailed arch, one in which the curved edge is indented with several small curves

Dalan: an arcaded verandah

Dargah: the tomb of a Muslim saint, or a shrine housing a sacred relic

Folly: an ornamental building with no practical function, often mimicking an exotic or old building

Gumbad: dome, or a domed building

Gumti: small dome or a small domed building

Hammam: bathhouse

Hijri: The Hijri calendar, also known as the Islamic calendar, is a lunar calendar consisting of 12 lunar months in a year of 354 or 355 days.

Imam: Arabic for leader; he is the head of a Muslim community who leads Muslim worshippers in prayer.

Incised plaster: limestone plaster carved and cut into decorative patterns

Jali: screen, usually carved out of stone

Jharokha: an oriel window; a decorative window projecting out of the wall

Kalash: a Hindu ritual vessel.

Kalima: the Islamic creed which states that 'there is no God but Allah and Mohammad is his Prophet'

Kangura: or merlon; an upright tablet-shaped construction, to be found in rows on top of a fort wall, behind each of which an archer or shooter can shelter

Khanqah: a Sufi monastery

Madrasa: an institution of learning, usually a college

Merlon: see kangura

Mihrab: literally arch; usually applied to the blind arches on that wall of a tomb or mosque that faces Mecca

Minar: tower

Minbar: pulpit in a mosque from where the imam leads the prayer

Mosalla: prayer carpet used by Muslims

Naubat Khana: a drum house located on top of a grand gateway, frequently attached to palaces. So named because of an open gallery on top that housed musicians who played ceremonial drums

Qalamdan: literally 'pen holder'; a ridge shaped piece of stone or masonry on graves of males

Qibla wall: the wall of a tomb or mosque that faces Mecca, in India it is invariably the western wall

Sarai: caravanserai, an inn

Scalloped arch: see cusped arch

Stucco: plaster coating often decorative; see also incised plaster

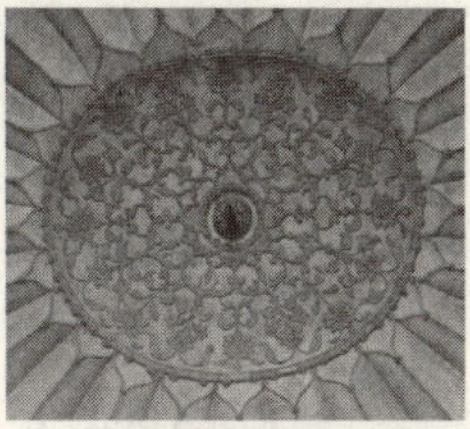

Takhti: literally 'writing tablet'; a flat ornament on a gravestone denoting a female's grave

Trabeate: in construction, covering space using vertical columns and horizontal beam

Wall mosque: a qibla wall with mihrabs, often next to a burial site

Wazir: minister; in Mughal times usually the prime minister

Wuzu: ritual ablutions performed by Muslims before prayer

TIMELINE OF EVENTS

This is not meant to be comprehensive, but just a ready reckoner of dates of the founding of the cities, key events and the reigns of the monarchs that figure in this book and during the period covered by these walk routes.

375-413: reign of Chandragupta II, during which the iron pillar at Mehrauli was set up

Circa 1060: Anangpal II of the Tomar dynasty founds the city of Dilli and builds Lal Kot

1150s: Chauhans displace the Tomars; extends Lal Kot to form Qila Rai Pithora

1192: Mohammad Ghori's armies defeat the forces of Prithviraj Chauhan

1202: construction of Qutub Minar begins

1206-11: reign of Qutubuddin Aibak

1212-35: reign of Iltutmish

1246: Balban becomes de facto ruler, with King Nasiruddin Mahmud ruling as a puppet

1265-87: Balban rules as Sultan

1290-1316: reign of Jalaluddin Firoz, founder of the Khalji dynasty

1296-1316: reign of Alauddin Khalji

Circa 1297: Alauddin Khalji founds the city of Siri

1320-25: reign of Ghiyasuddin Tughlaq, building of Tughlaqabad

1325-51: reign of Mohammad Tughlaq

1326-27: founding of Jahanpanah

1351-88: reign of Firoz Shah Tughlaq

Circa 1354: building of Firozabad

1398: invasion of Timur (Tamerlane)

1414-51: the Syed dynasty rules a weakened and shrunken Sultanate

1451-56: the Lodi dynasty rules, leaving behind monumental remains in Delhi, but no new city

1526-30: reign of Babur, who overthrows Ibrahim Lodi to found the Mughal dynasty

1530-40: first reign of Humayun

1533: construction of Dinpanah (Purana Qila) begins

1540: Sher Shah Sur defeats Humayun and drives him into exile

1555-56: second reign of Humayun, who defeats the last Sur ruler to regain the throne, but dies within the year

1556-1605: reign of Akbar

Late 1550s: Mughal capital shifted to Agra

1563-71: building of Humayun's tomb

1639-48: founding of Shahjahanabad and the construction of the Red Fort

1648: the capital moves back to Delhi

1658-1707: reign of Aurangzeb who deposes Shahjahan to become emperor

1719-48: reign of Mohammad Shah 'Rangila'

1739: invasion of Nadir Shah who plunders Delhi and seized the Peacock Throne—the golden throne of the Mughals

1748-1803: decline of the Mughal dynasty

1803: British East India Company occupies Delhi

1857: Revolt of 1857 or the Sepoy Mutiny—Delhi is an important centre of the great uprising against the British rule

1911: the transfer of the capital from Calcutta to Delhi is announced

1931: the inauguration of New Delhi as the capital

REFERENCES FOR QUOTES

The page numbers of the sources have been given in brackets.

Bernier, Francois. *Travels in the Mogul Empire, A.D. 1656-1668*. London: Oxford University Press, 1916: Pages—121 (257)

Dutt, R.C. *The Mahabharata Condensed in English Verse*. London: J.M. Dent & Co., 1899: Pages—79 (31)

Kaul, H.K. *Historic Delhi: An Anthology*. New Delhi: Oxford University Press, 1999: Pages—21 (34), 26 (317), 49 (186), 80 (40-41), 118 (279), 119 (280), 132 (96), 134 (96), 137 (105), 140 (101,102), 162 (152), 175 (176), 219 (53), 225 (51), 226 (54)

List of Muhammadan and Hindu Monuments: Delhi Province, Volume I. Calcutta: Archaeological Survey of India, 1916: Pages—154 (144)

List of Muhammadan and Hindu Monuments: Delhi Province, Volume III. Calcutta: Archaeological Survey of India, 1922: Pages—7 (9), 9 (12), 16 (14-15), 189 (92)

Nizami, K.A. *Studies in Medieval Indian History and Culture*. Allahabad: Kitab Mahal, 1966: Pages—54 (78)

Prasad, Pushpa. *Sanskrit Inscriptions of Delhi Sultanate, 1191-1526*. Delhi: Oxford University Press, 1990: Pages—13

BIBLIOGRAPHY

The list has been restricted to books in English that a non-specialist enthusiast may find interesting for further reading.

Barton, Gaynor and Laurraine Malone. *Old Delhi: 10 Easy Walks.* New Delhi: Rupa Publications India, 2014

Beg, Sangin. *Sair-ul-Manazil.* (ed) Swapna Liddle, (trans.) Nausheen Jaffery, New Delhi: Tulika Books, 2017

Blake, Stephen P. *Shahjahanabad: The Sovereign City in Mughal India, 1639-1739.* New Delhi: Cambridge University Press, 1993

Chenoy, Shama Mitra. *Shahjahanabad: A City of Delhi, 1638-1857.* New Delhi: Munshiram Manoharlal, 1998

Dayal, Mala (ed). *Celebrating Delhi.* New Delhi: Viking/Penguin and RAVI DAYAL Publisher, 2010

Hasan, Zafar. *Monuments of Delhi.* New Delhi: Aryan Books International, 2008 (reprint of the edition of *List of Muhammadan and Hindu Monuments: Delhi Province, Volume I.* Calcutta: Archaeological Survey of India, 1916)

Kaul, H.K. (ed). *Historic Delhi: An Anthology.* New Delhi: Oxford University Press, 1985

Kaye, M.M. (ed). *The Golden Calm: An English Lady's life in Moghul Delhi.* Exeter: Webb & Bower, 1980

Khan, Sayyid Ahmad, *Asar-us-Sanadid*, (ed and trans.) Rana Safvi, New Delhi: Tulika Books, 2018

Koch, Ebba. *Mughal Architecture: An Outline of its History and Development (1526–1858).* Delhi: Primus Books, 2013

Liddle, Swapna. *Shahjahanabad: Mapping a Mughal City*. New Delhi: Roli Books, 2023

Monuments of Delhi. New Delhi: Archaeological Survey of India, Government of India, 2010

Peck, Lucy. *Delhi: A Thousand Years of Building*. New Delhi: Roli Books, 2005

Singh, Upinder. *Ancient Delhi*. New Delhi: Oxford University Press, 2006

Spear, Percival. *Delhi: Its Monuments and History (Updated and annotated by Narayani Gupta and Laura Sykes)*. New Delhi: Oxford University Press, 1994 (originally published in 1943)

—., Narayani Gupta, and R.E. Frykenberg. *The Delhi Omnibus*. New Delhi: Oxford University Press, 2002

Stephen, Carr. *The Archaeology and Monumental Remains of Delhi*. New Delhi: Aryan Books International, 2002 (reprint of the 1876 edition)

INDEX

ALSO IN SPEAKING TIGER

CHANDNI CHOWK

THE MUGHAL CITY OF OLD DELHI

Swapna Liddle

What we know today as Chandni Chowk was once a part of one of the greatest cities of the world—the imperial city established by the Mughal emperor Shahjahan in the seventeenth century, and named after him—Shahjahanabad. This is the story of how the city came to be established, its grandeur as the capital of an empire at its peak, and its important role in shaping the language and culture of North India. It is also the story of the many tribulations the city has seen—the invasion of Nadir Shah, the Revolt of 1857, Partition.

Today, Shahjahanabad has been subsumed under the gigantic sprawl of metropolitan Delhi. Yet it has an identity that is distinct. Popularly known as Chandni Chowk, its name conjures up romantic narrow streets, a variety of street food and exotic markets. For Shahjahanabad is still very much a living city, though the lives of the people inhabiting it have changed over the centuries. Dariba Kalan still has rows of flourishing jewellers' shops; Begum Samru's haveli is now Bhagirath Palace, a sprawling electronics market, and no visit to Chandni Chowk is complete without a meal at Karim's, whose chefs use recipes handed down to them through the ages for their mouth-watering biriyani and kebabs.

Swapna Liddle draws upon a wide variety of sources, such as the accounts of Mughal court chroniclers, travellers' memoirs, poetry, newspapers and government documents, to paint a vivid and dynamic panorama of the city from its inception to recent times.

ALSO IN SPEAKING TIGER

CONNAUGHT PLACE AND THE MAKING OF NEW DELHI

Swapna Liddle

The origin of New Delhi can be traced to the Coronation Durbar in December 1911, where Emperor George V announced the transfer of the capital of the British Empire in India from Calcutta to Delhi.

Swapna Liddle traces in fascinating detail the events that led up to that historic day: the deliberations over the choice of location; the roles played by the Viceroy, Lord Hardinge, and the two principal architects, Edwin Lutyens and Herbert Baker; and, finally, the naming of the capital as 'New Delhi'—to distinguish it from the old city of Shahjahanabad.

Even as the new capital took shape, it was Connaught Place that gave life to the city. Designed as a shopping and commercial centre for the elite—both British and Indian—it boasted of the most exclusive shops, cinemas and restaurants.

While many of the old familiar haunts like Gaylord, Volga and Regal Cinema have shut their doors, Connaught Place continues to reinvent itself with shiny new multiplexes, branded stores and restaurants taking their place. A guidebook of the early 1940s described Connaught Place as 'indeed the most fashionable shopping centre...and, undoubtedly the most progressive part of the most progressive town in the country.' The crowds that continue to throng its corridors, both young and old, visitors to the city and residents alike, bear testimony to the statement.

Rare photographs and illustrations add to its value as a classic amongst city biographies, in keeping with Liddle's earlier book, *Chandni Chowk: The Mughal City of Old Delhi.*

ALSO IN SPEAKING TIGER

THE BROKEN SCRIPT

DELHI UNDER THE EAST INDIA COMPANY AND THE FALL OF THE MUGHAL DYNASTY, 1803-1857

Swapna Liddle

With a ground-level view of the workings of early British rule in India, *The Broken Script* describes in rich detail the complex tussle between the last two Mughal emperors and the East India Company, one wielding considerable symbolic authority, and the other a fast-growing military and political power. It is, above all, the story of the people of Delhi in this period, some already well known, such as the poet Ghalib, and others, like the mathematician Ram Chander, who are largely forgotten: the cultural and intellectual elite, business magnates, the old landed nobility and the exotic new ruling class—the British. Through them, it looks at the economic, social and cultural climate that evolved over six decades. It examines the great flowering of poetry in Urdu, even as attempts to use the language for scientific education faltered; the fascinating history of the Delhi College, and how it represented a radically new model for higher education in India; the rise of modern journalism in Urdu, and various printing presses and publications, exemplified by papers like the *Dehli Urdu Akhbar*; and the founding of remarkable institutions like the Archeological Society—all of which point to a fast-modernizing society that was being shaped to a significant extent by Western ideas and institutions, but was also rooted strongly in indigenous systems of thought and learning.

Combining immaculate scholarship with extraordinary storytelling, Swapna Liddle has produced an outstanding book of narrative history—on a great city in transition, and on early modern India—that will be read and discussed for decades.